An Illustrated History of the
University of Greenwich

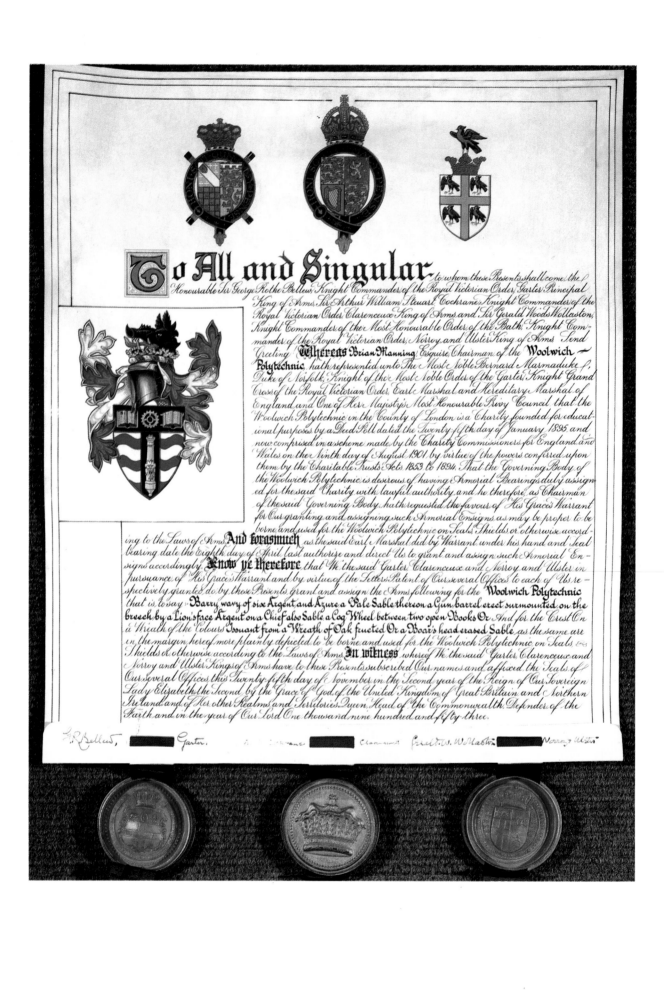

An Illustrated History of the

University of Greenwich

THOMAS HINDE

ISBN 0 907383 637
© University of Greenwich 1996
First published 1996

Printed and bound by Edelvives

Designed by Bob Speel

New photography by John Spragg

Published by James and James (Publishers) Ltd
Gordon House Business Centre
6 Lissenden Gardens
London NW5 1LX

PICTURE ACKNOWLEDGEMENTS

Most of the pictures are taken from the University archives at Riverside House in Woolwich, Avery Hill (including from the Colonel North archive), Dartford, Roehampton, the Rachel McMillan archive at Deptford, and various departments of University faculties. Thanks are due to the many employees of the University who took most of the photographs. The pictures on pages 10 (top) and 208 are copyright Guildhall Library, Corporation of London; those on pages 13, facing 19, 24, 30, 38, 39, 40, 44, 46, 49, 54, 63, 67, 72, 111, 118 and 124 are copyright Woodlands Library, London Borough of Greenwich; page 93 (right hand side) was provided by Hammersmith School of Arts and Crafts; page 100 is copyright Aerofilms of Borehamwood; the architect's drawings on pages 232, 233 and 237 are copyright Skidmore, Owings and Merrill in assocation with Derek Lovejoy Partnership, the photographs on pages 230 and 231 are copyright Nick Evans Architects, and pages 134, 137 and pages 138 (four pictures) are copyright Hulton Deutsch.

The Publishers wish to thank John Fisher at Guildhall Library, Jenny O'Keefe and Frances Ward at Woodlands, Michael Bampton at Manresa and Alison Goss at Woolwich for all their help and advice.

Half-title page: *Southwood House, centre of the University's administration.*
Facing title page: *The grant of arms to Woolwich Polytechnic, the forerunner to the University of Greenwich.*
Title page: *The Drawing Office, Woolwich Polytechnic, 1900s.*

Foreword

The century since the foundation of the institution which was to become the University of Greenwich has been a period of continuous and fundamental development in higher education. The pace of change has never been greater than in recent years. The University and its constituent parts continue to make a substantial contribution to this process.

With the Polytechnic becoming a University in 1992, and the departure of Norbert Singer as Vice-Chancellor a year later, the institution had truly reached the end of an era. Our centenary is therefore a particularly appropriate time to survey our history, to take stock of the present, and look forward to the future.

Since David Fussey was newly installed as Vice-Chancellor, and I was by now a long-standing member of staff, it fell to me to commission an author to carry out this work. The brief was to write an account which would be not only authoritative but also engaging to readers among students and staff past and present, and to the community we serve. Although I was aware that we had willing helpers and a storehouse of information (albeit sometimes chaotically organised) I had not fully appreciated the daunting size of the task. However, the choice of author was a good one. In my view he has done more than justice to the subject.

Thanks are due in particular to Denis Heathcote, the University Librarian, who was responsible for considerable organisation of the project and advice on the text and illustrations; to Alison Goss, without whose help we would not have been able to sort out the archive material; and to Keith Reed, Deputy Director until 1986, who provided invaluable advice on the text, and without whom the institution would have been a different place.

JOHN MCWILLIAM
DEPUTY VICE-CHANCELLOR
FEBRUARY 1996

Author's Acknowledgements

I would like in particular to thank Keith Reed for his early reading of the text, chapter by chapter, and his many helpful and knowledgeable suggestions, Denis Heathcote for his constant support throughout, John McWilliam for his special advice on the later chapters and David Fussey, the present Vice-Chancellor. Others who have given me invaluable help are Tom Appleton, Panos Arvanitakis, Alistair Baxter, Mark Cross, Sheila Cutler, Doreen Dickson, Alison Goss, Richard Holden, John Humphreys, George Jeffery, Angela John, Ivor Jones, Lisa MacDonald-Brown, Brian Manley, Sheelagh Mealing, John Mendham, Nunzio Mosca, John Parsonage, Valerie Pitt, Cheryl Saunders, Clive Seymour, David Shorney, Norbert Singer, Sara Spence, Valerie Stead, Jackie Taylor, Carla Walsh and Joyce Webb.

THOMAS HINDE

Contents

1

The Launch

1880–1901

WOOLWICH POLYTECHNIC OPENED ITS DOORS to students on 28 September 1891. It was the first to follow where Regent Street Polytechnic had led, and was itself soon to be followed by new polytechnics throughout the capital.

Five weeks later (3 November) its Council heard that so far 504 students had attended. These were men and women aged between 16 and 22, and were studying 38 subjects (though engineering, physics, chemistry, building, and, astonishingly, English language were for men only). The classes were being held in the evenings at the Polytechnic's newly acquired building, 47 William Street. So was born the direct ancestor of the University of Greenwich.

The birth had not been a simple one, the labour lasting four years, the gestation going back some 27 years to 1864 when a young man named Quintin Hogg left Eton. Hogg, born in 1845, fourteenth child of Sir James Hogg, had chosen not to follow his father into the Indian Civil Service, nor to go to Oxford, but to accept the offer of a job with a City tea merchant. For the next 18 years he remained in the City, soon becoming senior partner of a firm of sugar merchants and growing rich. During these years he also became one of the most active London philanthropists. Partly he did so as a result of strong Christian beliefs, partly in reaction to the ignorance he saw all around him in London.

His earliest attempt to remedy this suggests the spontaneity of his feelings. He found two crossing sweepers near Trafalgar Square and tried to teach them to read, but lost these first two pupils when they ran off calling out 'kool ecilop', words he later learned were a warning ('police look' reversed).

To get to know such poor boys better, Hogg bought himself a shoeblack's outfit and would spend whole nights on the streets, blacking shoes, holding horses, or doing other odd jobs. That same year (1864) he and the boy who had been his junior colleague at Eton, Lord Kinnaird, attempted to educate the poor on a larger

Facing page: Woolwich Dockyard viewed from the Thames.

Quintin Hogg, founder of the Polytechnic movement.

9

Children at a Ragged School, late 19th century. Picture by Percy Cruikshank.

Lord Kinnaird, who joined with Quintin Hogg to set up a ragged-boys' school.

scale by launching a ragged-boys' school. For this they rented premises in an alley near Charing Cross known as Of Alley, later York Place. Hogg would personally shave and scrub the boys before they were fit to be taught. Five of the first came naked except for their mothers' shawls pinned around them.

The ragged school was so successful that it soon needed more space and moved to Castle Street. Now, in 1870, the Government passed the Education Act which established School Boards throughout the country and made elementary education available to all (though not yet everywhere compulsory or free). This began to make ragged schools unnecessary and it would be easy to suggest that it was the reason for Hogg's next and more significant move: the separating of some of the boys of his school into an institute. But in fact he did this in 1871, before the Education Act could have had any significant effect, and he had other motives. According to his daughter, Ethel Wood, many of his ragged boys had so improved, and so many 'better-class boys' had joined the school that he had become 'seriously perturbed as to the advisability of letting them mix so freely with the ragged element'.

His institute was different in other ways. Its pupils were mostly older and at work during the day so it functioned, unlike the school, in the evenings. It also had a wider social purpose. 'What we wanted to develop our institute into', he wrote later, 'was a place which should recognize that God had given man more than one side to his character, and where we could gratify any reasonable taste, whether athletic, intellectual, spiritual or social.'

Hogg was not alone in wanting to provide the poor with something other than formal education. These were years when middle-class young men would spend their evenings in London's East End, helping at clubs where poor boys learned such manly sports as boxing. And though the so-called missions founded by public schools and universities had more of a religious purpose, they always included a boys' club at which sports and games were played. Interestingly, Winchester in 1876 and Eton soon afterwards had been the first schools to start missions of

Left: *The Regent Street Polytechnic grew out of Hogg's Young Men's Christian Institute.*

Below: *Work in the Polytechnic, and one of the 'character sketches' from the* Polytechnic Magazine.

this sort. But their dates show that school missions were not Hogg's model.

Nor does the suggestion made by Sidney Webb that Walter Besant's utopian novel, *All Sorts and Conditions of Men*, was an inspiration for the polytechnic movement seem relevant to Hogg's institute. True, Besant describes 'A Palace of Delight', designed to provide the poor with a place in which they could indulge in social intercourse and healthy recreation, and this led to the establishment of an actual 'People's Palace', later to become Queen Mary College, but the book was not published until 1882, 11 years after Hogg founded his institute.

This is not to deny that Hogg's vision was one to which society in general subscribed in those years. In 1894 the *Woolwich Herald* gave its own idea of that vision.

It is no use going to a man in the streets or the public house, and endeavouring to transform him on the spot. The first thing to do is to place him in a healthier environment, – to invite him for example to the reading room, where he will meet with cheerful company of higher character than that to which he has been accustomed. Then you will probably ascertain what is his hobby: perhaps he is a footballer, and will welcome the suggestion that he should join one of the teams. When you see that he is at home, and have shown him that someone takes an interest in his welfare, you may perhaps say 'There is a Bible-class upstairs; would you like to come up for half-an-hour' or 'Mr So-and-So is to give an address in the large hall on Sunday; I think you would be interested.'

The swimming bath at the Regent Street Polytechnic, fitted up as the winter reading room.

Francis (Frank) Didden.

The history of the first 14 years of Woolwich Polytechnic is in large part the history of a conflict between this vision of a social and religious institute and a vision of a further education college. Only in September 1903 did it drop the words 'Young Men's Christian Institute' from the name it gave itself in its prospectus.

Like Hogg's ragged school, his institute thrived, moving first to larger premises in Long Acre where it had space for 500, then in 1882 to the building which gave the whole movement its name: the Regent Street Polytechnic. This had been 'a well-known place of popular and semi-scientific entertainment' (Webb), and Hogg retained the name, though his Polytechnic Institute had little likeness to the original Polytechnic.

If the institute had flourished in Long Acre, in Regent Street the Polytechnic did so on what must have seemed a miraculous scale. In September 1882 it opened with 2,000 members and during its first winter these increased to 6,800. Though many came for its evening classes, it also quickly developed the social character which Hogg was determined it should have, forming a debating society, a savings bank, a Christian Workers' Union and even a Volunteer Rifle Corps. From 1886 it began to organize foreign visits at cheap rates for its members, to provide the poor, like the rich, with the chance to make the Grand Tour.

Hogg was the father of all subsequent British polytechnics (within 15 years there were nine in London), but more specifically he was the father of the Woolwich Polytechnic. To his institute when he first separated it from his ragged school in Castle Street had come a young man, Francis (Frank) Didden, who was strongly influenced by the experience. When Didden moved to Woolwich in 1884 to become a fitter in the Royal Arsenal he began to work for the founding of a similar institute there.

Woolwich, a small town of 7,500 at the beginning of the 19th century (left), *grew to 'a grand naval and military depot'* (below) *by the 1880s.*

Woolwich had grown from a small town of 7,500 at the beginning of the nineteenth century to a sizeable one of 36,000 by 1881, largely as a result of the Royal Arsenal. Though this was by far its largest enterprise, employing some 13,000 mechanics, it was by no means its only one. North of the Thames, connected to the town by the Free Ferry, were the Victoria and Albert Docks. South of the river were various factories, Siemens the largest, the Royal Military Academy, and the barracks. Though all this made the town a thriving one, it did not make it a civilized one. Its public houses were open from 5 a.m. till midnight, its slums were extensive and insanitary, some of its small houses occupied by as many as 20 people.

In the years following Didden's arrival at Woolwich various organizations – the Tenants' Defence and Fair Rent League, the Co-operative Movement – had

become active in the town, and from 1889 to 1894 the Revd J. Horsley, Vicar of Holy Trinity Church, wrote a succession of protesting articles for the *Woolwich Gazette*. Inspired by these Dr Smith, the Medical Officer of Health, took action and by 1891 he was able to write, 'In many instances, houses have been demolished and a better class of residence erected whilst, in all cases, the houses of the poor have been converted from insanitary to sanitary dwellings.' But he added, 'It is regretted that, in a great number of cases, the habits of the occupants do not contribute to the maintaining of this desirable change.'

It was against this background that Didden, two years after he arrived in the town, wrote to Hogg for advice. Hogg was encouraging. 'There is no place in England where you have a more certain clientele,' he replied. But he was anxious that anything Didden founded should, like his Regent Street Institute, be more than a school, and advised him,

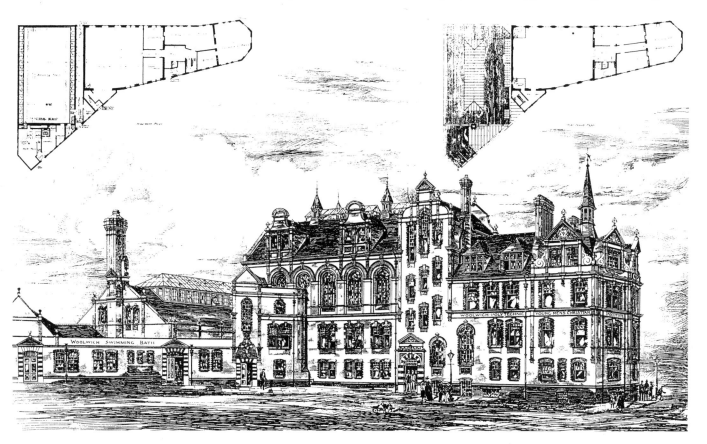

Design by W. Gilbert Scott for the proposed Polytechnic building (1888), including a swimming pool, on the old guardhouse site in Mill Lane. The War Office was not satisfied and the offer of the site was withdrawn.

You certainly require, as a minimum, a gymnasium, a few class rooms, a reading room and a coffee bar, besides some small hall where meetings could be held. These would necessitate no very heavy outlay, and I do not think the soul could be accommodated in a much smaller body.

At first Didden was less ambitious. He had already been looking for premises and hoping to get permission to use a small chapel at the Arsenal, later its reference library, in Plumstead Road. In July 1886 Hogg wrote again, telling him how sorry he was that this had not yet been given. When, however, the War Office finally refused, it suggested that it might grant the proposed institute a site on which to build. In 1887 two possible sites were found, one at the corner of Mill Lane and New Road, the other at the corner of Thames Street and New Road. Hogg wrote to Didden that the former (where the old guard house had stood) was 'practically granted'.

Plans were prepared (the War Office stipulated that it must approve these) and the group set about the more difficult task of raising the money. One attempt can be considered the first public emergence of the Woolwich Polytechnic: a sports meeting held at Charlton Park in July 1888 by a body calling itself the Polytechnic Athletic Club. The *Kent Mercury*'s description of this event suggests that Didden's efforts by now had wide support.

> The weather was fine, and there was a large attendance of visitors. The principal attractions were some amateur athletic sports and a gymnastic display, the latter by members of the London Polytechnic and the Royal Arsenal Gymnastic Society. The handicapping being good some capital racing was witnessed . . . while the various displays of gymnastics, boxing, sword exercises etc. were of a high order. A donkey race with the riders in costume caused much amusement.

Popular such events may have been, but they were never likely to raise the money needed and in 1889 Didden and his supporters applied to another source. Over the centuries the parishes of London had accumulated bequests which it was their duty to administer in favour of various charities. By 1870 many of these charities had disappeared. One bequest had required 6s. 8d. (33p) a year to be spent on the burning of heretics. Even some of the parishes no longer existed. And where charities were funded by income from London properties, this had often hugely increased, in one case from 8 guineas to almost £200. In total the parishes had around £100,000 to distribute annually. In 1883 the Government finally ended this confusion by passing the City of London Parochial Act. Charity Commissioners were given the duty of collecting the income of all such charities and, after allotting some to the Church for Church purposes and some to the five largest London parishes for poor relief, of handing the rest to a body known as the City Parochial Foundation for providing education, libraries, and open spaces for London's poor.

This body agreed to use some of its money to support educational institutes in South London, provided the sums it gave were matched by similar sums raised locally. As a result a public appeal was launched for the founding of three institutes. One of these, at New Cross, the Goldsmiths' Company agreed to support. This left the City Parochial Foundation free to support the other two, one at the Elephant and Castle, one at Battersea.

It seemed to Didden, however, that his embryonic institute at Woolwich was just as deserving and he wrote to the Charity Commissioners asking that 'some part of the funds of the City Parochial Charities, which the Commissioners propose to devote to technical education, may be allotted to this densely populated part of the Metropolis'. But when the Commissioners considered his

T. A. Denny, who largely paid for the site where the Polytechnic was to be founded. He became one of the founding governors, and was chairman 1891–94.

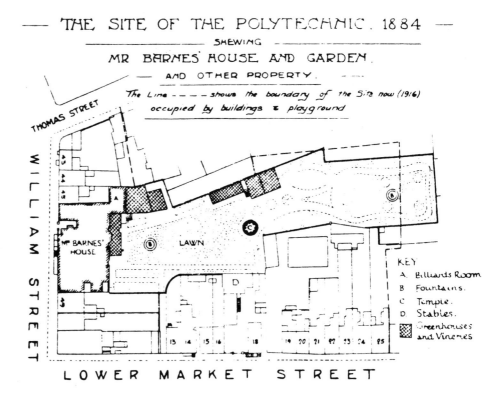

Map showing the original plot on which the Polytechnic was built, as reconstructed for the Magazine of 1916. Barnes's house at no. 47 was purchased in 1890. In 1892 a gymnasium and chemistry laboratories were built in the garden, while no. 49 was purchased, demolished and replaced by metallurgy and chemistry laboratories. This allowed the transfer of practical chemistry classes from the Royal Arsenal. The rear elevation of no. 47 can be seen to this day.

request they rejected it on the grounds that New Cross was close enough for the people of Woolwich to make use of the institute there, even suggesting that if Woolwich founded its own institute this should 'be affiliated to and worked in conjunction with the Goldsmiths' Institute'. (Ironically, it was Goldsmiths' which, almost 100 years later, surrendered its science departments to Thames Polytechnic – see Chapter 15.) That June (1889), Didden had worse news when the War Office refused to make the Mill Lane site available since it did not approve of the plans for the proposed building.

It was early next year that Didden,

> walking down William Street [now Calderwood Street] met Mr Samuel Barnes coming from his house. Naturally he asked whether Mr Barnes could tell him of anywhere likely. Mr Barnes, sympathetic, took him inside to talk the matter over, and there our pioneer, seeing in the comparatively spacious house and garden the means of an excellent beginning, ventured to suggest the possibility of such a use. (*Polytechnic Magazine*, 1916)

The same month, January 1890, T. A. Denny, a prosperous bacon merchant and one of Didden's most enthusiastic supporters, made Barnes an offer, and on 1 March Barnes replied, 'While I am making no inconsiderable sacrifice, knowing the purpose for which they [the house and garden] are intended I am prepared to accept the terms you name.' The price was £1,000, most of which Denny himself paid.

Students' and Members' Council, 1891.

Once it had bought Barnes's house, the Woolwich Polytechnic was a reality. Didden came to live with his family on the upper floor and a large gymnasium was built in its garden. In August 1890 its Athletic Club held a second fund-raising meeting in Charlton Park, and the following month Hogg gave it official status, together with the right for its members to use the new house. It also began to use a playing-field at Whiteheart Meadow, Plumstead. Soon a Cycling Club, a Photographic Section, a Chess and Draughts Club, a Minstrel Troupe, a Temperance Society, a Christian Workers' Union, and a Tract Band were formed, the latter to deliver religious tracts and undertake door-to-door Christian canvassing. A year later, August 1891, the Athletic Club held a third meeting, this time at Invicta Recreation Ground, Plumstead, watched by an audience of 3,000.

From January to July 1890 Hogg's *Polytechnic Magazine* had a correspondent at Woolwich calling himself 'The Stroller' who reported weekly on

During 1891, Samuel Barnes's house was altered and a new façade with an entrance on to William Street was constructed. The adjacent property at No. 49 was purchased and replaced by laboratories in 1892 (H. H. Church, architect). This frontage has remained virtually unaltered over 100 years.

events at Woolwich. On 9 January he wrote 'Frank Didden wishes me to state that on Tuesday January 20th, it is intended to hold a grand Social for Poly members and a limited number of members' friends. All sorts and conditions of good things are being arranged.' On 6 February he wrote, 'After thoughtful calculation I find this week's notes would fill nine and a half columns of Polytechnic Gossip.' And on 13 March, 'The new Swimming Club . . . will . . . start soon after Easter. Take comfort, O natatists! – and ye of the great unwashed, – for the limpid stream will be turned on, and there shall be rejoicing in the heart of our Poly swimmists.'

In the early years the Polytechnic's Governing Body continued to be its trustees. These included Hogg, Didden, Kinnaird, three Denny brothers and at least three other friends or benefactors. In 1891 however, it acquired two new managing bodies. First, probably in January, came a Council. At its earliest recorded meeting (5 February) its secretary described its constitution. It was to consist of representatives of each of the sections of the Institute, but also of so-called 'trustee representatives'. Apart from its other meetings, it was to meet monthly with the trustees, at meetings described as 'those of the Committee'. None of the Council proposals was to be put into effect unless agreed by the Committee. The trustees thus remained firmly in control.

For the most part the Council discussed the details of the running of the Polytechnic. Shove-halfpenny for instance it considered 'scarcely a fit game', and smoking, Hogg, as its Chairman, strongly opposed. (By stages smoking was allowed, first in the garden's bicycle shed, then at the far end of the main corridor, then in the main refreshment room between 8 and 10 p.m.)

Later in the year, to prepare for its first term, the Polytechnic acquired its second new management body: an Education Committee. This included Hogg, Kinnaird, two Denny brothers, Didden, a number of those who were to become the Polytechnics first teachers and two experienced representatives from Hogg's Regent Street Polytechnic. In choosing subjects to be studied this committee was to an extent limited; part of its brief was to include subjects previously taught in the district at classes supported by the Government's Science and Art Department, for only these could get the department's grants. But it seems not to have been unduly restricted since it was this committee which chose the 38 subjects that the Polytechnic provided for study by those first 504 students when it opened for its first session in September 1891.

William Street, now Calderwood Street, as depicted in an 1890s Prospectus. The main hall replaced the Duke of Wellington public house (bottom right) in 1935. The buildings in the distance on the other side of Thomas Street have gone, and Marks & Spencer now stands on the site.

2

Honeymoon Days – and a Rude Shock

1891–1894

⊢ ▓◈▓ ⊢•⊣ ▓◈▓ ⊢•⊣ ▓◈▓ ⊢•⊣ ▓◈▓ ⊢•⊣ ▓◈▓ ⊣

THOSE 504 STUDENTS – the forerunners of the University of Greenwich's 17,500 of 1995 – were not the only members of Woolwich Polytechnic. A further 121 were members of the Institute, making a total of 625. Indeed, those who were students only were at a disadvantage. While full members of the Polytechnic Institute could use the whole building including the gymnasium, formally opened that October, and could belong to the Polytechnic's many clubs, students who were not members had only the right to use the building's coffee room. Members of the Institute also paid reduced fees for classes.

Other activities in which Institute members could take part included Saturday evening concerts staged on a platform at one end of the gym, and 'Pleasant Sunday Afternoons', also conducted in the gym, where one C. J. Hunt would talk to audiences of five or six hundred men on religious themes. On weekday evenings the gym was used for sporting activities. From 6.30 till 8.00 members could practise gymnastics or sports on their own, from 8.00 till 10.00 there was formal instruction in fencing, boxing, single sticks and Indian club swinging. Soon the gym's equipment and instructors were augmented by its merger with the Royal Arsenal Mechanics Institute Swimming and Gymnastic Society, which had prospered under the brothers Arthur and Alfred Hutton. The Huttons became honorary assistant gymnastic instructors at the Polytechnic and brought with them their society's gymnastic equipment. Nor were gymnastics a male preserve at the Polytechnic, which in 1892 started a ladies' gymnastic class. This was only seven years after Madame Österberg had opened the college in Hampstead which was to give women for the first time systematic courses in the teaching of PE – the college which was to move to Dartford and merge with the Polytechnic in 1976.

The spirit of comradeship among early Poly members is suggested by its Christmas walk. In 1917, when the walk had become an annual event, one of the

In 1892 the Polytechnic started a ladies' gymnastics class. Clockwise from bottom right: *Sword exercise; wand exercise; the rather formidable-looking instructor, Miss Sims; a club solo; skipping drill; and dumb-bells.*

original walkers remembered how, on a 'typical December evening some twenty-three years ago when the usual closing notice was posted in the old Polytechnic building . . . a couple of the hardy ones' suggested a walk the following day – also an Arsenal holiday. At 10.00 next morning some 14 started from Plumstead Common and walked via Bexley, Crayford, and Dartford to Farningham.

The Bull at Farningham saw us demolish a whole dish of chops, etc., none of which had been previously ordered or prepared, indeed some of the party helped peel potatoes for the meal we wanted so badly. Another item which stands out vividly was the order, 'two chops each and one for the dog', said dog being George Golding's now defunct Gyp, whose obituary notice found a place in our Club Gossip in the old Magazine thus – 'Alas poor Gyp! – RIP'. A quiet hour after the meal, during which a piano and song played its part in the outing, thence onwards through the Crays . . . [and] back through Sidcup to Eltham and so to Woolwich brought our first jaunt to an end, but as we stood on Woolwich Common wishing each other a Merry Christmas and good night, each

voted the walk one of the finest days the Polytechnic Boys had ever experienced.

George Golding had been one of the earliest supporters of the Polytechnic's founders and a member of the Institute's first Council. The Athletic Club was his special enthusiasm and he was largely responsible for its athletic meeting in 1888. Subsequently he was its first life member and president, a position he held for 32 years. In 1933 his obituary in the Magazine described him as 'a man of great charm and inestimable worth, beloved by all with whom he came in contact.'

The 1891–2 session of the Polytechnic was so successful that Hogg even considered moving to Woolwich, writing to Didden in January, 'I have, I think, often told you that were I not so deeply engaged at Regent Street there is nothing I should like better than settling in Woolwich, and working in that same Institute as I used to work at Long Acre.' And in July, 'Supposing I should elect to come down to Woolwich, is there a reasonably good house at a reasonable rental which I could get, furnished if possible?' Though he did not come to Woolwich, he succeeded that summer in finding the Polytechnic a better playing-field, at Little Heath, Charlton, where soccer (but not rugger) could be played. He also encouraged his favourite nephew, Charles Campbell, to move to Woolwich. When Campbell arrived in November he wrote,

> It is just about fourteen months ago that, lunching one Sunday with Mr Hogg, I first met Frank Didden, and heard of the actual existence of the Woolwich Polytechnic, and so interested was I in what he told me that I asked my uncle the same afternoon whether he thought that I should be able to supply at all the need that was wanted. He at once seemed as anxious to see me there as I was to go.

The Athletic Club, given official status in 1890, was open to 'all young fellows with any taste or desire for outdoor recreation' (from the Prospectus of 1891).

Ladies' tailoring room, 1900s. By 1892–3 the Polytechnic offered classes in 80 subjects.

Right: *New Chemistry labs were built in 1892, and (below) Organic and Inorganic Chemistry syllabuses from a Prospectus of the 1890s described topics not out of place in courses of a similar level today.*

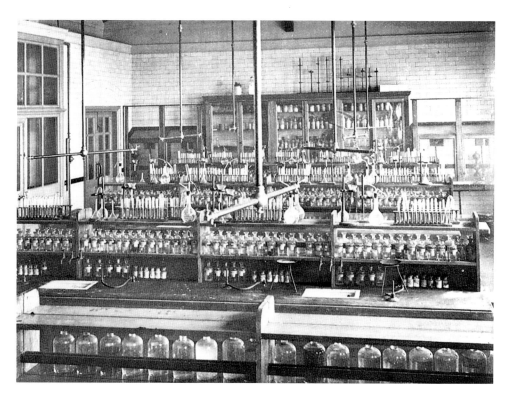

ORGANIC CHEMISTRY.

LECTURER:

LIONEL M. JONES, B.Sc., A.R.C.S., F.C.S.

ELEMENTARY.

On Tuesday at 7 p.m.

Scope of this Branch of Chemistry. Methods in use for Qualitative and Quantitative Estimation, &c. Boiling Point, and Melting Point Determinations.

Hydrocarbons, Homologous Series, Paraffins, Olefines, and Acetylenes. Their general formulæ and characteristics, with further study of the more important members. .

Saturated and unsaturated compounds.

The Halogen derivatives of paraffin and olefines, ALCOHOLS, ETHERS, ALDEHYDES, KETONES, ACIDS, ESTERS, or ETHEREAL SALTS, AMINES. The general properties and modes of preparation of these classes of compounds, with special reference to the more important members.

Mixed compounds, as Hydroxy Acids, etc.
Di- and tri-acid Alcohols, glycerol.
Di- and tri-basic acids.
The Carbohydrates :—Sugar, Starch, etc.
Cyanogen, and Cyanogen compounds, Urea.

PRACTICAL WORK will consist of the preparation of the more important compounds, and the detection of the commoner organic acids, &c., in salts and mixtures.

Text Book: "Organic Chemistry," vol. 1 (*Perkin and Kipping*).

Classes in ADVANCED ORGANIC CHEMISTRY will be arranged if a sufficient number of Students present themselves, and will be held at hours to suit the convenience of students.

Text Book: "Organic Chemistry," vol. 2 (*Perkin and Kipping*). Bernstein's "Organic Chemistry."

INORGANIC CHEMISTRY (*Continued*).

HONOURS STAGE.

Monday at 7 p.m.

In addition to the above subjects, the following will be studied :—

The properties of all the elementary bodies and their more important combinations (with the exception of the compounds of carbon).

Modern theories and laws relating to thermal phenomena of chemical combination, thermal unit, effect, and equivalent in mechanical effect, theory of flame and cause of luminosity, principles of spectrum analysis, dissociation, diffusion of gases, electrolysis, isomorphism, solution.

Recent discoveries and investigations in inorganic chemistry.

PRACTICAL INORGANIC CHEMISTRY.

ELEMENTARY.

Friday from 8 to 10 p.m.

Students in this course will themselves carry out the preparation of the elements and compounds enumerated in the elementary theoretical syllabus, and the experimental demonstration of their properties, and will receive instruction in the principles of qualitative analysis.

ADVANCED.

Wednesday or Monday, from 8 to 10 p.m.

The reactions of all the common metals and acids and methods of analysis for the examination of complex mixtures, &c., will be studied.

HONOURS.

In this course more difficult qualitative work will be dealt with, and the quantitative methods of estimating the more common metals and acids will be studied ; this will include volumetric analysis, the preparation and use of standard solutions, &c.

NOTE.—Students attending the Practical Classes are expected to attend lectures also, otherwise double fees will be charged.

During the next ten years Campbell was an active member of the Governing Body.

For the instructional session of 1892–3 the Polytechnic offered classes in 80 subjects and the number of 'class entries' increased by 50 per cent. Music, nautical astronomy and dressmaking (for women) were some now added. Already Woolwich students were winning medals and exhibitions. During the 1892–3 session two won Whitworth exhibitions, out of the 30 competed for throughout the country, and the following year so did three more, a number equalled only by the Provincial School, Glasgow. That year three students won Queen's Prizes, also competed for nationally. The Polytechnic itself gave silver and bronze medals, the majority in these two years for metal-plate work, although, in the words of the 1893–4 annual report, 'we have not, hitherto, been able to devote very much attention to the teaching of so-called "Technical Subjects".'

The metal-plate work teacher, James Moir – responsible for the successes in this subject as well as a continual agitator for a library – was one of a loyal staff, most of whom did evening work at the Polytechnic in addition to their daytime teaching, for low fees. Moir was paid £1 a week for three evening classes. Other teachers included Henry Angle, almost stone deaf, author of geometry textbooks, and J. Howard Hale, whose art lessons at 2.30 on Tuesdays and Thursdays were the first daytime classes. Science, however, had been the Polytechnic's 'chief task', the 1893–4 report explained, and it was science teaching that made more space essential.

In 1892 new laboratories for chemistry were built in what remained of No. 47's garden. At the same time the Council decided to buy 49 William Street which was demolished and replaced with laboratories for chemistry and metallurgical studies. Part of the aim was to bring to the Polytechnic classes in practical chemistry which were being held at the Royal Arsenal.

In 1893 the Council also built a new small hall and established a library. The cost of these improvements and extensions was heavy, but now at last the Polytechnic was given a grant by the City Parochial Foundation and an implied commitment to continue this annually. In the same year the Technical Education Board of the London County Council (of which Sidney Webb was the chairman) gave it £750 for equipment. The Board was established in 1893 as a result of the 1889 Technical Instruction Act. This in turn had been a consequence of general anxiety throughout the country that Britain would fail to compete successfully with countries like Germany and France unless it gave its people a better education. Nineteen years earlier, Forster, when introducing his 1870 Education Bill, had told Parliament, 'If we are to hold our position . . . among the nations of the world, we must make up the smallness of our numbers by increasing the intellectual force of the individual.'

The 1889 Act was specifically intended to create a technically literate working class. It gave local authorities the power to spend money raised by a one-penny rate on 'technical or manual instruction'. Technical instruction meant 'instruction in the principles of science and art applicable to industries' (though not 'the teaching of the practice of any trade or industry or employment'). Manual instruction meant 'instruction in the use of tools, processes of agriculture, and modelling in clay, wood, or other material'. The local authority was empowered to establish a committee to put the aims of the Act into practice, hence the LCC's Technical Education Board.

By chance, the funds available to the Board were increased. In 1890, Parliament considered a bill putting a tax of 6d. per gallon on spirits, the money to be used to compensate the owners of public houses when these were compulsorily closed by the local authorities. By the time the clauses concerning compensation had been deleted, as a result of opposition from the temperance party and the public house licence holders, the tax had already been voted, so the Chancellor of the Exchequer persuaded Parliament to give the money it raised to local authorities, and allow them to spend it on technical education. The LCC had failed to take advantage of the permission until Hogg, as an alderman, persuaded it that this was its duty. Woolwich and other Polytechnics were then given important grants from what became popularly known as the 'whisky money'.

The Technical Education Board, however, only made its grant along with a significant condition: that the Polytechnic appoint an Educational Principal, something it had not previously had. Frederick Garrett was appointed in the same year. It was the education which the Polytechnic could provide that interested the TEB. Nor did the two grants prevent a financial crisis. At the conclusion of the 1893–4 session the Polytechnic was apparently well established and functioning in all the ways its founders had hoped. On the one hand it was holding classes in a widening range of subjects; on the other its many social, sporting, and quasi-religious societies and clubs were flourishing. The annual report on the year's session (which dealt exclusively with educational matters) gave no hint that anything was wrong. It was therefore a considerable shock not only to members and students but to the whole Woolwich community when, in June that year, it was announced that the Polytechnic would close.

The 1889 Technical Education Act aimed to create a technically literate working class. Syllabus for shorthand (below), and (bottom) notice of a competition, both from a Prospectus from the mid-1890s.

3

Salvation and its Price

1894

━━━━━━━━━━━━━━━━━━━━━━━━━━━━━━━━━━━━━━

I F THE ABRUPT CLOSURE of the Polytechnic in July 1894 was a shock to its students and the public, it did not surprise the trustees who had seen a crisis coming at least eight months earlier. Then (December 1893) they had decided not to appeal to the public for funds because of 'the state of trade, agricultural depression etc.'. Their problem was a simple one: the Polytechnic had run out of money. By this time its trustees had spent between £16,000 and £18,000 on buildings, sites, and running costs, and were supporting an overdraft of £6,000 which was almost exhausted.

In January 1894 a scheme of rescue and proposals for an 'incoming Governing Body' were already being discussed with the London County Council's Technical Education Board, to which the trustees had inevitably gone for help. During the next six months, however, they discussed appeals to the City Parochial Foundation and the War Office and the raising of a mortgage on the Polytechnic's buildings as ways of paying off its debts and so avoiding handing over all control to the TEB. Only when these schemes had failed did Hogg write, on 11 July, to the TEB's secretary, offering to negotiate the handing over of the Polytechnic with all its assets, its overdraft paid off, provided the TEB would meet certain conditions. These included 'That the Institute be carried on under a scheme to be approved by the Charity Commissioners . . . exactly similar to that under which the Polytechnic (Regent Street) is worked,' and that the trustees:

> be given the free use of the hall and such adjoining rooms as may be necessary on Sundays for the purpose of holding . . . unsectarian religious services. . . . Furthermore, that the general lines of the Polytechnic (Regent Street) as to the admission of religious and social work, are to be followed as closely as possible.

Facing page: Icebound boats on the River Thames in Woolwich Reach during the winter of 1894–5.

Finally, I must report myself once more *hors de combat*, having met with an accident which I fear will incapacitate me for some weeks. Soon after Christmas I slipped on the pavement, and in recovering myself jarred my leg, and must have severely injured an important muscle of my thigh. The pain soon abated, and I thought no more about it. On Saturday, 21st, I went down to Merton Hall to play football as usual, but while I was walking to pick up a ball and not actually playing at all, the injured muscle snapped in two, and I had incontinently to desert my team, and make tracks for a surgeon. Since then I have been in bed, from which place I am writing this letter, and I mention my accident to account for my absence from the Poly. As the mountain can't come to Mahomet, however, I am bound to confess that Mahomets galore come to the mountain, and we have been having high times up in my bedroom.

Just as I was writing these last words a letter from Mr. Studd arrived, dated Venice, January 29th. He writes me: "A priest at Rome was highly amused to think that I, an Englishman, had indulged in such 'child's play' as football, and could hardly credit that in a few rare cases English sports actually resulted in fatal injuries. I don't know what he would have said to so grave and reverend a signor as yourself indulging in such follies." It turned out, however, that Mr. Studd's friend, the priest, was janitor of the Catacombs, so he may be excused for taking somewhat sepulchral views of life and its pleasures. On 8th inst. we shall see our old friend among us again, just in time, I am sorry to say, to miss Gap's tea. I hope soon to be able to get into the Poly. again in a "dot and carry one" kind of fashion. Meanwhile, good friends, farewell. I only hope you are all having as good a time on your ten toes as I am having on my back.

Part of an article by Quintin Hogg complaining of a football injury, in the Quintinian Supplement *to the* Polytechnic Magazine, *1893. Hogg was the editor of the* Polytechnic Magazine, *which covered all the Polytechnics.*

In response the Technical Education Board agreed to receive a deputation appointed at a public meeting, which included the local Member of Parliament, the rector of Woolwich and representatives of the Local Board of Health, of the Royal Arsenal, of the London and Provincial Bank, and of the Polytechnic. The delegation took with it recommendations from the meeting that the TEB should increase its annual grant to £1,500 for two years provided the City Parochial Foundation (or some other body) did the same and the Local Health Board contributed £500 a year; and that the TEB would also provide £2,500 for new buildings if some other body did the same.

These recommendations were accepted by the TEB and as a result the Polytechnic was able to reopen on 1 September and start its 1894–5 teaching session on the 24th, thus not missing any part of the new term. The Technical Education Board, however, imposed new, significant conditions. The new Governing Body would still have Hogg as its chairman, and the original trustees would be able to appoint three members, but they would be much outnumbered by the remainder who would be appointed by the TEB (6), the City Parochial Foundation (4, of whom Hogg was one), and the Local Health Board (3).

It was while this settlement was being devised that A. J. Naylor was appointed First Clerical Assistant at the Polytechnic, to become Clerk to the Governors a year later, a position he held for no less than 37 years. He had first become interested in the Poly in 1890 when he booked through Didden for one of its early foreign trips, this one to Madeira. When Naylor retired the then Principal wrote that it was almost impossible to visualize the Polytechnic without him. In Naylor's opinion the man who deserved special credit for solving the Polytechnic's 1894 problems was William Garnett, secretary to the TEB. To commemorate Garnett's contribution to London education the LCC in 1953 named the further education teacher training college which subsequently moved to Roehampton, Garnett College. It was an appropriate coincidence that, in 1987, the college that had been given his name was to merge with the institution which he had done so much to rescue (see Chapter 15). 'For a full year', Naylor wrote, 'Garnett attended all the meetings of the Governors and it was he who persuaded the TEB, City Parochial Foundation, Local Health Board and War Office to agree to their contributions.'

Early in 1895 as part of the settlement the Polytechnic was given a new charter which read:

The object of this institution is the promotion of the industrial skill, general knowledge, health and well-being of young men and women belonging to the poorer classes, by the following means:
I. Instruction in:
    (a) The general rules and principles for the arts and sciences applicable to any handicraft, trade or business.
    (b) The practical application of such general rules and principles in any handicraft trade or business.
    (c) Branches or details of any handicraft, trade or business, facilities for acquiring the knowledge of which cannot usually be obtained in the workshop or other place of business. The classes or lectures shall not be designed

or arranged so as to be in substitution for the practical experience of the workshop or place of business, but so as to be supplementary thereto.

II. Instruction suitable for persons intending to emigrate. [In the 1890s there was much unemployment at Woolwich. One young workman, Bill Oxley, remembered queuing outside factory gates from 5 a.m. in the hope of a day's work, fearing that he would be forced to join the army.]

III. Instruction in such other branches and subjects of art, science, language, literature and general knowledge as may be approved by the Governing Body.

IV. Public lectures or courses of lectures, musical and other entertainments and exhibitions.

V. Instruction and practice in gymnastics, drill, swimming and other bodily exercises.

VI. Facilities for the formation and meetings of clubs and societies.

VII. A library, museum and reading room or reading rooms.

The order in which these were placed, 'Instruction' first, 'facilities for clubs and societies' sixth and 'reading rooms' last, indicates all too clearly what were now to be the Polytechnic's priorities. There was also pressure to increase certain sorts of instruction. Just as the grants from the Arts and Sciences Department had been limited to classes in 'art, science, language, literature and general knowledge', so grants from the Technical Education Board were limited to classes providing 'technical and manual instruction as defined by the Technical Instruction Acts'.

These changes were not imposed on the Polytechnic without protest, both public and private. On 14 September 1894 the *Woolwich Herald* warned that they would 'mar in a very large degree the usefulness of the Polytechnic, and render it, in comparison with what it has been . . . a comparative failure'. The reformed Polytechnic might become 'a mere machinery for instructing in the sciences those young people who have already realised the importance of such studies, and who would pursue them whether the Polytechnic existed or not'.

A. J. Naylor, first clerical assistant and, from 1895–1932, Clerk of Governors.

The Charter of 1895 laid down that the Polytechnic should instruct the poorer classes in 'the general rules and principles for the arts and sciences . . . [and their] practical application to any handicraft, trade or business'. Below and left: Syllabuses from the late 1890s for Steam and the Steam Engine, Metallurgy, and Female Telegraph Clerks.

22

STEAM AND THE STEAM ENGINE.

LECTURER:
C. J. TOPPLE, M.I.M.E.

ELEMENTARY.

Wednesday, at 8.30 p.m.

HEAT.—Its nature and effects, measurement and mechanical equivalent, transmission.

STEAM.—Generation of, causes which influence boiling point, temperature, pressure and volume of steam, latent heat, saturated and superheated steam.

EXPANSION.—Mean pressure, gain by expansive working, condensation.

DISTRIBUTION of steam by slide valve, lap, lead, traver, valve diagram, simple forms of expansion valves.

ENGINES.—Early forms, modern non-condensing and condensing, simple and compound: indicator and indicator diagrams.

BOILERS.—Land, marine and locomotive; general construction.

DETAILS OF Steam engines and boiler fittings.

Text Book—Jamieson's "Steam and the Steam Engine."

METALLURGY.

LECTURER:
J. B. FARLIE, F.C.S.

ASSISTANT LECTURER
A. H. MUNDEY.

ELEMENTARY.

Tuesday at 7 p.m.

Definition and scope of metallurgy. Physical properties of metals, explanation of metallurgical terms. Slags and fluxes; refractory materials Classification and construction of furnaces and fuels; peat, wood, various kinds of coal and coke, charcoal, gaseous fuel. The calorific power of fuel. Methods of preparing coke; description of the ovens employed.

The metallurgy of iron and steel; copper, zinc, lead, tin, mercury, gold, and silver; their properties, ores, and methods of extraction from their ores.

Text Book.—Bloxam & Huntingdon's "Metals" (*Longmans*).

ADVANCED.

Thursday at 7 p.m.

In this course will be included all the subjects enumerated in the Elementary Syllabus, but treated in a more exhaustive manner.

The chemical principles involved will be closely studied, and the details of construction of Furnaces, &c., explained.

Electro-metallurgical processes will be experimentally demonstrated.

In addition to the foregoing metals, the properties, extraction and uses of the following will be studied—Platinum, Cobalt, Nickel, Arsenic, Antimony, Bismuth.

Text Book.—As above, and also Roberts & Austen's "Elements of Metallurgy" (*Griffin*).

56

SYLLABUS OF CIVIL SERVICE CLASSES—Continued.

FEMALE TELEGRAPH CLERKS.

Age, 15 to 18. Subjects of Examination—Arithmetic, Dictation, Handwriting, General Geography, Composition.

Candidates who have passed the Examination attend the Post Office Telegraph School to receive instruction in Telegraphy for which no charge is made. The instruction lasts three months, when they receive 10s. per week, rising to 14s. on taking full charge of an instrument, followed by annual rises up to 27s. per week. These appointments are very popular, and are eagerly sought after.

FEES   -   15s. per Term of 12 Weeks.

GENERAL INSTRUCTION.

Students who do not intend to compete for the Civil Service, but who wish to join the Classes for Dictation, Arithmetic, or other subjects, can do so at a special scale of fees on application to the Tutor.

'Instruction and practice in gymnastics, drill, swimming and other bodily exercises': the Polytechnic gym in the 1890s, from a Prospectus. Standing on the site of the garden of Barnes's house, it is still in daily use 100 years later.

Facing page: Advertisements from the Polytechnic Prospectus, 1900.

F. C. Garrett, Educational Principal 1893–5.

Next month a correspondent drew attention to a significant contrast: 'Under the old policy to draw new members to the Polytechnic was the first principle. Under the "new policy" the first aim is more students.' Both Webb and the Educational Principal, Frederick Garrett, replied, Webb pointing out that the Technical Education Board had saved the Polytechnic and that the purposes for which it could give grants were limited by law, Garrett denying that 'the vitality of the place had largely disappeared'.

Garrett, inevitably, because of his position, was a supporter of the new order, while Didden resisted it. At a meeting of the trustees four days before the new charter was published (25 January 1895):

the relative positions of the secretary Frank Didden and the educational director F. C. Garrett were discussed, Mr Hogg giving it as his opinion that one would have to go. The general feeling of the meeting was that Garrett was not very much in sympathy with the main objects the Trustees had in view when they founded the Institute, namely to influence the morals of the members both by unsectarian religious teaching and healthful athletic exercise. Under these circumstances it was thought that Mr T. A. Denny and Mr Campbell (the representatives of the trustees on the Governing Body) should endeavour to influence those members of the Governing Body who are in sympathy with them, so that in the event of the question of Garrett and Didden arising at any meeting, they may have sufficient following to secure the retention of Didden even at the expense of Garrett leaving.

At first they seemed to fail. It was to replace Didden that Naylor was appointed Clerk to the Governors, while Didden was demoted to Head of the

Social Side and forced to give up his top floor of 47 William Street so that it could be used for classrooms and a laundry. But this did not end the matter, which was discussed at length, first by a special committee of the Governing Body, then in April at two long meetings of the Governing Body itself. The issue was whether the Social Side under Didden was independent or merely a department under Garrett's control.

On 29 April Denny, defending Didden as the trustees had suggested, told the meeting:

> There would be bad feeling among the members if Mr Didden were put out. But for Mr Didden there had been no Polytechnic. He had worked earnestly for many years and the Governors could not desert him now. In the abstract one head was best but Mr Garrett would not work with Mr Didden.

When another Governor asked 'on what authority it was stated that Mr Garrett would not work with Mr Didden', Governor Campbell 'replied that Mr Garrett had said to him "If I stay I must be first – if I am first Didden must go."'

Eventually Didden himself was called and asked 'whether he would or would not accept a position subordinate to a Principal if desired to do so by the Governors'.

> Mr Didden replied that he could not answer the question in that form. The chairman then asked Mr Didden whether he would serve under a Principal only if the Principal were approved by him.

> Mr Didden replied that he would require to know who the Principal was and would be willing to work under him only if he were in sympathy with all the branches of the Polytechnic work.

The meeting finally voted 8 to 6 that the Governors should advertise for both a new Principal and a new Head of the Social and Recreative Side (after an amendment to advertise only for a new Principal had been rejected because of the injury this might do to Garrett). The outcome was surprising. From 91 applicants for the position of Principal a special committee selected Andrew Ashcroft, Demonstrator of Engineering in University College, London. Garrett had not applied and a suggestion by one Governor that he should nevertheless be considered, was rejected. Didden, however, was one of 81 applicants for Head of the Social Side, and it was he whom the same committee chose. Ultimately the Governors, perhaps persuaded by the arguments of Denny and Campbell, had decided that if one of the two must go it should be Garrett.

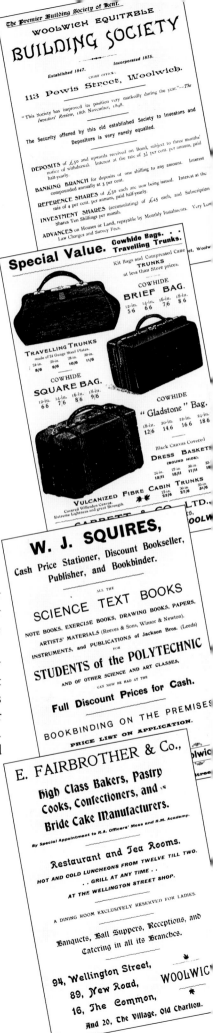

4

The Social Side Capitulates

1894–1904

━━

THOUGH THE INSTRUCTIONAL SIDE of the Polytechnic was now firmly established as its main business, this had also suffered during the hiatus, as Garrett made clear in his final report on the 1894–5 session. 'The closing of the Institute last summer,' he wrote, 'and the uncertainty during the autumn as to whether it would not again be closed at Christmas caused a number of Woolwich students to join classes at New Cross [Goldsmiths'] and other places and fully accounts for the decrease in the membership of most departments.' However, he considered that

> Bearing in mind the special difficulties . . . there is every reason to be satisfied with the work of the Session . . . 70 classes (exclusive of those in the School of Art) have been held in various Science, Technical and Commercial subjects, and have been attended by 1,252 students, while the Art department has been open on two afternoons and four evenings, and its classes have been joined by 171 students; the totals for the year being 1,423 'class entries' made by 717 individuals (518 being men and 199 women).

In the rest of his report Garrett noted other difficulties. One was the tendency of students to come to classes 'insufficiently equipped for their work; . . . never having learned to think exactly, or to express their ideas correctly, and almost ignorant of mathematics, they do not hesitate to join classes in advanced subjects by which it is almost impossible for them to profit.' To correct this the first meetings of classes had been 'thrown open to all' so that students could meet the lecturers and 'ascertain their fitness or otherwise for the class'.

More important was lack of teaching space. Most badly needed were physical, electrical and engineering laboratories, and two 'well equipped lecture

Facing page: 12.5 inch rifled muzzle-loader weighing 38 tonnes, outside the Royal Gun Factory in the Royal Arsenal, 1877–8. The Royal Arsenal and local industry furnished many students.

31

rooms each to accommodate about 80 students'.

Finally he wrote about the teaching staff,

> The present system whereby the Polytechnic only occupies teachers for a few hours during the week is not satisfactory, as they come here at the close of a day's work elsewhere, and consequently – though with the best will – cannot give their best energies to their classes . . . it is very desirable that at least the Heads of the chief departments should be in the service of the Institute only.

He nevertheless ended by thanking them warmly.

> It is difficult to particularise but I must specially acknowledge the services of Dr Draper and Mr Evans among the teaching staff, and of Mr Naylor in the office; that the institute has come so well through a period of such difficulty is in great part due to the hard work and valuable advice of these gentlemen.

He did not mention Didden.

During the four-year regime of Garrett's successor, Ashcroft, the Polytechnic expanded in two ways which, for clarity, are best described separately. Vital, if it were ever to prosper, was a response to the problem which Garrett considered most serious, the 'lack of proper accommodation' from which all departments were suffering. Garrett's opinion was backed by others. The head of the Art Department complained that in his classrooms 'the noises and foul language which frequently rise from women in William Street render it hopeless to get together satisfactory day classes.' In March 1896 George Golding formally protested that the Athletic Club committee could not meet because it had no room allotted to it. In a statement during his first session, the new Principal wrote 'we are holding some classes in the Laundry and Kitchen of the Domestic Economy School, and one in a room under the

The general art room and a corner containing sculptures, 1906.

Gymnasium which is little better than a cellar.' At the end of the session he added, 'we have now come to the limit of our present accommodation. It seems quite possible that during next Session we shall either have to engage outside rooms, or refuse to accept a number of students.' He admitted that in this next session (1896–7) new chemical and physical laboratories, a new art room and two large classrooms would probably be opened. These were to be in Lower Market Street (later Polytechnic Street) where the Governing Body had bought a group of houses which backed on to the garden of 47 William Street. A year later, however, he could still only report that the Governors had got as far as making a contract for the new buildings, and they were not finished until the 1897–8 session.

By then the engineering laboratory on the existing site was also ready. The dramatic difference these expansions made to the Polytechnic's teaching accommodation is suggested by the increase in its floor area, which more than doubled, from 7,100 sq. ft. to 16,000 sq. ft.

The new buildings were paid for largely by the Polytechnic's two principal supporting bodies, the Technical Education Board (£3,500) and the City Parochial Foundation (£500), but partly by subscriptions from Governors, staff, students, other members of the Institute, and the public, a demonstration of the continuing local enthusiasm for the Polytechnic. The War Office, on the other hand, gave nothing beyond its miserly annual grant of £200, although the Governors had written to the Marquess of Lansdowne, Secretary of State for War, pointing out the benefit which the new buildings would bring the Royal Arsenal by providing it with better-trained workmen. To mark the opening of the new buildings by Dr Collins, Chairman of the London County Council, the Polytechnic staged an exhibition to which five other Polytechnics, Birkbeck Institution and the People's Palace all contributed. The following year the Technical Education Board gave a further £978 for equipping the engineering laboratory. The main item bought was a small steam-engine plant consisting of a Cornish boiler 12 ft. long and 4 ft. 6 in. in diameter and a horizontal engine of about 10 horsepower.

The new engineering laboratory of 1897 contributed to a near-doubling of the teaching accommodation. Above left: Engineering workshop in the 1900s. Above: The heat engine laboratory, which remained largely unchanged from the 1900s through to the 1970s.

Mrs A. A. H. Gillanders, head of the School of Domestic Economy and Superintendent of all women's classes.

Alongside these vital increases in accommodation and equipment there were important additions to the variety of teaching the Polytechnic could offer, one of them significantly extending its daytime activities. The Art Department's afternoon classes had already been followed in March 1895 by a School of Domestic Economy for Girls. Within a few days the class of 45 was full. The following year Mrs A. H. H. Gillanders, till then teacher of laundrywork, took over the new school, also becoming Superintendent of all women's classes, positions she held for 24 years with such success that an LCC inspector named her in his report, regretting the loss the Polytechnic would suffer by her retirement.

Now in September 1897 a day school for boys was also opened. Starting with 72 boys, its numbers rose to 92 by the end of the session and to 102 the following year. For its third session (September 1899) girls were admitted and a mistress appointed. So, too, was a headmaster, T. F. Bowers, previously Head of the John Ruskin Board School, Camberwell. Though still under the Principal, Bowers had considerable powers of his own, including the right to dismiss any student 'whose attendance at the School is, in his judgement, detrimental to its welfare'.

At first the school was divided into two sections, technical and commercial, but the latter proved more popular and it was this which the Governors planned to expand. For the 1900 session, however, they decided to register it as a Science School, so that it would qualify for the Technical Education Board's grants and there would be no need to raise the fees. The Day School, as it was generally called, was the first secondary school in Woolwich and the Polytechnic's Governors deserve credit for their enterprise in launching it.

Facing page (above): *Spread from an illuminated book presented to Archdeacon Escreet, who succeeded Hogg as Chairman of the Governing Body in 1903, on his retirement in 1907; and* (below left and right) *the coats of arms of Woolwich Polytechnic and Thames Polytechnic.*

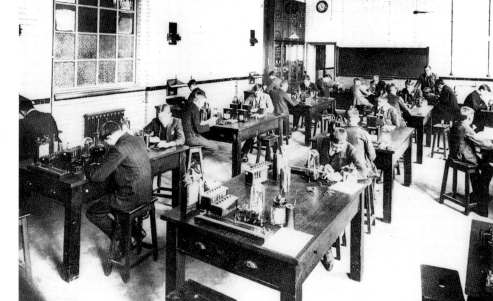

The elementary electrical laboratory in the 1900s.

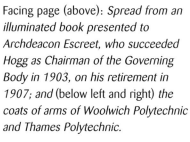

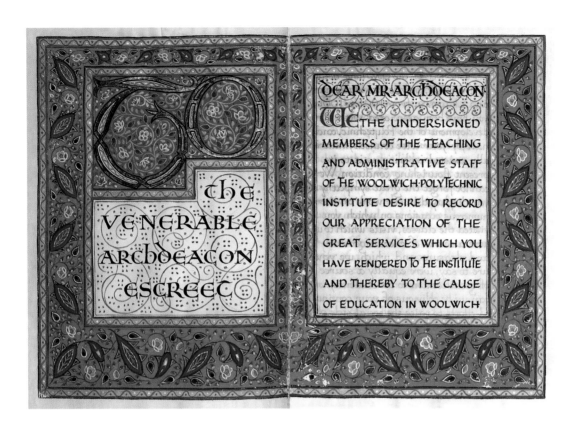

TO THE VENERABLE ARCHDEACON ESCREET

DEAR MR ARCHDEACON

WE THE UNDERSIGNED MEMBERS OF THE TEACHING AND ADMINISTRATIVE STAFF OF THE WOOLWICH·POLYTECHNIC INSTITUTE DESIRE TO RECORD OUR APPRECIATION OF THE GREAT SERVICES WHICH YOU HAVE RENDERED TO THE INSTITUTE AND THEREBY TO THE CAUSE OF EDUCATION IN WOOLWICH

DISCERE AGERE CONFICERE

The Armorial Ensigns of

THAMES POLYTECHNIC

It was at the teaching of engineering, however, that Ashcroft believed the Polytechnic should aim to excel. From his arrival he lectured in the subject himself. 'Woolwich', he wrote, 'is said in some respects to resemble a Provincial town; may we hope that it will follow the example of some Provincial towns, and produce men who will help to meet the urgent needs of the district.' The urgent need of Woolwich, with the Arsenal as easily its main employer, could only be for well-trained engineers. One result of his promotion of the subject was that engineering classes enrolled 398 students in his last complete year, compared to 244 in his first, another that in the following year a matriculation class in engineering was launched.

During Ashcroft's time some rivalry between the teaching and social side of the Polytechnic continued. In July 1895 the Governing Body had reprimanded Didden for arranging a student trip to Switzerland without obtaining the permission of the Social and Recreative Committee, and the following February it ordered the Head of the Social Department to act under the direction of Governor Campbell and to consult the Principal before arranging trips. In September 1895 the Governing Body told Didden that he did not have a consultative seat at its meetings, adding that they considered it desirable for the Head of the Social Side to be about the Institute in the evenings. In 1897 the *Woolwich Herald* printed a letter complaining of 'a continuous starving and encroachment of the social side for the benefit of the educational'.

But the new accommodation eliminated one reason for friction. In June 1898 the secretary of the Athletic Club wrote to the Governors thanking them 'for many kindnesses shown during the past year and especially with regard to Room No. 11 which has recently been handed over to the club'. And on the whole these were years of harmony. Typically in July 1898 the Governors gave way to Didden when he objected to the phrase in the following year's prospectus which stated that the religious services at the Polytechnic were held 'by permission of the Governors' and agreed to delete it. In his early statement (January 1896) Ashcroft had declared his support for the Institute's societies, which

> being all self-governing, give the members very valuable practical experience in the principles of government. The members of the various Committees and Heads of these Societies learn that it is not always, or often, an enviable position to be a responsible manager; that those in high places have often to sacrifice their own personal interests for the general good. I believe that a great deal can be done by the managers of such institutions as this, by rightly influencing the members in the management of their societies.

In marked contrast to Garrett's final report which had made no mention of the social side, Ashcroft each year gave details of its fortunes. In 1896 he reported that during the year membership had risen from 249 to 308. The popular Saturday concerts were being held again and had incurred a much reduced annual loss (£10 against £63). The Athletic Club's best supported activity was swimming (68 members), the least popular cycling (25 members). Next year there was a further 8½ per cent increase in membership. Almost twice as many

Facing page: *The formal entrance to the Polytechnic following construction in 1916, this block is at the corner of Thomas Street and Calderwood Street. After refurbishment in 1995, it was christened the Calderwood entrance in memory of William Calderwood, Chairman of the Governing Body 1910–13 and 1930–4. Calderwood, a local industrialist, was also an active trade unionist and the LCC's representative governor. He was also a governor of Avery Hill College.*

Men's Club Room, early 1900s, part of which can still be seen, although without the billiard table.

were attending the gymnasium classes. (The instructor reported that the ladies' class had more than doubled, due to an excellent display they had given in April.) But swimming was again the most popular and cycling the least popular sport. In 1898 membership fell but by July 1899 it had recovered most of the loss.

In general Ashcroft's four years saw a steady revival and expansion of the Institute's core evening classes, now numbering around 100 and covering not only the sciences, engineering, technology, languages and the arts, but book-keeping, typewriting, and elocution, class entries expanding from 1,423 in Garrett's last year to 2,295 in Ashcroft's, the number of students attending these classes from 717 to 1,111. If the Woolwich Polytechnic's character had changed it was proving no less valuable to the town it served.

The calm of Ashcroft's four years did not last. On 4 August 1899 he wrote to the Governors,

> Having been appointed Assistant to Professor Unwin I am compelled to tender you my resignation of the post of Principal of the Woolwich Polytechnic. I shall be glad if arrangements can be made, at any rate in the day time, for me to be free at the end of September next.

The Governors minuted no explanation of Ashcroft's unexpected resignation. They were, perhaps, preoccupied with the problem of what to do seven weeks later when on 24 September the new session would start – far too soon for a successor to be appointed. As late as 20 November they were still asking Ashcroft to 'retain his office as Principal until the new Principal takes up his duties'. The man they had by then chosen from 49 applicants was John Ryan, Professor of

Engineering at University College, Bristol. Ryan did not accept the position without being assured that their vote for him had been unanimous.

The second disruption of the 1899–1900 session was even less to be expected or avoided: the Boer War. Most schools and colleges were to some extent affected by this faraway event, but none so immediately and seriously as the Woolwich Polytechnic. In his first annual report (July 1899) Ryan wrote that it had been

> an exceptional year in which the most serious difficulties have been encountered. The South African War has made unusual demands upon the energies of those employed in the Royal Arsenal, and . . . seriously affected the regularity of their attendance throughout the Session. And in cases where students who were working overtime made a special effort to attend the classes, they were at times physically unable to do full justice to such studies as called for sustained attention or involved some mental strain.

Ryan used his own mechanical engineering class as an example. Of the six students who had entered it, 'one had to give up because he was working till 9 o'clock on weekdays, in addition to Sunday employment', another failed 'through the strain of extra hours at the Arsenal', another did not attempt the examination, and another failed through 'omitting the practical work'. In contrast the fifth not only passed Part I but gained 'the distinction of a First Class in Part II', while the sixth 'who was not required to do overtime, occupied the highest place in the Honours List and gained a Silver Medal, with a Prize of £3'.

This did not prevent the people of Woolwich, students of the Polytechnic no doubt among them, from celebrating the relief of Mafeking.

> I had never witnessed such signs of joy and hilarity in the streets for it was a night of all nights . . . I remember that the Star and Garter, next door to our premises in Powis Street, that day housed most of the influentials of Woolwich. Starting about midday with loud expressions of loyalty and riotous choruses interspersed with liberal consumption of whisky and other beverages, the company in the end became too intoxicated to utter even the faintest 'Hoorah'.

During the following years the Polytechnic was embarrassed by another problem. This was a result of the increasing interest which the Government's Board of Education began to take in its teaching and its premises, sending inspectors to visit these. On the whole their reports were favourable, but one inspector criticized the School of Art so severely that the Board withdrew recognition.

The decision was perhaps a fair one. The school's life class, for example, had been discontinued (during the 1899–1900 session the Governors had resolved that it be confined to the study of the male figure). And when the Governors protested to the Board it replied, 'from Mr Ryan's letter of 27 March, it seems that there is no legitimate demand for such a class in this engineering neighbourhood;

The Arsenal gate adorned for celebrations of the relief of Mafeking by British forces after siege by the Boers, 1900.

where, he writes, "the small available Art Room space should obviously be dedicated to the legitimate needs of the locality".' The Governors, nevertheless, resolved to maintain the School of Art for at least a further year, and in 1903 another inspector reported that he had visited 'A very satisfactory class, carefully and efficiently taught . . . though the number attending is very small for a town the size of Woolwich.'

The School of Art continued to be a problem. In March 1904 Ryan's successor wrote. 'This department is one of the least satisfactory in the institute', and recommended the appointment of a full-time headmaster. It was only in the following year that the LCC successfully supported an application to the Board of Education that it should be recognized again.

Though other departments adapted themselves to the war and resumed their steady growth, the Arsenal and its varying fortunes were a background to the Polytechnic of which it was always aware and sometimes violently reminded. At 8.10 a.m. on 18 June 1903 there was a 'terrible Lyddite explosion' in the Danger Buildings. 'All morning relatives of workers in the danger area crowded into Arsenal Square, seeking information, asking questions yet fearing what might be the answer.' Sixteen died and 15 were seriously injured.

The Arsenal's domination of the town before the First World War is suggested by Margaret Skelton in her novel, *Below the Watchtowers*, 1926:

He stood outside the station . . . The noise! Terrific! Waggons, guns, lorries, horses, trams, workmen, soldiers, women, struggled in the roadway from or towards the Arsenal. The air throbbing with strange sounds, seemed to move audibly in his ears and to swathe him from his fellows, except as they afforded a spectacle of other isolated atoms struggling in the palpable

The equally imposing entrance of the Chatham Dockyard, from a slightly earlier date. Nearly a century after this picture was taken, the University would move into premises there in the former naval quarters.

atmosphere. The revolution, the countless wheels hummed and purred unendingly, and below that sound – throb, throb, throb – deep, ominous, and barbaric, the tom-tom beat of a colossal hammer fell at relentless intervals.

In these latter days there crashes out at intervals from beside the river a rending shattering sound. 'Beware!' screams a voice into the shuddering air.

The buildings thrill and palpitate in acknowledgement of that warning; the gulls pause for a second in their wheelings and scream answeringly; the startled stranger makes hasty enquiry of the inhabitants who smile with pitying casualness upon the questioner, half proud of the great Gun that is the god of Gunton [Woolwich]. For these same inhabitants are his thralls: they make him, they train in his service, they eat by him, they drink by him, and in due time maybe they die by him.

In the year of that explosion the Technical Education Board, which had already played such an important part in the Polytechnic's development, made an equally significant contribution to its future when it named Avery Hill as a suitable site for the sort of teacher training college which the LCC should found. Some 80 years later the Polytechnic's merger with Avery Hill was to be its most important – probably securing its survival (see Chapter 14).

Meanwhile, in 1901 the Governors had established the Penfold Medal, with funds raised by the people of Woolwich to commemorate Abel Penfold, who had died the previous year while still serving as a Governor. The gold medal was to be awarded to the most distinguished student each year. The Wiseman and Withers Exhibition was first awarded three years later to provide £100 a year for

Abel Penfold, member of Governing Body 1895–1900. The Penfold Medal was created in his memory.

three years to support the education at the Polytechnic of a young Arsenal or factory worker of the town.

In the summer of 1901 the Governing Body agreed to absorb the Woolwich University Education Association into the Polytechnic by forming classes which would carry on the association's work. Members were to be granted equal privileges with Polytechnic students. This was the sort of extension into advanced teaching which Ryan favoured. Towards the end of the 1901–2 session, however, he made it clear that he considered the Polytechnic's problems could not be solved by such minor expansions, and were more fundamental than those caused by the Boer War. He was not alone in recognizing that things were wrong. In May 1904 a correspondent wrote to the *Kentish Independent*, 'The Woolwich Polytechnic does not compare with its sister institutions, considering the date of its foundation and the large district in which it is placed' – a view probably becoming common.

As a consequence, in June 1902 Ryan presented the Education Committee of the Governing Body with an eight-page pamphlet containing his analysis of the Polytechnic's weaknesses and proposals for putting them right. Most serious was the way in which individual students were entirely free to take as many or as few classes as they liked, in any combination. During the session then ending, out of 398 who could loosely be called (by their employment) engineering students, 187 had taken one course only. Just as 'deplorable' was the fact than only 97 had studied mathematics during the previous winter. Many were thus coming to physics or engineering courses with far too little mathematics to benefit from them.

After giving details of the numbers taking particular courses, Ryan wrote,

By the above Analysis the need for systematic organization in the Engineering Department is abundantly clear. . . . Profiting by experience I now propose to offer courses involving say three or four Subjects, at a compound

Originally built 1716–20 by Sir John Vanbrugh for the Crown, this building was used as the Board Room for the officers of the Ordnance, and from 1741 as the Royal Military Academy. More recently, it was used as the Royal Artillery Officers' Mess. It is to become the Educational Centre and Library for a proposed Artillery Museum. (Picture from 1969.)

fee for the whole Course, which will offer some immediate and tangible advantage to Students. I strongly recommend the establishment of such Courses, which may be provisionally arranged to consist of four Subjects at a compound fee of 15/-.

It would be much more convenient if we could wait until the New Buildings are available, before attempting to reorganise our teaching. Nevertheless I feel that the time for action is now. The War being at an end it is very probable that the hours of work in the Arsenal will revert more or less to the normal. . . . This then is the time for bringing forward arrangements which may be enduring and which may bear fruit in the future.

Six weeks later he presented his recommendations to the Governing Body, along with his annual report, in which he wrote,

Taking a general survey of the Results I consider them better than those of last year, though still lamentably short of what they should be. Unless next year's work brings about a very significant improvement I think you would be justified in contemplating a large measure of reconstruction, to take effect on commencing the Session 1903–4 with New Buildings.

The 1902–3 prospectus duly included eight compound courses of the sort Ryan proposed, and when he came to write his account of the session he considered them to have been its great success. But by half-way through the session in mid-March he had clearly concluded that the 'very significant improvement of the Polytechnic as a whole' for which he had hoped was not occurring and that a further 'large measure of reorganization' was needed. The proposals he made for this had as their most important feature the appointment of full-time heads of the departments of engineering, physics, mathematics, and chemistry. Twelve days later the Governors voted their approval.

All this suggests that Ryan was a man with radical plans for reform which he was keenly promoting. In two years he had proposed two major groups of changes which were to prove vital to the Polytechnic's successful growth. Nor, more importantly, does it suggest that his efforts were being frustrated by conservative Governors. Indeed, on 24 May he attended a Technical Education Board meeting at which the Board was to discuss his proposals for heads of departments which the Governors had sent to it with their recommendation.

At their meeting next day they were not a little astonished when he told them that this matter had not been discussed because at the meeting he had been appointed Principal of the Paddington Technical College. As a consequence he would cease to be Principal of Woolwich Polytechnic.

The Governors at once asked him for a statement about the reasons for his resignation. When they met again he merely provided them with an uninformative letter in which he restated his resignation. By this time, however, he had met two of them, who now reported that their discussion had centred on Clause 8 of his conditions of employment. This read: 'The Principal will be responsible to the Governors for the maintenance of discipline throughout the whole institution at all times, and all officers, teachers and assistants will be under his general direction.'

This makes Collin Brooks's suggestion (*An Educational Adventure*, 1954) that it was 'temperament, or circumstance, or a combination of both, which did not permit Dr Ryan patiently to await the acceptance of his reforms and their implementation' seem a misleading explanation of his resignation, and strongly suggests that the real reason was the problem which had troubled the Polytechnic since 1893 when the Technical Education Board insisted on the appointment of an Educational Principal in return for rescuing it financially: the semi-independence which the Social Side had continued to claim.

Earlier events of Ryan's time hint at this interpretation. In March 1900 the Governing Body set up a subcommittee to report on the expenditure of the Social Department. When, the following month, they were told that the London County Council had resolved 'that the attention of the Governing Body of the Polytechnic be called to the large expenditure of the Social Side', they urged their subcommittee to report as soon as possible.

This it did in October that year when it made detailed recommendations about the membership of the Social Side and the subscriptions members of its various societies and clubs should pay. But such proposals failed to answer a more important part of the problem, and a year later the Governing Body resolved somewhat testily that 'the subcommittee previously appointed to consider the question of the division of Establishment Charges, should go into the matter forthwith.'

The matter had, indeed, become urgent. The Governors were currently hoping for a £2,000 grant from the Technical Education Board towards a further and larger extension of its buildings in Lower Market Street, but less than a month later they were told that the TEB had referred back the proposed grant

Drawing Office, 1900s.

in consequence of certain statements . . . respecting the expenditure of the Social Department of the Polytechnic, which statements his Board desired to investigate before sanctioning the grant. The Board's Officers had therefore been authorised to investigate the accounts of the Polytechnic with a view to ascertaining how far the statements made were correct.

The problem was the old one, that grants from the Technical Education Board had to be for the Polytechnic's educational, not social, activities.

By then Ryan himself had been carrying out his own investigation, and on 28 November he produced for the subcommittee twelve pages of 'Statistics of Social Uses of the Polytechnic as bearing on Social Proportions of Establishment Charges', which offered calculations based either on space used, time used, or attendance of members. In his introduction he wrote that he was merely giving the committee 'the means of coming to a conclusion without unnecessary delay and without prolonged meetings'. Three weeks later the subcommittee reported that it had used Ryan's figures to help it decide that 25 per cent was the Social Side's appropriate share – a figure which apparently satisfied the Technical Education Board, since the following February it approved the grant.

Modelling room in the School of Art.

Events which followed Ryan's unexpected resignation provide stronger evidence that it was caused by difficulties with the Social Side. At their next meeting the Governors widened their discussion to include the early resignations of Ryan's two predecessors, and resolved:

> That a committee be formed with power to act to revise the memoranda as respecting the position and duties of the Principal so as to emphasise the authority of the Principal in the Polytechnic.
>
> To report upon the position of the Institute Council and the Question of reorganization raised by Dr Ryan's resignation.

Nominally this committee was, thus, to enquire into the vestigial 'Council' which had survived alongside the Governing Body created in 1894, and it duly recommended that the council should be abolished. But its third and fifth recommendations revealed its real purpose by proposing a far more significant change.

> 3. That the committee is of opinion that the time has now arrived for such a reorganization of the Social work of the Institute as will bring it into line with the present facts of Polytechnic life . . .
>
> 5. That having carefully considered the condition of affairs now obtaining at the Polytechnic the Committee is of opinion that it is a matter for serious consideration of the Governors whether it is desirable to continue the office of the Head of the Social Side.

Not surprisingly, the full Governing Body took over six months to bring itself to dismiss the man who had been Woolwich Polytechnic's founder. Twice it

The Arsenal Gate and Beresford Square, 1904. Although its surroundings have much changed, the gate itself has lasted, and underwent a major restoration in 1995.

deferred discussion of the committee's proposals, then appointed a fresh committee to reconsider paragraphs 3 and 5. Finally, however, on 21 December 1903 it resolved:

> As the placing of entire responsibility for the due and proper control of all Sections of the Polytechnic directly and completely in the hands of the Principal renders the retention of the office of Head of the Social Side unnecessary . . .
>
> (a) The services of the Head of the Social Side be dispensed with.
>
> (b) Formal notice be given him to vacate his office at the expiration of 2 years from 1st January 1904.
>
> (c) He be relieved from all further work in connection with the Polytechnic, on, and from, 1st January 1904 [in just ten days' time].

Resolutions which, by implication, criticized Didden so severely suggest that he had been, to put it mildly, a nuisance to the three Principals who had left while he was Head of the Social Side. The Technical Education Board showed no more gratitude to the man who had founded the Polytechnic. When asked to approve the payment of his salary for two more years (£400) it reduced the amount to £250. Hogg, if present, would perhaps have protected him from such ingratitude, but Hogg had died the previous January. The Governing Body had duly launched an appeal to raise £500 for a 'Quintin Hogg Scholarship' in mechanical engin-eering. Its final reference to Didden's dismissal was half a sentence explaining why he deserved *any* continuation of his salary.

Hogg's successor as Chairman, Canon Escreet, *was* present. Escreet (who later became an archdeacon) believed, according to Brooks, that the Institute should 'care for the minds and bodies of the young men and maidens and the care of their souls could safely be left to the priests, parsons and other clerics . . . appointed, and anointed for that very purpose.' Certainly this would have made him unsympathetic to the religious functions of the Polytechnic. Present, too, was Ryan's successor, William Gannon, previously Principal of the Norwich Technical Municipal Institute. He had been appointed on 21 July, and the dis-missal of Didden (finally confirmed on 26 January 1904) cannot thus have been a formal condition of his agreement to take the job. He may well, however, have been told unofficially by Escreet and others that it would follow.

This was not quite the last of Didden. Surprisingly, considering how he had been treated, he became one of the three Governors whom the original trustees were still entitled to appoint, and began regularly to attend Governing Body meetings. He was also secretary of the Pleasant Sunday Afternoons organization which continued to use the Polytechnic's hall for its religious meetings though numbers were falling and by 1911 only about a hundred would attend instead of the many hundreds of 15 years earlier. In this position within six months he was giving new offence by disobeying the Governors' instructions that (1) he should describe its services as 'being held at the Polytechnic' and not as 'Woolwich Polytechnic PSA services', and (2) that he should submit all its notices to the Principal for his approval.

In November 1905 the Governors threatened to cease to let Pleasant Sunday Afternoons use its premises. In response Lord Kinnaird, representing the trustees, sent letters of apology and promises of correct behaviour in future, but they only relented on condition that the trustees 'withdraw Mr Didden from the post of Governor and also from that of Honorary Secretary to the PSA'.

5

Gannon Takes Charge

1904–1912

WILLIAM GANNON WAS A MAN of greater determination and persistence than his three predecessors, but he was not at first an impetuous one. Though he had been appointed in July 1903 he attempted no major reforms for the session which began that September but waited six months longer. It was not until 3 March 1904 that he sent the Governing Body a 30-page document dealing with every aspect of the Polytechnic's teaching activities.

'The Woolwich Polytechnic does not compare favourably with its sister organizations,' he began. On the other hand he considered its potentialities were great and that it 'should aim to be regarded as the local college of London University'.

At present it had certain 'prominent and unfortunate features: the small number of whole-time teachers, the absence of organized departments and the existence of separate evening and day staff. Out of 42 teachers, only one was full-time. As a result virtually all of them came to the Polytechnic 'for a few hours in the evening', and had 'no opportunity of making the necessary preparation for lectures or laboratory work; they cannot meet one another for the purposes of discussion, and as there is no Head teacher to supervise this work, there is much duplicating, waste of energy and friction.'

The absence of heads of departments led to unnecessary duplication of apparatus for day and evening classes, and prevented 'co-ordination of the work carried on in these classes'. As for the existence of separate day and evening staff,

in all the Polytechnics, except Woolwich, subjects like mathematics, chemistry, physics, drawing, technical work, and housewifery (and English, French, Geography etc., in some of them) are taught by teachers who are either the Heads of, or Assistants in, the various departments, and . . . are available for day or evening classes.

Facing page: *A 1914 view of the Polytechnic building in William Street (later Calderwood Street), built in 1891. The central block remains unchanged, but the nearest part was replaced by the 1917 development (see pages 35 and 61). The Duke of Wellington public house, at the other end, was replaced by the Hall in 1935.*

William Gannon, Principal, 1903–12.

THE WOOLWICH POLYTECHNIC.

Principal - - - - - WILLIAM GANNON, M.A.

LECTURES FOR THE PEOPLE.

A Course of 25 Lectures, in connection with the University of London, on

" SOCIAL FORCES IN NINETEENTH CENTURY LITERATURE "

Will be given at the Polytechnic by

PROFESSOR W. H. HUDSON,

Late Professor of English Literature, Stamford University, California,

On FRIDAY EVENINGS, Commencing October 7th, 1904.

The Lectures will be divided into three series—

I. Ten Lectures (October 7th—December 9th) on the Age of Revolution, and the Democratic and Humanitarian Movement.

II. Ten Lectures (January 13th—March 17th) on the Scientific Movement, and the Religious Upheaval and its Idealistic Movement.

III. Five Lectures (April 7th—May 12) on the Artistic Movement, and further Development of Democracy and Humanitarianism.

Syllabus of the Lectures may be obtained free at the Polytechnic, or will be forwarded by post free if application is made.

Admission Fee : 1s. for each series, or 2s. 6d. for the full course of Lectures.

A LIMITED NUMBER OF RESERVED SEATS CAN BE BOOKED AT 5s. FOR THE FULL COURSE.

A. J. NAYLOR, Clerk to the Governors.

'Lectures for the People', 1904.

Gannon's proposed reorganization was similar to the second of Ryan's (set aside by the Governors after his unexpected resignation). Like Ryan, Gannon wanted engineering to be the Polytechnic's speciality. 'This department must, on account of local industry, be given the premier position,' he wrote, and he recommended that it should have a head and two full-time assistants rather than just one full-time teacher. There was also to be a mathematics and experimental physics department of which he would become head with three full-time assistants; a chemistry and metallurgy department with a head and one full-time assistant; and an art department with a full-time head.

Gannon warned the Governors that his reorganization would 'involve a displacement of several members of the present staff,' but added, 'I feel it equally my duty to say that the reorganization is imperatively necessary, and cannot be delayed. It is of importance that the Governors should come to a decision on an early date, as the posts should be advertised by the end of April so as to secure the best men.'

The Governors were persuaded and three quarters of the staff for the 1904–5 session were full-time. Of the previous part-time teachers, only A. Coomes (building instruction) and James Moir, the long-serving teacher of metal-plate work, became full-time, the rest not being rehired. Though the Polytechnic was entitled to treat them in this way, many felt aggrieved.

Another of Gannon's proposals was equally significant: that the Polytechnic should start a daytime technical school to teach mechanical and electrical engineering, chemistry and metallurgy to 15–19-year-olds who had come from a school of science. There were successful technical schools at other polytechnics, he argued, and there were good if not better reasons for one succeeding at Woolwich. Its purpose would be to train apprentices, 'a subject which is being much discussed of late'. He did not add that Woolwich had an additional reason for increasing its daytime teaching. The next new block of classrooms in Lower Market Street would be ready in November 1904, and another was to be completed in May 1906. Until now virtually all the Polytechnic's classrooms and laboratories had been empty except in the evenings; day classes were needed to justify its investment in increasingly extensive premises.

Two years later technical schools of this sort were established, one of science and engineering, another of commerce. For the first there were a total of 16 scholarships (though in 1906–7 it only attracted 15 students). For the second there were three scholarships but 45 joined.

Behind Gannon's reorganization lay a belief in the importance of what colleges like the Polytechnic could do for the country. This belief was entirely different from that of Hogg and Didden, but close to that of the framers of the 1889 Technical Instruction Act. When the 1904-5 prospectus was published in the summer of 1904 one paragraph read:

The paramount importance that education and exact knowledge will exercise in the future on the supremacy of the nations cannot be doubted, and with the stress of actual, and prospective, foreign competition, it becomes a pressing necessity for those engaged in industrial and commercial processes to become acquainted with the fundamental principles of science, of economics, of philosophy, and of art, and of their application to manufactures.

Forging a gun at the Arsenal. Trade lads from the Arsenal were sent to the Polytechnic from 1904 onwards as part of a scheme to supplement the apprentice system. The release by the War Office of the trade lads was the first example of 'day release' in the UK.

The thoroughness of Gannon's investigation of the Polytechnic is suggested by his final recommendations which included: (2) the wood required for lighting fires to be purchased ready cut; and (3) the windows to be cleaned by contract.

They did not, however, include one proposal, probably because its final details were already being agreed: a scheme for the training of youths described as trade lads from the Arsenal. This was also intended to be a substitute for the country's declining apprentice system. The Arsenal expected to send 40 lads at first and eventually 140. In the spring of 1904 after consultations with Gannon and a good deal of cautious deliberation, the War Office finally agreed to take part. One of the scheme's significant features was that the lads, besides attending evening classes, would come for one afternoon each week. Woolwich Polytechnic was thus the first college in the country to establish the equivalent of today's day-release courses. Curiously, the scheme was not mentioned in the 1904–5 prospectus, the year when it began, though the prospectus observed in its Engineering Department section,

> Enterprising employers of labour now insist on all their apprentices attending courses of technical instruction as they recognise that they must have technically trained men on their staff, and craftsmen of a high degree of intelligence, otherwise they will not be able to meet the fierce present-day competition at home or abroad.

At first Woolwich did not apparently have enterprising employers of this sort and it was some years before any took part. For the Arsenal lads, however, the scheme worked well and at the end of the session the Governors reported that various superintendents of the ordnance factories of Woolwich had taken a keen interest. The War Office, besides paying the lads' fees and their wages during their afternoon of instruction, increased its annual grant to £500.

Early in 1905 Gannon submitted his reorganization of the Polytechnic's Institute – in effect its Social Side. This proposed changes which could make the Institute more decisively an offshoot of the Polytechnic's teaching side. Young men or women who wished to join the Institute, for example, but were not students could now be told by the Governors, on the Principal's recommendation, that they could only do so by becoming students. Other proposals indicated the firm control Gannon intended to take of the social side: 'The Principal and the Clerk to the Governors shall be *ex-officio* members of all Institute clubs and societies and have a seat at all business meetings. . . . Any printed matter in connection with any Institute club or society must be submitted to the Principal for approval before it is issued.'

Along with these internal changes of Gannon's first few years there was an external one which in future would have the greatest influence on the Polytechnic's development. In 1903 an Act of Parliament extended the well-known 1902 Education Act to London, giving the London County Council control of all London education. The Technical Education Board was abolished and the Polytechnic's chief supporter became instead the LCC's Education Committee. By this time the Governors of the Polytechnic were accustomed to dealing with

Facing page: *The view from Woolwich, looking upriver towards Docklands, with the Thames Barrier* (centre) *and Canary Wharf* (far right).

50

the TEB, with which they had developed a good relationship and the change caused them anxiety, but its main early consequence was far from damaging since it gave the Polytechnic a more secure source of funds.

The same year Sidney Webb, chairman and vice-chairman of the TEB between 1893 and 1902, published *London Education*, in which he included an enthusiastic description of the sort of London polytechnic which, by the time Gannon's reorganization had been put into practice, the Woolwich Polytechnic began to resemble:

> The visitor who goes over one of the larger and more highly developed polytechnics will find within the institution on the day of his visit all kinds and grades of educational work simultaneously going on. In one room he will see boys of fourteen learning arithmetic, or girls being taught to sew; in another wing of the same building he will come across classes of plumbers or bricklayers, compositors or tailors, receiving practical training in the processes of their respective crafts; close by will be seen the smithy or the fitting shop, crowded with young engineering artisans; in other class-rooms he will find groups reading Dante, or studying economics; and presently he will enter a splendidly equipped physical or chemical laboratory, where he may discover . . . the professor, with a selected band of students working out a Royal Society grant for original research, or . . . graduates of more than one university preparing their theses for the doctor's degree. The typical London Polytechnic does not belong exclusively to elementary, to secondary or to university education; it is not distinctly a day college, nor yet an evening institute; it is particularly affected neither to science nor to the arts, neither to technology nor to literature. Its remarkable growth and success is due to the fact that it combines and includes them all.

Facing page: Sculpture in the University. Top: carved keystones in the Wardroom, HMS Pembroke, at Chatham; middle: Galatea from the Winter Gardens at Avery Hill (left) and (right) bronze statue representing Spring in the boardroom, Southwood House; bottom: portrait statues of Colonel and Mrs North, Avery Hill.

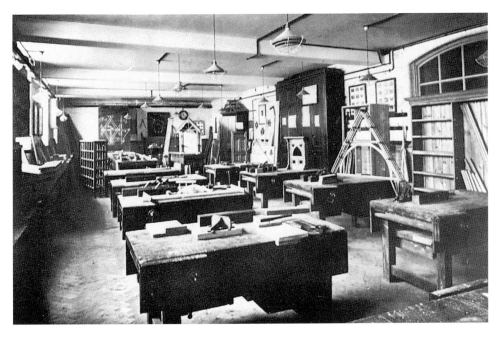

Carpentry workshop at the Polytechnic, 1906. As the Prospectus had observed in the previous year, 'Enterprising employers of labour now insist on all their apprentices attending courses of technical instruction as they must have technically trained men on their staff, and craftsmen of a high degree of intelligence'.

One matter did not go smoothly in these years, indeed it ended in a scandal which today would make tabloid headlines: Gannon's connection with the headmaster of the old Day School. It was Gannon's right to bring the school more directly under his control, but this involved depriving headmaster Bowers of powers he had long exercised. Early differences between the two men seem petty but suggest what was to follow. In November 1903 the Education Committee imposed a settlement by which Gannon won one point – he had the right to enter any Day School classroom whenever he wished – but Bowers won another – Gannon must only communicate with members of the Day School staff via Bowers.

The first crisis came four weeks later when Gannon brought a list of complaints against Bowers to the Education Committee. 'The Principal', its minutes recorded,

> further stated difficulties with the Headmaster were continually occurring and a state of affairs was created in consequence which made it absolutely impossible for him to administer properly the affairs of the Polytechnic, and he asked that he should receive a further definitive statement from the Committee that he had their unqualified support in his action regarding the Headmaster as otherwise he felt bound to say to the Committee . . . that he must at once place his resignation in the hands of the Governors.

After calling in Bowers and listening to his far-from-persuasive answers to Gannon's complaints, the Education Committee minuted that it 'commends the action taken by the Principal, and that the Headmaster be informed that he must conform to the requirements of the Governors as required by their representative officer, the Principal.'

This satisfied Gannon provided the Headmaster was called back and 'the terms of the resolution at once conveyed to him'. But again the settlement only lasted a month. By 14 January Bowers had a new grievance: that he was no longer allowed to submit his monthly reports direct to the Governing Body but only via the Principal, with *his* comments. At Bowers' insistence the matter was brought to the Governing Body, but Bowers had nothing except custom to support his case. Naylor, the ever-loyal Clerk to the Governors, noted in his dead-pan minutes, 'After some discussion during which the condition of Mr Bowers' health and mental condition were mentioned the chairman stated had he known in time that the complaint of the Headmaster was so trivial he would not have allowed it to be brought to the notice of the meeting.'

Two months later Gannon submitted his general plan of reorganization which included various important changes to the Day School, and though Bowers did not make objections to these, there is little doubt that sooner or later he would have been dislodged by Gannon. In practice the opportunity for this came quickly, as a result of the 'alleged misconduct of certain boys of the School'. On 2 June the Governing Body voted that six boys should be asked to leave and if they refused be expelled, another boy should be suspended, and 13 more admonished. Arrangements should be made for these 13 'to be addressed by the Medical Officer of Health for the district on the serious results attending such misconduct'. Furthermore, Mrs Gillanders, supervisor of Women's Studies, should 'see the mothers of the three girls whose names have been mentioned'.

Exactly what happened is never said but the minutes of the Education Committee's meeting of 10 June make guessing fairly easy.

Recommended

1. On two mornings per week the girls shall be taken between 9.30 and 9.50 . . . in a separate room from the boys, by the senior mistress or other mistress, who will treat of such subjects as can best be dealt with by a woman, in addition to religious instruction.

2. That it be an instruction to the senior mistress that the Governors hold her responsible for discipline in the girls' cloak rooms and lavatories . . .

3. That organised excursions on Saturdays or other days in which the boys and girls take part be forbidden.

4. That it be the duty of the gymnastic instructor to attend in the dressing room while the boys are changing clothes. . . . Any misconduct on the part of the boys to be reported to the Head Master.

5. That it be the duty of the gymnastic instructress to attend in the dressing room while the girls are changing clothes. . . . Any misconduct on the part of the girls . . . to be reported directly to the senior mistress.

On 25 July the Education Committee recommended that Bowers be asked to resign and if he failed to do so, be dismissed. No doubt it was right to hold Bowers responsible, but the incident had provided a convenient reason for getting rid of the less valuable of two men who could not co-operate with each other.

The 1906–7 session was probably Gannon's most successful. He was firmly in charge of all Polytechnic activities, both the Social Side and the Day School (now known as the Secondary School) having been reduced to departments. His reorganization of the other departments was in place, giving each of them a Head who, with full-time assistants, did most of the teaching. Total student numbers during the previous four years had risen from 1,068 in the last of Ryan's sessions (1902–3) to 1,807 in 1906–7, and class entries from 2,300 to 4,387.

Originally the door to the Polytechnic on Lower Market Street (now Polytechnic Street), built 1904, later transformed into a window. The room was used as an office by R. T. Smith and T. B. Vinycomb.

Part of a cartoon from the Polytechnic's handwritten magazine, Pom-Pom, 1906.

Wellington Street, c. 1910. New Polytechnic buildings were later built just beyond the town hall clock tower on the left-hand side of the road.

Polytechnic prospectus of 1906–7, including the new Day Schools and the trade school of dressmaking.

PAMPHLET No. 3.
For information as to other pamphlets published see back of cover.

WOOLWICH POLYTECHNIC.
SESSION 1906-7.

PARTICULARS
OF THE

Day School of Science & Engineering,

Day and Evening Classes Preparing for the Examinations of London University,

Day Commercial School,

Day School of Art,

Day Trade School of Dressmaking,

Day School of Domestic Economy,
AND

Day Secondary School.

The Polytechnic is situated in Lower Market Street and William Street. Entrance in Lower Market Street. Nearest Stations :—Woolwich Arsenal (S.E. & C.Ry.), North Woolwich (G.E. Ry.) and Ferry. Telegraphic address :—"Polytechnic, Woolwich." Telephone No. 272 Woolwich.

PRICE 1D., BY POST 3D.

In 1906–7, besides the two new technical schools for 15–19 year olds in science, engineering and in commerce, a trade school in dressmaking was opened, 'to offer to girls such instruction in dressmaking as will enable them to adopt this trade as a means of livelihood'. 50 girls joined. Interestingly, an analysis carried out that year of the future occupations of 400 out of the 655 girls who had been at the School of Domestic Economy since its foundation showed that, after domestic service (170), by far the largest number (70) had become dressmakers; 18 had become typists and 14 teachers, while the rest had taken up 18 different occupations, one becoming an 'artificial tooth maker'.

During the 1906–7 session there were also two developments which foreshadowed on the one hand the great expansion of the Polytechnic's activities into teacher training in 1976 and 1985 when it merged first with Dartford and second with Avery Hill teacher training colleges, and on the other hand its transformation into a university in 1992. The Secondary School was recognized by the Board of Education for the preliminary education of elementary school-teachers, the Governors arranging for the admission of bursars for this purpose, and in subsequent years of pupil teachers and student teachers. And at about the same time seven members of the mathematics, engineering and science departments, including Gannon himself, were recognized as teachers for internal degrees of London University.

Unfortunately the usefulness of this move in the direction which the Polytechnic was ultimately to take was at first smaller than it might have been because four other teachers suggested by the Polytechnic were rejected by London University. This meant that some students who had enrolled for a group of classes which would qualify them to take London University degree examinations found that certain of their classes did not do so, and several were forced to transfer to other institutions.

During Gannon's remaining five years the Polytechnic's fortunes were more

A room in the trade school of dress-making, from the Prospectus of 1906–7.

mixed. In most ways it continued to prosper. The London County Council approved of the quality of its evening classes, reporting in 1908 that the work seemed altogether to be 'in a very sound and healthy state', and the Board of Education wrote that the courses for Arsenal trade lads proceeded 'very satisfactorily' and the Engineering Department was becoming 'capable of good advanced work'. About the Art Department it was equally complimentary. This – now fully recovered from its problems of a few years earlier – was benefiting from its new full-time head, William Evans, who had taken over as part of Gannon's reorganization and was to remain its head until 1925. Already in 1908 it had 173 students and had 'developed considerably in scope and usefulness'. That year, on four days in September, the Polytechnic was opened to the public, 3,757 of whom came. A further opening was planned for September 1911.

By 1912 the Governors were able to claim in their annual report that 'the Polytechnic had indeed become one of the most principal (*sic*) centres of Engineering instruction in the metropolitan area.' Furthermore the School of Domestic Economy continued to prosper, its numbers rising from the 45 or 50 to 67 by 1911–12, while the boys and girls of the Secondary School now numbered over 400. There was also a new venture in 1909 in the form of a second girls' trade school, for teaching them ladies' tailoring.

Against all this, in 1907–8 the evening classes were seriously affected by a reduction in staff at the Arsenal, numbers of students falling to 1,178, class entries to 3,587, both remaining at around these figures until the end of Gannon's time. And while the two trade schools for girls prospered and the commercial day school survived, the science/engineering school for boys collapsed.

The other problem was the recurring one: lack of space. The staff, for example, had no common room and were forced to use part of the committee room. Though some of the new classrooms and laboratories in Lower Market Street were of an acceptable quality, the converted living-rooms in the original William

From the Prospectus of 1909.

Woodcut of the Polytechnic facing on to Lower Market Street (later Polytechnic Street), by Horace Wooler of the Polytechnic, in an illuminated book presented to Archdeacon Escreet in 1909.

Notice of the Engineering Society's annual event for 1910. Two years later, the Governors were able to claim that the Polytechnic was 'one of the most principal (sic) centres for Engineering instruction in the metropolitan area'.

Street building by now seemed to belong to another century. The problem was still unsolved by the time Gannon left, though the Governors were at least able to report that they had 'given most careful attention to the scheme for the extension and partial rebuilding of the Polytechnic' and express their sincere hope that 'in the near future the London County Council may be in a position to enable them to carry into effect this most urgently needed attention'.

In their next paragraph the Governors announced Gannon's resignation, to become a Board of Education Divisional Inspector, and expressed their thanks for his nine years of 'most effective work'. Again the departure of a Principal after a longer, but still comparatively short, period in office asks for an explanation. Brooks, who wrote in the 1950s and must have known some who took part in the events of Gannon's time, suggested that the cause was friction between the Principal and the Governing Body. 'Not all the Governors,' he wrote, 'and sometimes not the Governors collectively, commanded his [Gannon's] real respect. . . . He acted on the highest principles, he felt that he knew what was best for those in his care . . . but he was impatient and intolerant of opposition, and a little contemptuous of those who had not his own academic qualifications and standing.'

More specifically, Collin Brooks suggested in his 1955 history of the Polytechnic, it was Gannon and William Calderwood, Chairman of the Governing Body from 1910 to 1913, who could not co-operate with each other. In 1907 Escreet had been succeeded in this position by Henry Butter, engineer and worthy alderman, then by Calderwood. 'Gannon's severance with the Polytechnic', Brooks wrote discreetly, 'would undoubtedly have come sooner or later under any chairman.' The fact remains that it came under Calderwood.

The difficulty these two had in co-operating was an irony, since, after Hogg and Didden, they were the two who before the mid-1930s did more for the

56

Polytechnic than anyone else. Like Didden, Calderwood had begun his working life at the Arsenal, then crossed the river to work for Palmer & Co., soon becoming its managing director. At first he was an active trade unionist and when, in 1895 at the age of 25, he was selected to be a Polytechnic Governor, it was as the London County Council's 'industrial representative'.

Among innumerable ways in which he helped the Polytechnic, it was he who in 1904 played a large part in arranging the scheme for the training of Arsenal trade lads. He was much involved in negotiating the major extensions of its premises in 1915–16 and 1931–2, and in securing a site in Lower Market Street for a large and worthy hall. He was also involved in educational work outside the Polytechnic, becoming a chairman of the King's Warren School to which the girls of the Polytechnic's Secondary School went in 1912. His membership of the Board of Governors of Avery Hill Teacher Training College was to be another connection with the Polytechnic's future, though he was not to know it. His commitment to the Polytechnic is shown by the regularity of his attendance at meetings. Of the 181 meetings of the Governing Body and its committees in the five years before he first became chairman he missed only two, a record to which no other Governor came anywhere near. William Street, site of the Polytechnic's first home, was justifiably given his name.

If it was likely that two such determined and active men as Calderwood and Gannon would fail to work together, this should not detract from Gannon's important contribution to the Polytechnic's history. He was to remain a Board of Education Inspector for the rest of his working life and be rewarded with an OBE when he retired.

William Calderwood, Chairman of the Governing Body 1910–13.

6

War

1912–1928

To succeed Gannon the Governors chose Alexander Hogg, aged 44, for the previous 12 years Principal of the Municipal Technical Institute, West Ham. As a mathematician and chemist, Hogg had previously taught science at four schools, then become Principal of Darlington Technical College. One of his referees credited him with a 'genial and considerate character', another wrote that at West Ham he had been 'a good disciplinarian but tactful enough to be always on the best of terms with the teaching staff and the large body of students'. In no sense was Hogg chosen to halt or reverse Gannon's reforms, indeed he was to extend them, but with greater tact, his underlying aim being, like Gannon's, to move the Polytechnic towards becoming a University College. He had frailties, one of them fussiness about the positioning of furniture in staff offices. Late one evening the head porter heard muffled cries for help. In trying to shift a heavy cupboard, Hogg had toppled it, trapping himself behind. But on the whole co-operation with his staff as well as his employers marked his 20-year regime, this extending over the most difficult period the Polytechnic had yet experienced: the First World War.

During Hogg's two pre-war sessions he and the Governors aimed in particular to expand the ways in which the Polytechnic provided Woolwich with educational opportunities for its poorer citizens. In 1912 the trade lads scheme for the lads of the Arsenal was reformed to double their daytime classes, these now to become one whole day or two half-days a week, so enabling them 'to pursue their theoretical studies under conditions which give to them and to the teaching staff far better opportunities of progress than could possibly be secured by attending evening classes alone.'

The Governors appealed to local employers to take advantage of this improved scheme by granting their 'promising apprentices from among whom they may hope in the future to select those suitable for more responsible positions' the

Facing page: *Children from the Polytechnic Day School, 1910.*

59

Alexander Hogg, Principal 1912–32.

Boys from the Arsenal in the trade lads scheme had their daytime classes doubled in 1912. (Drawn by trade lad E. C. Andrews and engraved on the block by trade lad W. Clothier, Woolwich Polytechnic Magazine, 1916.)

chance to attend. Now at last the employers responded and by the end of the session six firms were co-operating with the Polytechnic.

In addition a new daytime Junior Technical Department was set up, also for selected boys of ability, to give them a training which would enable them 'to enter Engineering Works under favourable conditions'. In its first year 30 boys attended the Engineering Trade School, as it was named, and in the second year 62.

The co-operation which now developed between the Polytechnic and local employers included the sending to them of monthly reports on employees who were attending day classes, and on the younger ones attending evening classes. These not only kept the employers informed about their boys, but also, the Governors noted, 'contributed very materially to the success of the work undertaken'. For their part the employers were increasingly allowing their employees who were taking courses to leave early in the evenings, while some were refunding their fees and others were 'taking satisfactory progress as a qualifying factor for promotion'.

At the same time the Governors criticized employers (and parents) for allowing their young employees (or children) to give up all education for a period after leaving school before they started evening classes. The sort of classes which they would then start were run by the Evening Institutes of the London County Council, and had grown up in parallel to the Polytechnic's evening classes.

From the time when the LCC's Education Committee had taken charge of London's education in 1904, it had set about bringing order to the city's many and often overlapping educational establishments. In 1905 it had arranged for the transfer of most of the Polytechnic's commercial and literary evening classes to the Bloomfield Road Evening Science, Art and Commercial Centre, which at the same time transferred some of its science classes to the Polytechnic, to which it became affiliated. Now in 1912 the LCC proposed a further rationalization: the co-ordination of its Evening Institutes' classes with those of the Polytechnic, so that the former would lead naturally to the latter. This was successfully put into practice in September 1913. One result was that the Polytechnic received better students, specifically taught at the 12 Evening Institutes taking part in the scheme with the idea that this was where they would go next. Another was that the Polytechnic was able to direct potential students who were not ready for its courses to those of the LCC Institutes.

At the more learned end of its activities, the sort of advanced scientific and engineering work which students were now undertaking is suggested by papers they delivered during the 1912–13 session. These included: 'Acetyl Halogen Sugar Compounds and Other Sugar Derivatives', 'The Estimation of Small Quantities of Lead', and 'The Determination of Oxygen in Steel'.

Accommodation remained a problem. The Governing Body knew what it wanted but became involved in long and frustrating arguments with the LCC, with the aim of trying to persuade it to provide the money. In the Governors' opinion the two greatest needs were the rebuilding of the old William Street premises and the erection of a new building on the corner of William Street and Thomas Street which would provide more classrooms as well as proper offices for the Principal, the Superintendent of Women's Classes (still Mrs Gillanders), and the administrative staff. There was some relief in 1912–13 when the girls of the Secondary School were sent to a school of their own at Plumstead; it was this which left space for the new Engineering Trade School for boys. On the other hand in January 1914 there was a fire which put out of use four classrooms in William Street, forcing the School of Domestic Economy temporarily to close.

In 1913–14 the Polytechnic at last received the financial help it had been asking for, in the form of one generous loan and another generous grant. The £10,000 loan was from the City Parochial Foundation, to enable the Governors to buy the freeholds of their premises. The £26,000 grant was from the LCC, for the much-needed extending and re-equipping of its premises. Already by November 1914 various improvements had been made including the fitting-out of a group of rooms for the teaching of photography, the installing of a new heating system in the gymnasium and the converting of lighting in the William Street buildings from gas to electricity. Despite the start of the war, the Governors hoped that the erection of new buildings would start early in 1915.

This it indeed did, and at the end of the 1914–15 session the Governors were able to write,

> The outstanding feature of the work of the past year was the completion of a further scheme of alteration and extension of the Polytechnic premises. The oldest and most inconvenient portions of the original buildings were demolished, and in their place were erected a new and well-equipped school of Domestic Economy . . . , a suite of rooms for administration, and an excellent series of laboratories, workshops, lecture rooms and drawing offices for the Engineering Department, while the whole of the previous detached buildings were brought under one roof and connected by well-lit and spacious corridors. . . . Further . . . alterations . . . secured good rooms for the Teaching Staff, additional accommodation for the School of Art, a remodelled Physics Department, a suite of rooms for Metallurgy, as well as rooms for the use of the Polytechnic Clubs and Societies . . . which are of such benefit . . . in the formation of character and in the development of a feeling of fellowship.

The new buildings were formally opened on 6 July 1917 by the Marquess of Crewe.

Apart from the special grants of the sort which financed these buildings, the LCC continued to be by a long way the largest contributor to the Polytechnic's general running costs, giving £11,423 in 1913–14 and in addition granting scholarships to 283 students to help pay their fees. Next largest was the Board of Education which gave £4,600.

Though lack of space had held back the development of the clubs and societies which the Governors were keen to promote, an Engineering Society had existed since 1899 when the Principal, Ashcroft, had encouraged its founding. This published its own magazine and held about seven meetings a year at which it would discuss papers on such subjects as 'Variable Speed Gearing', or 'The Evolution of Modern Gun Carriages and Mountings'. In 1906 Gannon had considered that its proceedings were more suited to men of over 30 than those of 18–25 and proposed the founding of a junior branch. His aim was to encourage Polytechnic students to join, alongside representatives of the Arsenal who now

The new Thomas Street entrance, 1916. Extending and re-equipping of the Polytechnic premises had begun after a large loan and grant two years earlier. After refurbishment in 1996, it was renamed the Calderwood entrance.

Plan for the new Engineering Department of 1916.

The Engineering Society

This had existed since 1899 and produced its own magazine and papers, typically with a military bias.

Right: Picture taken on a visit by the Society to the cables section of the Siemens factory to see lead-covered telephone cables being manufactured.

Below: A typical Engineering Society paper, 1911.

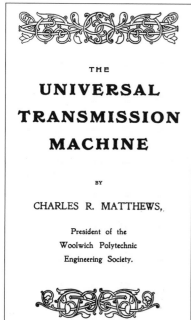

THE

UNIVERSAL TRANSMISSION MACHINE

BY

CHARLES R. MATTHEWS,

President of the
Woolwich Polytechnic
Engineering Society.

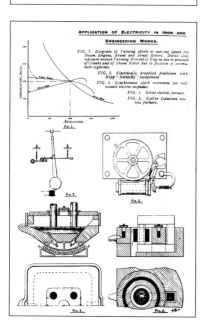

dominated it. Despite his reforms it continued to be much preoccupied with military matters. In 1910 it heard a paper on 'The Motor as a War Store'. Captain Haynes, its author, did not foresee the tank but he did reject the Pedrail system (fitting wheels with sliding spokes, with feet at the end of each spoke) and favoured caterpillar tracks for 'special work with heavy guns and in siege operations'.

The effect the Boer War had had on the Polytechnic was minor compared to the effect of the First World War. Not only did Arsenal employees have to work overtime in the evenings but, even before conscription was imposed in 1916, many joined the armed forces. In Woolwich no less than in the rest of the country, women took their places in munitions factories. In 1914 the Arsenal employed 125 women munition workers – by 1917 it had 25,000.

Two of the schools for girls suffered most severely. In September 1913, at Hogg's suggestion the Commercial School had ceased to admit boys. 'Boys', he wrote,

quite easily secure Civil Service appointments direct from the Secondary School. With the girls the case is different. For well-educated shorthand-typists and other girl clerks the demand much exceeds the supply and for girls who wish to secure these positions it is necessary to have some specialised instruction after completion of the ordinary school course. The number of qualified girls applying for admission increases.

But numbers had declined in 1914–15 to 13 and eventually to 10 in 1917–18. It was probably this decline which precipitated the closure rather than 'lack of suitable accommodation', the officially minuted reason.

The School of Domestic Economy (which, apart from the School of Art, had been the first to hold daytime classes) struggled on, but its numbers had fallen from 43 in 1914–15 to 30 by August 1920, when it too closed. In contrast numbers at the girls' dressmaking and tailoring schools held up fairly well as did those at the boys' trade school, the Secondary School and the part-time classes for trade lads from the Arsenal and other local firms. At the evening classes, however, still the core of the Polytechnic's activities, there was a steady fall in numbers for the first three war years, though surprisingly a marked recovery in 1917–18.

The Social Side suffered even more severely. In August 1915 the Athletic Club lost its playing-field near Church Manorway, Plumstead, requisitioned by the War Office for railway sidings for the Arsenal, with the result that all its sporting activities came to an end. After the 1915–16 session the Governors reported that the Social Side had become 'little more than a name'. Next year the clubs and societies were 'again almost entirely in abeyance'.

By 1917–18 however, they became 'more active', as a result of two developments. In the new buildings they had been given a group of rooms for their activities, to become known as 'the Den' and at Eltham the Governors had bought 20 acres of land for a new playing-field, part of which was already being used.

The Polytechnic itself also took part in the war. In May 1915 the Education Committee resolved that 'all the resources of the Polytechnic be placed at the disposal of the Arsenal for the manufacture of whatever [munitions] the Chairman of the Governors and the Principal think can be made.' During the 1916 summer holiday, when the disastrous First Battle of the Somme was being fought in France, the Engineering Workshops of the Poly were kept open. About the 1915–16 session the Governors reported that the Polytechnic's premises had been 'largely utilised in the actual production of munitions'. The Chemical Department had in addition carried out analyses and estimations of metallic alloys, the workshops had made articles required by various departments of the Arsenal, and the Engineering Department had trained semi-skilled men to become effective gauge-makers, and given special training to the mechanics of the Royal Flying Corps. Two months after the Armistice the Chief Superintendent of Ordnance Factories thanked the Polytechnic schools for their help in making tools for munitions.

The Polytechnic was involved in munitions production during the war. Below: *One of the Arsenal factories in about 1916, and (below left) women workers at the Woolwich Dockyard in 1918.*

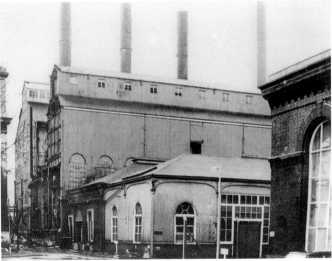

'Found in the School of Art, January 1917' (from the new Magazine established during the war).

Facing page: *The number of students and staff who served in the armed forces during the war is suggested by this illustration from the* Woolwich Polytechnic Magazine *(1917) entitled simply 'Four Polytechnic boys of one family'.*

Meanwhile in November 1915 the Polytechnic allowed the Bread and Food Reform League to give special classes in War Economy Cooking; and in April 1917 when food was at its scarcest, the Polytechnic engaged Miss Florence Pelly to give 'special free public demonstration lectures upon War Time Cookery'.

In 1916 the Polytechnic celebrated the twenty-fifth anniversary of its first teaching session with the publication of a new magazine. There had been a single issue of a magazine by the Athletic Club in 1894 and a longer series of magazines had appeared in 1896–7, but this, too, had collapsed and no copies can be found. Inevitably, the first issue of the 1916 Magazine was much concerned with the war. It listed 13 staff and 175 ex-students or members of the Institute who were in the armed forces. Among the staff were A. J. Naylor, the long-serving Clerk to the Governors, now a Captain in the Royal Army Medical Corps, and another clerk, H. J. Sisley. More staff were to follow them, including T. B. Vinycomb, Head of the Physics Department. Among the ex-students and members, only 21 were officers, two captains the highest in rank, but many were sergeants or corporals. Twelve were sappers.

This and later wartime numbers regularly carried letters from 'Somewhere in France', describing experiences on the Western Front. Typically, Sapper T. M. Calcutt wrote:

> Wiring is our worst job as it is between the German and English lines that you have to [work]. The first night I went wiring I was not feeling at all comfortable but as soon as you get to work you forget all about the Germans. The rotten part about it is that they don't forget you and when the starlights go up and they spot you they put a few whizz-bangs over just to liven you up. Luckily for us we saw the flash of the gun and were all flat on the ground when the shell burst. . . . The Infantry have an awful time in the trenches. They have to stick it day after day, but we only go up there for, at most, twelve hours. . . . While I was in this place I met Private Drake, he was carrying a dixie of soup for the men's dinner. We had a chat about old times.

Calcutt was later killed.

These wartime magazines show that in some ways life at the Polytechnic continued as before. A girl student of one of the trade schools writes to insist that 'stitching' only occupies a fraction of her school life which also includes learning 'illuminating facts of Industrial History' and 'brave attempts at dramatic representation' of the works of Shakespeare and Sheridan 'with very comical and inadequate "stage-properties"'. The Football Club and the Ladies' Hockey Club were still finding places to play matches, but the secretary of the (groundless) Athletic Club was reduced to giving general advice, warning members, for example, that 'Marriage is, unfortunately, one of the most destructive accidents of club life', but reassuring those who suffered such an accident that they could rely on members for alibis.

The second number of the new Magazine gave an idea of the later lives of early members of the Institute. Out of 12, four had gone to India, one as a missionary, three had worked at the Arsenal, one of them becoming a manager, one was a factory inspector, two were foremen or engineers in manufacturing companies, another was a surveyor, another a Baptist minister. At the Poly the missionary and the Baptist minister had both been harriers, the Arsenal manager a cricketer and swimmer.

Throughout the war, the Magazine also carried obituaries of staff and ex-students who had been killed, eight in the first number, 53 in total. Earliest of the staff to die was the Welshman, A. I. W. Horlock, one of the oldest of the Secondary School masters, a much-liked teacher of mathematics and music lover. The Magazine commemorated him with a poem, a photograph, and a long obituary which recalled him once saying that 'if all else failed he could make a living travelling along the by-ways of the world with his violin'. Like many from the Poly, he had joined as a private in the infantry. Another to die was Eric Naylor, elder son of the Clerk to the Governors.

The Polytechnic commemorated its dead with a memorial tablet, hung in the main corridor, unveiled there in May 1921 by the Bishop of Woolwich. The Athletic Club placed a tablet to its own 13 dead in the Den.

Peace produced a welcome surge of activity at the Polytechnic. By 1919–20 numbers of students taking evening classes had risen to 2,032, close to double the 1913–14 figure, and there had also been encouraging increases in numbers at its three trade schools – engineering, dressmaking, and ladies' tailoring – in the apprentice scheme for the Arsenal and other local businesses, and at its Secondary School.

But 1918 also brought a new Education Act, the so-called Fisher Act, and as a result in July 1920 the LCC published its London Education Scheme. This considerably extended the LCC's powers over the Polytechnic. In a sense it had the right to claim these. By 1919–20 its grants to the Woolwich Polytechnic had risen to a total of £18,850 a year. In return the LCC required the Polytechnic to make regular reports on its activities, to obtain approval for the appointment of its Principal and for the amounts of all staff salaries, and not to extend or reduce its activities without LCC consent.

Continuing attempts to bring order to London education were equally justifiable but ultimately the place its new scheme gave to the Woolwich Polytechnic was not the place its Governors believed it should have. In October 1920 they submitted a reply which made clear their ambitions for the Polytechnic and how these differed from the LCC's. Essentially the LCC saw the Polytechnic remaining what it was, mainly an evening-class institute, concentrating on engineering and science, but with attached trade schools, secondary school, and apprentice classes. The Governors on the other hand wanted it be freed from all except the evening classes and to be allowed to extend these into the daytime and to direct them towards higher education, so ultimately transforming it into a university college.

Among their other comments, the most important was that the LCC scheme made seriously inadequate provision for higher education in Woolwich (now a town of some 140,000) with the result that many students found they had to travel for three hours a day to reach the courses they needed. And, that

PERCY W. STURTON,
R.N.A.S.

Private FRANK STURTON,
ROYAL MARINE ARTILLERY.

Private HARRY STURTON,
ROYAL SUSSEX REGIMENT.

FRED. C. STURTON,
R.N.A.S.

educational establishments should be divided horizontally rather than perpendicularly. For the Polytechnic this meant not only that it would be freed from its day schools and apprentice schemes but that it would be allowed to expand sideways from its narrow science and engineering specializations into higher education of all kinds.

Spelling this out, they recommended that Woolwich:

should be given a scheme of Education which shall be locally more complete . . . and . . . be treated as a more self-sufficing and self-contained Educational unit.

That in the local arrangement of Continuation work, both Day and Evening Courses, the separation should be according to grade . . .

That all higher work in Science, Technology, in Art and in Commerce, should be concentrated at the Polytechnic, and that more extended provision should be made for the proper preparatory work to be done elsewhere, and, above all, that adequate Secondary School accommodation should be at once provided.

That the local scheme should be so framed that it may allow the greatest possible freedom in the arrangement of subjects of study, and so that it shall not in any way hinder the possible ultimate formation of a Local College of University standard . . .

They feel that owing to the great distance from the present centre of University activity, a strong Local College, including several faculties, may become an absolute and recognised necessity. They would aim at provision of University teaching for all capable of profiting by it, and giving the widest possible University outlook, and would encourage every form of study and corporate life.

Regrettably the Governors' comments, foreshadowing as they did events some 40 to 70 years ahead, failed to persuade the LCC, which was content to let the Polytechnic retain its existing shape. Within the old framework, however, it soon began to make significant progress of the sort which the LCC was reluctant to support. In 1920–1 there was a notable increase in the number of students over 21, who now numbered almost a third of the total, and in the School of Art over half the total – proportions roughly maintained the next year, though numbers as a whole fell, partly as a result of an LCC-imposed increase in fees, partly because of local unemployment. In the 1920s this became severe at Woolwich. One of its other great institutions, the Royal Arsenal Co-operative Society (50 years old in 1918) supplied food parcels for the poor as part of the Metropolitan Boroughs' relief scheme, and gave the remains of its War Relief Fund to needy members.

Reporting on the 1922–3 session, Hogg took the opportunity of looking back over his first ten years as Principal. The most important development had been the new building (though still more accommodation was needed). Among other changes for the better had been the great increase in the number of students

Memorial tablet to the staff, students and members of the Polytechnic who died in the First World War.

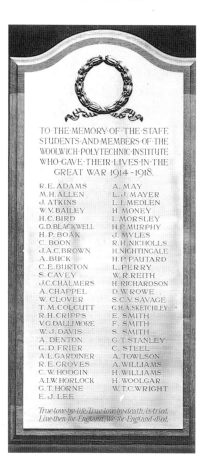

taking the sort of integrated courses of study introduced by Ryan; now they made up three-quarters of the total. But mere statistics, he continued, did not give a true index of development.

> What is more important in taking this longer view is the very great increase in the volume of the more advanced work so that higher classes which could be barely run ten years ago have now in many cases to be duplicated, and in some cases triplicated, while another outstanding and important change is the increased demand for language study on the part of Engineering and Science students, so that in place of two meagre classes ten year ago, we now have nine well filled.

That year 24 engineering students, and 19 science students were registered as internal students at the University of London.

Two years later Hogg considered that the 1924–5 session had been the best since the war:

> Almost every record showed an increase, and the standard of work and the result obtained were highly gratifying. . . . In all departments a considerable increase in the volume of advanced work was shown and the attendance of these advanced students was remarkably good, especially in the higher mathematical classes.

The School of Art (now usually consisting two-thirds of women students) shared in this post-war prosperity, and was doing interesting advanced work. In 1922–3, for example, it was 'experimenting with firing glazed pottery in reducing atmospheres' with the aim of obtaining 'the fine smoke lustre effect which is associated with certain old Persian and Italian ware'. The trade lads schemes also flourished. The arrangement with the Arsenal had been in operation for 20 years and 'produced many men now holding high positions in the Engineering world'. (In 1923 the lads were given the more dignified name of Arsenal Engineer Apprentices.) 'We have some similar schemes', Hogg continued,

School of Art Post-War Work

Tempera panel by H. Shimmell (above left); poster by B. Pluckrose (above); and (below) book illustrations by M. Allington.

Quality Street.

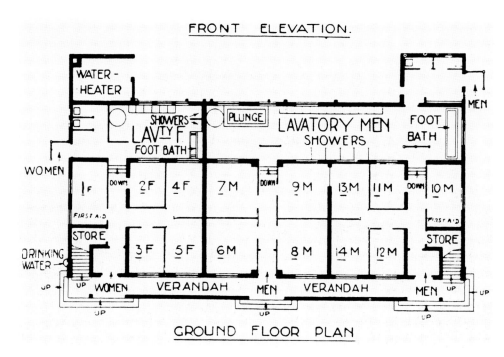

FRONT ELEVATION.

GROUND FLOOR PLAN

Plan for the ground floor of the new Sports Pavilion at Eltham Well Hall. The upper floor was entirely designated as a tea room.

Miss Hatt, a Woolwich Polytechnic student, winning her place in the First Women's Olympiad at Monte Carlo.

WOMAN "SPRINTERS."—Miss H. M. Hatt, of Woolwich Polytechnic, winning her heat in the 100 yards scratch race at Stamford Bridge. Many of the girls showed very good form, running extremely well.

'in operation with the Western Electricity Co., with Messrs Siemens, with the Silvertown Rubber Company and with Messrs Colliers.' So too did the Day Schools which the Polytechnic would have willingly shed. In the Secondary School there were now 47 boys (out of 282), who were over 16 years old.

About the trade schools the Governors had written in 1920, 'From the standpoint of further educational opportunities, they are blind-alley schools. After a two years' course, boys and girls have no definite road to some further course of study.' Though Hogg had been able to note in 1923 that boys who left were being selected by the Arsenal for its apprentice scheme, a more important change which would give the boys a better chance of obtaining further education was made in 1927 when the School's two-year course was extended to three years.

Most pleasing to some Governors was a strong revival of the Social Side. By 1924–5 the Athletic Club had some 500 members who were making good use of the new playing-field. This, the third the club had had, replacing the playing-field taken by the War Office for railway sidings during the war, had at first seemed dauntingly unsuitable. In 1923 the club's president T. W. Higgs wrote,

I suppose there are not six people who know the trouble that was taken to find a suitable substitute for the recreation ground we were compelled to vacate. I recall visiting the field we now occupy when a railway track ran across the ground carrying material for building the munitioners' hutments, when slush was boot-top high and water lay in sheets near the viaduct which lies on the south side. . . .Visualise, if you can, all the disadvantages – an undulating meadow, once arable land and never levelled, full of sedge grasses and pitted with cattle hoofholes and badly water-logged in places. Yet the best to be obtained in view of the . . . conditions which prevailed.

Opening of the new Sports Pavilion at Eltham Well Hall, 1930. It was extended in 1939, unfortunately losing the fine balcony.

By now cricket, football, and ladies' hockey were all being played on this once-derelict site. And seven years later (1 February 1930) the Club celebrated the civilizing of its new ground with a fine pavilion. Now it had four football fields, three cricket pitches, two hockey grounds, eight grass tennis courts, and a quarter-mile running track. The total cost, including a groundsman's cottage, much of it contributed by the City Parochial Foundation, was £5,370.

Meanwhile, in 1921, ten female Woolwich Polytechnic athletes and ten from the Regent Street Polytechnic represented England at the first International Women's Olympiad at Monte Carlo – a further example of the Polytechnic's involvement in women's physical education which reached a climax when it merged with Dartford College in 1976. 'So far as our team was concerned, the results passed expectations, for out of the ten events in which they competed they gained eight firsts and one second' (*Woolwich Polytechnic Magazine*, May 1921). Seventy years later one of the team, Miss Beatrice Look, then aged 90, was interviewed by the *Kentish Times*. She still had her heart-shaped silver medal and 'a rather dog-eared scrapbook' in which she could be seen correctly dressed in white jersey with union jack, black pants and stockings held up by garters. Most successful was Miss Hatt who was placed in four events.

Throughout the early post-war years, it was for the removal of the Secondary School from its premises that the Governors of the Polytechnic campaigned most steadily. Eventually in October 1924 the LCC invited a deputation from the Governing Body to meet its Higher Education subcommittee and discuss the building of a new school.

Another four years passed before a new Secondary School was at last completed, to be known as the Shooters Hill School and there the Polytechnic's Secondary School moved in 1928. The space it vacated left the Polytechnic still short of accommodation, and it was made more so by the founding of a Junior

Beatrice Look from the Polytechnic representing England in the First Women's Olympiad.

FOR MONTE CARLO.—Miss Look, one of the twenty-six women athletes to represent England at the international sports meeting at Monte Carlo, practising the high jump.—(*Daily Mirror.*)

School of Art in 1930 and the creating of a Building Department in 1931. Only the following year did it get the enlargement of its premises which it so badly needed.

Part of the extension completed in 1916 had consisted of the impressive entrance on the corner of what were then William Street and Thomas Street, recently renovated as the principal entrance to the Woolwich island site. The new building, ready in January and February 1932, formed an extension along Thomas Street and provided among other things an electrical engineering laboratory and classrooms for the girls' trade schools. On its flat roof a playground was created. The opening of this new block was an appropriate event to mark the end of Hogg's 20 years as Principal, years in which the Polytechnic had made steady if gradual progress in the direction in which he wished to steer it, towards becoming a university college.

The Polytechnic and those institutions with which it later merged had a long tradition of women's physical education. Left to right: *PE 1970s, Avery Hill; outdoor gym, undated, Dartford; swimming gala, 1950s, Avery Hill; natural dance movement, 1935, Dartford.*

From top: *Gym, 1920s, Rachel McMillan Teacher Training College; gymslip from 1917, Avery Hill; tennis team, 1910s, Avery Hill; Avery Hill gym, 1912.*

7

A New Regime, Another War

1932–1950

+·+ ⊠◆⊠ +·+ ⊠◆⊠ +·+ ⊠◆⊠ +·+ ⊠◆⊠ +·+ ⊠◆⊠ +·+

I̲T̲ ̲W̲A̲S̲ ̲N̲O̲T̲ ̲O̲N̲L̲Y̲ HOGG who retired in 1932 after 20 years as Principal, but also Naylor after 37 years as Secretary and Clerk to the Governors. The figures suggest how important these two had been in providing the Polytechnic with continuity of management and purpose while Governors came and went. Other figures suggest the importance of the choice of their successors. The new Principal, Edward Mallett, was to stay 18 years and the new Secretary, Joseph Halliwell, 33 years, their regimes like those of their two predecessors spanning a world war.

Mallett's appointment was a strange affair. Early in 1932, when Hogg informed the Governors that he would reach retiring age at the end of the session, they duly appointed a subcommittee which short-listed nine out of 52 applicants to succeed him. After taking the advice of the LCC Education Officer, G. H. Gater, the subcommittee reduced these to six whom it interviewed on 8 February. It then rejected all of them and resolved to readvertise the position. Nevertheless on 22 February it interviewed three of the six again and asked Gater's opinion. 'Mr Gater dealt with this question at some length,' the minutes reported, and was presumably not encouraging, for the whole matter was postponed for a month and the Chairman (Calderwood) was empowered meanwhile to make his own search for someone suitable.

A month and a half passed before, on 11 April, the subcommittee began the process again, short-listing ten of 32 new applicants then reducing them to six. These included Dr E. Mallett, Assistant Professor of Electrical Engineering at the City and Guilds College since 1921, who had not previously applied. Even on 18 April, however, when the subcommittee voted for their preferred candidates Mallett had only five supporters against another candidate's six, and it was not until 2 May that the Governing Body interviewed three of the six and finally chose Mallett.

Facing page: *Powis Street, Woolwich hung with decorations for the Coronation, 1937.*

73

Dr Edward Mallett, Principal 1932–50.

Joseph F. S. Halliwell, Secretary 1932–65.

Halliwell's appointment had been a simpler matter. On 7 March the subcommittee reduced 511 candidates to eight, to whom Hogg added four. A week later it reduced these to two and on 21 March 1932 the Governing Body chose Joseph F. S. Halliwell, Registrar of the Wigan and District Mining and Technical College.

Eighteen years later G. Leslie Wates, Chairman of the Governing Body from 1945 to 1947, wrote of Mallett, 'He was most direct in his thought and in his approach to all his problems, so much so, that he ran the risk of being misunderstood by those who might have expected a more diplomatic approach to some thorny problem. But he was completely fearless in facing up to his problems, and however high and mighty were those taking an opposite view, he took his stand on the right, as he saw it, and maintained his position against all opposition.' 'On Committees,' the Magazine's editor wrote, 'he could be ruthlessly logical – particularly when discussion became irrelevant – and could hack his way with ease through the most tangled red tape.' Here was the sort of Principal the Polytechnic – indeed any institution – needed.

'He liked dealing with individuals, not committees,' Wates wrote, and the Magazine added, 'As members of the Union we knew him not so much as a principal or colleague, but as a friend.' The Woolwich Polytechnic Union of Clubs and Societies was one of Mallett's most significant contributions to the Polytechnic.

In proposing it he aimed to correct what he believed to be 'a serious lack of co-ordination ... between ... the students and the older members of the Athletic Club'. He perhaps also wanted to give the Polytechnic a feature which at least in name seemed appropriate if it was to become, as he hoped, a university college. But his underlying purpose was to draw the Athletic Club back into the general life of the Polytechnic. In 1929 there had been a previous attempt to do this when a Students' and Members' Council was formed, consisting of representatives of the Governors, staff, students, and the Athletic Club, but he considered that 'there was a general feeling that this Council had not met the situation'.

His problem was that the Athletic Club, as the oldest feature of the Polytechnic, with a clear identity of its own, not to mention its own constitution and assets, had fiercely loyal members, who disliked the idea of being swallowed by some new, traditionless organization.

In July 1933 the Governing Body formed a subcommittee to discuss the proposed Union and the attitude of the Athletic Club. In October this subcommittee reported that it found the scheme 'a very desirable one from all points of view' and drafted a constitution. In November the Governing Body voted to give all clubs and societies notice that the Union would come into operation on 1 September 1934. Though some members of the Athletic Club were willing to discuss the proposed constitution of the new Union, others were not, in particular the secretary, and at a special meeting of the Club in May 1934 called to settle its attitude to the Union, the members backed the secretary, voting 66 to 33 against joining.

When Mallet reported this result to the Governors the Chairman proposed that he and Mallett should discuss the matter with 'a few members of the Athletic Club' and that meanwhile the report of the Athletic Club's meeting and vote should be censored. The Club's secretary now wrote to the Governors to tell them that the club viewed 'with misgiving and disapproval the method adopted by the Principal in endeavouring to persuade members by individual letters to support the Union'. But the Governors were unmoved, resolving after 'a lengthy discussion' that their intention to launch the Union on 1 September should be reaffirmed, and that the Athletic Club should be so informed. They subsequently instructed the Principal to cease to allow the Athletic Club the use of Polytechnic facilities.

This was the sad end of the Athletic Club. Its various sporting clubs survived as parts of the Union, indeed they thrived. The Swimming Club, for example, using the town baths which were many years later to be floored over and become the Students Union building, regularly won individual and team prizes. In 1935 its secretary, G. W. Manley, typified the connection between the Arsenal and the Polytechnic. Starting there as a messenger boy, he had risen to head its administration, one of his jobs to break the news to wives whose husbands had been killed in accidents, another to organize the wartime dispersal of the Arsenal throughout the country, completed in September 1940, just one week before the Arsenal was first hit by German bombs.

Of the old Athletic Club, however, all that remained was the Den, with no more importance than the Dramatic Society, the Engineering Society, the Rambling Club, or the Sketch Club. This long room just inside the Thomas Street entrance on the right, later the Union Bar, was remembered by G. W. Manley's son, Brian (student and later Governor), as a quiet, civilized place with somewhat the character of a London club, but the sporting activities of its members were reduced to billiards, snooker, and darts tournaments.

The amalgamation of the Polytechnic's sporting clubs with its other societies in a single Union by no means reduced the support the Governing Body gave them. In 1936 the scheme for the addition to the sports ground of a bowls green, tennis pavilion, and football and cricket shelters was approved and in 1939 an extension of the main pavilion was completed. Meanwhile a Badminton Club and a Rugby Union Club had been formed. Other societies, known collectively as House Clubs, also multiplied. In 1935 came the Table Tennis Club, Debating Society, Orchestral Society, and Scientific Colloquium, and in 1938 the newly formed Operatic Society staged its first performance: Gilbert and Sullivan's *The Gondoliers*, with elderly but still active Professor Lewis Cairns James as producer. 'Jimmie', as all knew him, had first appeared in a Gilbert and Sullivan opera in 1886. 'Who will ever forget his early work with us on *The Gondoliers* when at the age of 75 he demonstrated to the chorus of *contadine* the correct way to dance the Ca-chu-ca?' In the following years the society acquired a reputation for its Gilbert and Sullivan operas. Secretary Halliwell was an addict, and contrived to enrol its members who were not all genuine students as a Polytechnic class in choral music.

The Union soon took over the editing of the *Polytechnic Magazine*, which in September 1936 appeared in a blue rather than a grey cover, and announced that in future it would publish two issues instead of one a year. Its contents were not notably more adventurous than those of earlier numbers, but showed what a quantity of clubs and societies the Union was now supervising – over 20. It duly reported the retirement of the Union's first president, George MacDonald, someone whose connections with the Poly went back to its earliest emergence;

Scene from The Mikado*, Woolwich Polytechnic Operatic Society.*

he had attended the Athletic Club meeting of 1888. 'At that time he was a member of a local cricket club called the "Fernwood". This club decided to join the Polytechnic en bloc, and so formed the first cricket team to play under the name of the Polytechnic.' MacDonald became a student in the engineering department; later he was for seven years General Secretary of the Athletic Club, then from 1933 its last President. His appointment as first President of the Union represented a reconciliation between the Club and the Union.

MacDonald's successor, Frederick White, had also been connected with the Poly for over 30 years, first attending evening classes in 1903, then enrolling in a four-year course as an Arsenal trade lad. During the First World War he had taken charge of a munitions factory at Park Royal which employed 6,000 men, women and boys. In 1934 he had been one of the long-time members of the Athletic Club who had 'made a strong fight against the change', but he now believed that the Poly's sports clubs had gained more than they had lost. White was a singer who for many years helped to supply 'the vocal items at club dinners'. That two such staunch members of the Athletic Club should have become the first two Presidents of the Union seemed at the time highly appropriate, but was also ominous, as events which followed the war were to show.

It was of great advantage to Mallett in founding the 1934 Union that it soon had a place in which to operate: the fine hall which opened in 1936. This was another of several important extensions of the Polytechnic's premises during the 1930s. Building it became possible when the Governors were at last able to buy the Duke of Wellington public house which stood at the corner of Lower Market Street and William Street (now Polytechnic Street and Calderwood Street) and divided the original William Street houses from the Lower Market Street blocks. An equally significant development was the recognition by the Governors that the island site, formed by Calderwood Street, Polytechnic Street, Thomas Street, and Wellington Street should be reserved for the Polytechnic's expansion. This they first suggested in 1935. The new hall (which had a refectory below and chemistry laboratories above) was an essential element in such a plan. So, too, were the acquisition of 34/35 Thomas Street and their transformation into workshops, laboratories and lecture rooms in 1936–7 and of 26/27 Polytechnic Street and their similar transformation in 1938–9. But the main 1938–9 extension was the building within the quad of the three four-storey block which became the library. Formal application to the LCC for further development of the island site was not, however, made until 1944, and that was only the beginning of a long story.

Though the extensions of the 1930s were primarily important for the much needed classrooms and laboratories they provided, they had the second function of making the Polytechnic's premises less of a rabbit warren. 'The rooms, labs and dungeons of this rhapsodical building,' Halliwell had called them in 1934. During the past year, he continued, many changes had already been made, and this 'is where we introduce you to Mr W. S. K. Edney, the Poly carpenter [later Clerk of the Works], who has proved to be a wonder at pulling down or putting up partitions, and no room looks the same after he has had a few hours in it. Take a stroll in the dungeons and see how the classrooms and labs have evolved from lumber rooms and store houses of long forgotten rubbish.'

Wall-hanging by millinery girls of the trade school, shown at the Victoria and Albert Museum and in Copenhagen (The Polygon, 1933).

Mallett's first annual report, delivered on Speech Day in December 1932, concerned the 1931–2 session, a time at which he admitted that he 'knew nothing of the Woolwich Polytechnic except that there was such an Institution'. The Depression was now at its height and Woolwich suffering even more severely than it had in the 1920s. Then, in 1928–9, the Woolwich Council of Social Service, a body consisting of representatives from the town's philanthropic groups, had formed the Woolwich Unemployment Council, which among other things sponsored allotments. In 1931 the largest of these, consisting of 550 plots on Erith Marshes, was also the largest in the country. Four years later there were 80 societies in Woolwich helping the unemployed. Nevertheless, in 1932 Mallet was able to report that the Polytechnic was in comparatively good health. The decreases in student numbers and class entries were of less than 4 per cent, and in total student hours of a mere 0.7 per cent.

'It would appear therefore,' he continued, 'that although somewhat fewer students were enrolled their attendance was better, and this is more to be desired than a large number of students who enrol and attend irregularly.'

After listing the progress of the physics, chemistry, engineering and newly formed building departments, as well as the School of Art and the technical schools, he observed significantly, 'It has been said that what is wanted in Woolwich is a University College, but I find that there is already within the Polytechnic organization a University College in the faculties of Science and Engineering.' These now had 80 undergraduate students and 22 postgraduate students. Whatever the LCC might want, the Poly was relentlessly taking a course which, for at least 30 years, its Principals had wished it to take.

The following year, Mallett's first, the educational side at the Polytechnic developed in so many directions that Halliwell tried in the Magazine to summarize them. Most important were the full recognition of the Polytechnic by the University of London for the preparation of students for internal degrees; the launching of part-time day courses in a variety of subjects, some of which led to degrees; and the formation of an electrical engineering department, with Mallett himself, an electrical engineer, as its head. Interestingly, at this time one of the services which the Polytechnic provided was the teaching of science to female students from Avery Hill Teacher Training College three miles away at Eltham – another early connection between the Polytechnic and the college it was to join 50 years later in its most significant merger.

Two years later (1934) Mallett was chosen to deliver the annual Faraday lecture – the subject he chose: television. It was an appropriate honour for the Principal of Woolwich Polytechnic. Faraday, just over 100 years earlier (28 October 1831), while staying at the house of a friend on Woolwich Common, had discovered a natural phenomenon which has had as much effect on modern life as the internal combustion engine: that a current can be induced in a coil of wire when this is rotated in the field of a magnet – hence the dynamo. For some years Faraday was also a visiting Professor of Chemistry at the Royal Military Academy, Woolwich.

It must be added, however, that Mallett mistakenly put telecommunications, on which he had published respected textbooks, into the physics department, partly because of his already well-formed ideas about the subject and partly

because it was also a subject in which the physics department's head, Vinycomb, had a special interest. For almost 30 years this had an adverse effect on related teaching at the Poly, years during which it became increasingly apparent, with the vast expansion of electronic applications, that it should have been in the electrical engineering department. The mistake was not corrected until the mid-1960s when new heads of physics and electrical engineering were appointed.

In 1934 came an even more important development: the launching of sandwich courses in engineering – often described as the first in the country though in fact Northampton Polytechnic had already started something similar. They were largely of Malletts's personal devising and some 20 years ahead of their time (in the mid-1950s sandwich courses were revived nationwide by the National Council for Technological Awards). Under Mallett's 1934 scheme local factories sponsored students from among their employees, who would spend two months at a time at the Poly, alternating with two-month periods at work. The course was to last two years at the end of which they would be qualified to sit University of London B.Sc. degree examinations. Seventeen boys from the first group completed the course and the success of the scheme is suggested by their achievements, three getting first-class degrees, nine second-class degrees, and one a pass. At the end of their time this first group showed their gratitude by entertaining Mallett and the other staff who had taught them to supper.

At this point (November 1936) Mallett made a full report to the Governors on the sandwich scheme. By now two further groups had enrolled, and he admitted that their quality had been less satisfactory, particularly the second. Five members of this had had to repeat their first year. The fact was that some of those who entered the scheme were not well enough advanced to benefit. 'It is really asking too much of the average student', he wrote, 'to start in the course without a knowledge of engineering drawing and applied mathematics.' He therefore recommended that the adding of a third, preliminary, year to the course.

That December Mallett attended a conference at County Hall at which the scheme and his suggestion were discussed, and as a result received a letter from the LCC's Education Officer. He, too, believed that the scheme needed modifying but not in the way Mallett had suggested.

It appears to the Council [he wrote] that an undue emphasis has been given to preparation for university degrees, and that entrants to the course have been chosen, to an undue extent, from amongst those who . . . are capable of proceeding to university degrees . . .

With regard to the Governors' request to increase the length of the course . . . to three years . . . the Council would be unwilling to agree to this extension if the preliminary year were merely devoted to those aspects of formal science and mathematics which would enable the last two years of the course to be treated academically.

Commenting on this, Mallett told the Governors. 'Previously, on the 9th November, I had been called up by Mr Rich and severely reprimanded for the success of the sandwich students in the B.Sc. (Eng.) examination. This reprimand I refused to accept, as I pointed out that everything that had been asked for by the Education Officer had been done faithfully and well.'

He then defended at length and vigorously all that he had been doing to promote degree work at the Polytechnic, including regaining University of London recognition of Polytechnic teachers, abandoned by Hogg. In his defence he described a parallel piece of obstruction by the LCC Education Committee.

'At about the same time, and in order to facilitate the progress of our boys towards a degree by putting them in a better position to obtain matriculation, it was asked that French should be included in the curriculum of the [Technical] School. . . . This was not agreed at the time, but French classes out of school hours were permitted. Since then, however, all that was asked for has been granted.'

He concluded, 'It would appear from the above that the LCC have throughout been most helpful in increasing our opportunity for doing degree work. The attitude now seems to be a complete reversal of this policy.'

Throughout 1937 the Governing Body and the LCC's Education Officer exchanged a succession of letters, both obstinately maintaining their positions. In October the Education Officer wrote, 'The proposals now submitted, more particularly the suggestion of a three-year course, do not comply with the Subcommittee's request. The Subcommittee have definitely decided not to approve an extension of the present course for three years, and they will not be prepared to consider an alternative scheme which sets up a separate three-year course.'

Commenting on this letter, Mallett told the Governors that it 'showed a complete misunderstanding of the Governing Body's proposals'.

Students' Art of the 1930s

Facing page: *Engravings by Edward Wood* (top three), *and* (below) *H. Shimmell* (The Polygon, *1934–7).*

This page (left to right): *Engravings by Ida Bayne, G. Ransom and Marjorie Essex.*

Polytechnic Personalities

Left to right: *Walter Alfred Scoble, head of the Civil Engineering Department; George MacDonald, last president of the Athletic Club and first president of the Union; Thomas Vinycomb, head of the physics department.*

Rather over a year later Mallett told the Governing Body's Education Committee than 'at an interview at County Hall on 13 January 1939 with the London County Council officials and Board of Education inspectors, it had been decided to extend the sandwich course to three years by the addition of a preliminary year.' What had happened during 1938 is not recorded, but clearly Mallet's persistence had overcome LCC obstinacy.

Outstanding among the Polytechnic staff of the time, both academically and as a personality, was the Irishman, Thomas Bernard Vinycomb, head of the physics department. To students (and fellow staff) he seemed the archetypal, absent-minded professor, and the Magazine in its profile hoped that he would stay until the Poly became a university and he could be a genuine professor. 'Not a few Poly people must have been greeted by him as if faintly remembered, even though they had been in consultation together but an hour or two earlier. This state of abstraction is a sign of considerable mental activity and, presently, the fruit appears as a new way of teaching the useful habits of the imaginary number 'j' (the square root of minus one), or another device of his famous wave model.' A colleague, travelling to work on the top deck of a bus, found T. B. (Vinycomb) scrabbling about on the floor below his seat. Asked what he was doing, he replied that he was looking for a sixpence he had dropped there the previous morning. Vinycomb had been at the Poly since 1908, apart from serving as a Captain in the war when he won the MC. The University of London acknowledged his quality by making him a recognized teacher of his own speciality, electrical communications.

Second of the Magazine's Polytechnic personalities was Walter Alfred Scoble, eventually to retire in 1944, head of the civil and mechanical engineering department. Scoble had begun his working life as an engineering apprentice at HM Dockyard, Devonport. After winning many prizes for mechanics, engineering, and mathematics at the Royal College of Science, he had first taught at Plymouth Technical School. In 1907 he undertook research which led to a successful, power-driven aeroplane, and various aspects of flight continued to interest him, but at the Polytechnic, which he joined in 1919, it was wire ropes that became his chief interest and he carried out valuable research on them for the Institution of Mechanical Engineers. During the Second World War he was to be attached to the Royal Naval Air Service at Greenwich, then to the RAF as OC Kite Balloon Research. To the Magazine's interviewer he described himself (after removing a coil of cable from his chair and using a slide-rule) as 'say twenty-five next birthday; build slim; hair, well slimming too'. The chief impression he gave his interviewer, however, was that of a man distressingly distracted from his research which (along with golf) was his passion by meetings, visiting girl students, and a colleague who wanted his cocktail shaker repaired.

On 28 January 1938 the University of London inspectors visited the Polytechnic for the first time since 1932. Their concluding comment read,

> As a result of our inspection of Woolwich Polytechnic we were impressed by the progress made during the past five years and by the general standard of efficiency. We recommend the renewal of recognition of the Polytechnic for a period of five years as a public educational institution offering satisfactory provision for the instruction of Internal Students and for the instruction of students pursuing courses of advanced study or research.

The report's only criticism was of the library, which they considered 'inadequate for the volume of work carried on in the Polytechnic'.

Among its interesting comments were that the course fees were 'extremely low' and that 95 per cent of the students came from elementary schools. It was thus, the report claimed, still doing what it had been originally founded to do, 'provide education for students from the "poorer classes"' – only half the truth.

The Second World War disrupted the Polytechnic as seriously as the First but in different ways. At once boys and girls of the technical schools and of the Junior Art School were evacuated. 'After standing by for a week,' Mallett told the Governors,

> the Junior Schools were finally evacuated on September 2nd, by train at 1.10 p.m., from Woolwich Dockyard Station to Snodland. . . . At Snodland we were met by a fleet of motor buses and taken to four villages: Burham, Eccles, East Malling, and West Malling. With the Girls' School at Burham, the Art School and 60 of the Boys' School at Eccles, and the remainder of the boys at the two Mallings and no suitable school premises available, it was evident at once that organised schooling would be difficult, but the weather was fine and all were kept busy and happy hop and apple picking, trench digging, walking and games.

About 100 of the 400 who had said they wished to go hadn't turned up. Teaching did eventually start, but in 1940 when alarm had subsided all three schools

The Second World War

The Second World War affected all of the institutions that eventually united to form the University of Greenwich.

Clockwise from this page:

Bomb damage to the 1938–9 Wellington Street extension (later the library of the Polytechnic), 12 January 1941.

Refugees from the Rachel McMillan Teacher Training College nursery.

Bomb damage at Garnett College.

Contents of the library at Manresa House heaped for safety in the dining hall.

Entering and inside the air-raid shelters at Dartford College of Teacher Training, 1940.

Sid Drake, a Polytechnic student killed in action in 1940, in whose memory a Memorial Trophy was established.

reopened in London (later to be evacuated again to Gainsborough, Trowbridge, and Northampton).

Meanwhile at the Poly air-raid shelters were dug in the playground, others were created in basement workshops, a demolition squad and a first-aid squad commandeered classrooms, 109 officers and men of the Queen's Own Regiment were billeted in the gymnasium (later taken by Woolwich Borough Council for a furniture store), and a barrage balloon unit established itself on the sports ground. The Ministry of Education had anyway decided that no schools or colleges of any sort should open in London. But during the next three weeks it changed its mind and the Poly's part-time day classes and sandwich courses opened on time for the 1939–40 session, the evening classes following on 9 October.

Student numbers, however, fell dramatically, from 4,635 in 1939 to a low point of 1,570 in 1940–1, the chief reason that as soon as the bombing of London began in the autumn of 1940 all evening classes were stopped and held instead at weekends. Since these provided less time, many had to be cancelled. Even for the 1944–5 session numbers were still some 1,200 below the pre-war figure. To an extent members of the armed forces replaced normal students. Some were instrument mechanics, some engine artificers, some tool room operatives, some servicemen taking specially arranged radar courses. In all 2,451 military personnel, 235 employees of the Royal Ordnance Factories, and 284 students sent by the Ministry of Labour took courses at the Polytechnic during the war, and in 1944–5 over 800 of them remained. Apart from providing such courses the Polytechnic's most significant war work was the making of gauges; its Gauge Testing Centre was recognized by the National Physical Laboratory.

The first bombs fell on the Polytechnic in 1940. These were incendiaries and extinguished before they could do damage, and it was not until Sunday, 12 January 1941 that it suffered seriously. Then, at 7.30 p.m. a bomb fell in the car park at the centre of the island site. During the afternoon students, staff, and friends had been attending one of the Polytechnic's wartime dances, and this had ended about 6.30. If the bomb had fallen then many must have been killed. In fact there were no casualties.

On fire-watching duty at the time on the roof of the hall were the two porters, Mr Warn and Mr Boyle. Secretary Halliwell had just visited them and

was on his way down, at library level. Here the library doors fell over him and over the balustrade. After extracting himself he and the porters made their way down the stairs, deep in fallen bricks and plaster, to the car park where they found Union members using hoses to prevent an outbreak of fire. Most seriously damaged was the block at the south end of Polytechnic Street, but in addition the engineering laboratories and the gymnasium lost their glass.

Repair work began early on Monday to replace windows, clear debris, stretch tarpaulins over damaged roofs, shore up one unsafe wall, and demolish another. Soldiers taking part in a course at the time gave help and most classes had begun again by Wednesday. A fortnight later bombs fell in Calderwood Street, blowing out the Polytechnic's windows here and also in Thomas Street.

Meanwhile many young men and women who might have been Poly students were in the forces. It lost fewer staff than in the previous war, since their occupations were mostly 'reserved'. A few, however, did fight, and a young member of the Art School staff, Jack May, died as an RNVR lieutenant. Curiously little other information survives about the wartime activities of staff or students; there was no Magazine to list casualties, as there had been in the First World War. The Union Council, however, raised money for memorial gates which were erected at the sports ground, and dedicated to the dead of both World Wars by the Bishop of Woolwich on 7 November 1948. They replaced the plaque to First World War dead which had gone when the wall to which it was fixed was removed in one of the Poly's many rebuildings, but unlike the plaque, they carried no names. They were designed by L. S. M. Prince, head of the School of Art since 1929. His most important work at the Polytechnic had been the establishment of the Junior School of Art, which, by the time he left, was receiving more applications for admission than it could accept. During the war it was he who had led the Junior School of Art on its evacuation pilgrimages 'in great triangles across the country, from Maidstone to Trowbridge . . . and finally to Northampton.' As well as contributing revealing caricatures of Poly staff and Governors to the Magazine, Prince regularly exhibited his water-colours at the Royal Academy. His memorial gates had been inspired, he wrote, by childhood memories of gates built in 1714 for John Morley, a member of the Butchers' Company 'on the outskirts of a small town on the northern fringe of Essex'.

The Polytechnic celebrated victory in Europe with a party on a Friday night in June 1945. Many 'concert acts' were staged in different classrooms, and these

Photograph taken after the war, of the 1939 extension, viewed from Wellington Street. The left wing was largely rebuilt after bomb damage (see picture on previous page); the repair is indicated by the lighter coloured brickwork.

The memorial gates at the Well Hall Sports Ground, Eltham, dedicated in 1948 by the Bishop of Woolwich to the dead of both World Wars.

were followed by community singing then dancing to the music of four bands until 2 a.m. It was on this occasion that a stuffed, gold-painted cockerel (the Chanticleer), once the property of the School of Art, was adopted as the Poly Union's mascot.

Once the War ended the Polytechnic quickly re-expanded. By 1946–7 there were in total 200 more students than in 1939. The increase in those working for degrees was more dramatic, from about 80 to over 300. This was largely the result of an influx of demobilized servicemen on war-service grants, many of them unable to find places at the country's universities, and of students from overseas.

In response the Polytechnic started, in addition to the engineering degree courses, new full-time courses for University of London general degrees and for special degrees in physics, chemistry, and mathematics. Soon, too, an Economics and Management Department was created. Some of the training arranged for servicemen during the war was also developed into permanent full-time courses.

On the other hand during early post-war years the Government gave polytechnics no clear idea of the way in which it wanted them to develop. The Butler Education Act of 1944 had classified all post-school education (part-time as well as full-time, at colleges as well as at universities) as 'further education'. And it had given local authorities not merely the right but the duty to provide 'adequate facilities' for further education. The new Ministry of Education (which the old Board of Education became) now had the power to compel them to do this.

At the same time the Government had once again been persuaded, this time by the war, of the importance of technical education, since the prosperity of the country would depend on the production of a steady and far larger stream of recruits with technical qualifications for industry. As a result it had set up the Percy Committee, 'to consider the needs of higher technological education in

England and Wales and the respective contributions to be made thereto by universities and technical colleges; and to make recommendations, among other things, as to the means for maintaining appropriate collaboration between universities and technical colleges in this field.'

In 1945 the Percy Committee's first three recommendations read

1. Industry must look mainly to universities for the training of scientists, both for research and development, and of teachers of science.

2. [Industry] must look mainly to technical colleges for technical assistants and craftsmen.

3. Both universities and technical colleges must share responsibility for educating the future senior administrators and technically qualified managers of industry.

This was a recognition of the important part technical colleges must play in higher education. The Committee also suggested the selecting of a limited number of technical colleges to do degree work, but neither this report, nor the Barlow Report (1946) said which colleges, nor gave guidance on the question which was to become vital to Woolwich during the following years: whether or not such colleges were exclusively to undertake advanced teaching. Even the LCC's Scheme for Further Education, published in 1949, which named Woolwich among the eight colleges to be encouraged to concentrate on advanced technical courses, did not say how exclusive this concentration should be.

Throughout Mallett's five post-war years his purpose remained what it had always been: to turn Woolwich Polytechnic into a college of the University of London, on the model of Queen Mary's College, Mile End, once the People's Palace. The great increase in students taking degree courses in these years was a satisfying move in that direction. But even apart from the Polytechnic's three secondary schools the great majority of students were still enrolled on non-advanced courses.

The typical non-degree Poly student of these years would be aged 15 to 18, in his first, second, or third year of part-time study for ONC (Ordinary National Certificate), or aged 18 to 20, preparing for HNC (Higher National Certificate). His subjects would be mathematics, engineering, physics, chemistry, and drawing. These exams were roughly the technical equivalent of GSE O-level or GSE A-level, for which other students would also be studying, mainly in the same science subjects.

It was to cater for its much increased advanced teaching, however, that the Polytechnic now employed a third again as many full-time staff (65 in 1939, 86 in 1947). Among long-serving senior staff, Vinycomb remained head of physics, Arthur Vogel of chemistry (see below), and Hugh Lowry of mathematics.

Both Lowry and Vogel had reputations in their subjects which extended far beyond the Polytechnic. During the years ahead Lowry was to become the first Vice-Principal, and for two interregnums Acting Principal. In the opinion of one colleague he was 'the most truly honourable man I have ever met' (Keith Reed).

'In the lecture room', *Chanticleer* wrote, when he retired in 1958, 'Mr Lowry may on occasion have left some of his students aghast at the rapidity with which

Dr A. I. Vogel, head of chemistry and author of the standard texts on analytical chemistry, still used and updated regularly by University staff.

his chalk covered the surface of the blackboard. Indeed it has been rumoured that the erasing board-rubber in his left hand sometimes out-stripped the fast moving chalk in his right hand.' An equally apocryphal tale – but just as true in spirit – was of an occasion when the Poly's porters came to take his blackboard to another room. As they carried it out, Lowry went with it, still busily writing on it with his right hand and erasing with his left. Lowry was no dry academic. 'The students', *Chanticleer* wrote, 'benefited from his sociable nature. Mr Lowry frequently attended their social evenings.' Fellow staff remembered that 'In fire-watching days (or nights) Mr Lowry established himself as a formidable opponent at the billiards table.'

In 1947 Prince was succeeded as head of the School of Art by Herbert Buckley. There followed one of the Polytechnic's saddest losses when, a few months later, Buckley died suddenly after attending that year's Christmas party. He had taught at the Polytechnic for 27 years and *Chanticleer* printed an impressive three pages of tributes to him. Students remembered particularly his broad-minded approach to their work, never imposing his own ideas on theirs. Seniors remembered him best from the war years when he had taken charge of the part of the school which had remained in London. All had admired him as much for his character as his teaching; they remembered too, his devotion to the Polytechnic. About his own work his successor, Heber Mathews, wrote, 'His paintings, done during the Summer vacations in the brilliant sunlight and warmth of Southern France, recreate in terms of painting, through their reverberant colour, the very life of the country, revealing to the full the richness of his soul. Inevitably, such a man must at times suffer frustration, bringing great agony of spirit.'

Heber Mathews's time also ended sadly since he presided over the School of Art, during the first phase of its destruction (despite his passionate protests) by the LCC. He had trained as a painter, but abandoned painting for pottery.

> To have watched him throwing [a colleague wrote], and to see how the clay seemed to grow beneath his hand was indeed to witness creative activity . . . To have worked in close co-operation with him (he would never tolerate the attitude that his staff worked 'under' him), for nine years is . . . an experience which gave me an understanding of the real function of education. For Mr Mathews education meant the awakening of the mind, as very distinct from the storage of factual knowledge. . . . As a young boy, Mr Mathews' great interest was in music, which he never lost, and few people realised that one of his favourite relaxations was to sit at the piano and abandon himself in music of his own composition.

Mathews had come to the Polytechnic in the mid-1920s and in total taught there for 30 years.

Chanticleer had become the Polytechnic's magazine in May 1948. Ten years earlier the old *Polytechnic Magazine* had announced that its issue of April 1938 would 'mark the end of the journal in its present form'. During the two previous years, since its take over by the Union in 1936, its general appearance and contents had remained little changed, 'but the time has now come' the 1938 editorial continued, 'when something bigger and better is called for. Preparations are already in hand and we hope that September will see the beginning of a new magazine series, having contents worthy of the big organization it represents.'

The bigger and better magazine was called *Woop* (Woo-lwich p-olytechnic) but how many issues were published remains obscure since the University archives have no copies. Indeed, its existence is known only because it is mentioned in a slim, coverless *Woolwich Polytechnic Magazine* which was now published alongside *Woop* and was concerned entirely with the doings of clubs and societies. It described *Woop* as 'literary'. Both probably disappeared in September 1939 at the start of the war.

In 1945 a clubs and societies journal and a *Woolwich Polytechnic Magazine* of 1930s style both reappeared. 'After six years of war . . .', the Magazine began, 'it was a pleasant surprise to find that we were now allowed a certain amount of paper to have this magazine published.' Style and contents were traditional, and despite the Union's clubs and societies journal, it too included reports of their activities. The Operatic Society had recently staged *Iolanthe*, and one of the cast described the alarm he had experienced, when being made up as a peer of the realm below stage while the chorus of fairies were 'tripping hither, tripping thither' above his head.

After five issues this magazine also disappeared, and it was now that *Chanticleer* appeared. Later its editor wrote that the Magazine Board remembered Mallett with gratitude 'for it was Dr Mallett who fought for us when the question of discontinuing the publication of the magazine arose'. Though again of paperback format, it was better produced and no longer printed on yellow-tinged wartime paper. Its title was significant. This was the polite version of Corky Prior's Cock (see below), the Union's mascot and symbol of student power.

Twelve issues were published, numbers 10, 11, and 12 (1956, 1957, and 1959) of larger size ($7\frac{1}{2}$ by 10 ins). Throughout its life it made a serious attempt to include articles, poems, and photographs by students, eventually reducing to five pages out of 40 accounts of the doings of clubs and societies.

On 31 January 1947 the inspectors of the University of London visited the Polytechnic for the first time since their pre-war 1938 visit. They found the engineering laboratories adequate 'but the equipment is much the same as in 1938'. The physics laboratories were also adequate though there were relatively few students taking degree courses in this subject. About Vogel's chemistry department, however, they were enthusiastic. 'The Inspectors were favourably impressed with the equipment of the chemistry department. The apparatus is up-to-date and there appears to be no difficulty in obtaining grants for research purposes. The staff, five full-time lecturers in addition to the Head of Department, is adequate.'

The inspectors' main criticism was of the Academic Board. This had been established in 1932 to advise on all aspects of the teaching of students taking internal degrees at the University of London. It consisted of the Principal, all teachers recognized by the University (at this time seven), and two other teachers elected by the staff. But it was, in the Inspectors' opinion, 'not a very active

The active social life of the Polytechnic quickly resumed after the War. The cycling club issued its own magazine.

Crowds on Wellington Street waiting for Princess Margaret to leave the Town Hall on the occasion of her visit to Woolwich in October 1951, the year after the Polytechnic celebrated its Diamond Jubilee.

body'. In particular it did not recommend or have power to appoint new members of staff, and it had 'inadequate control' over the admission of students to degree courses. Such criticisms were based on a view that, if the Polytechnic was to have university-style degree courses, it should have other university features, one of the most important that teaching staff should take an active part in its management.

With the non-academic features of the Polytechnic the inspectors were better pleased. 'We gained the impression that there was an active social and corporate life.' They also noted an indication that the Polytechnic was already becoming more than a local college in so far as it was taking an interest in how its students survived when not at their books. 'The Principal informed us that a hostel near the Institution is available for a small number of students and many others live in approved lodgings.'

Unlike the 1938 inspectors, those of 1947 drew no general conclusions and made no specific recommendation that the Polytechnic should continue to be recognized for University of London internal degrees – this was apparently now assumed.

In 1950 the Polytechnic celebrated its Diamond Jubilee. Throughout the year numerous special sporting events were staged, from a table tennis tournament in March to a ladies' hockey tournament in October. There was also an exhibition, a fancy dress ball, a 'Youth Hostel Association Moonlight Hike', and a performance of *Merrie England* by the Operatic Society.

On 31 March about 225 members, staff, Governors, and friends sat down to a Jubilee Dinner. The menu may have had a three-course, wartime simplicity (some foods were still rationed) but the band of the Royal Artillery played, toasts were drunk to the Polytechnic and its founders, and the occasion was altogether a splendid one. In his speech Sir Thomas Spencer, Chairman of the Governors, said that 'the Polytechnic must develop into an Industrial University College, not in ten years time, not in five, but now.'

Chanticleer's comment on the contrast between the Polytechnic of 1890 and that of 1950 captures more of the transformation that had taken place than its flippancy suggests. 'Certainly some members might profit from a rein-auguration of the "W. P. Temperance Society". The Sectarian Ban unfortunately now excludes such activities as the "W.P. Tract Band". But what an elevating touch it would be if now, as in the Naughty Nineties, Union Council Meetings "commenced and closed with prayer".'

Nine months later Mallett, probably the most influential of the Polytechnic's first five Principals in guiding it towards university status, died while still in office. He had been unwell during the year, but as active as ever – a member of staff who came in 1947 retains as his main impression, Mallett speeding down a corridor, the gown he always wore streaming out horizontally behind him. He also had an excellent relationship with Secretary Halliwell, not something easily achieved since the LCC's block grants were in fact under the control of the Secretary and he, not the Principal, was responsible for disbursing the monies. Their offices were on opposite sides of the 1916 entrance, and Mallett would say that no unwanted visitor ever got past, referring in particular to local or national officials. To name just a few of his contributions to the Polytechnic's development, he had helped to give it its first worthy hall, established its sandwich courses, formed the forerunner of its Students' Union, and successfully seen it through five years of World War.

8

Local or National

1950–1956

THE YEARS 1950 TO 1970 saw an almost total transformation of Woolwich Polytechnic. By the end of this time barely a feature (the maze-like buildings of the island site excepted) from students and staff to the work they did, the exams they took, and the Governing Body, which up to a point, governed them, was what it had been 20 years before. Three new Principals had come, and the third had been transformed into a Director. At the same time the Woolwich Polytechnic had even lost the name to which thousands of past members felt so much loyalty. True, the signs of the changes to come can now be seen in earlier years, but at the time there were other signs which suggested other futures and might have proved better forecasts.

There was another difference between these 20 years and earlier ones. Then, too, the way in which the Poly developed was never fully under the control of its Governors or Principals, but men like Calderwood, Gannon, and Mallett had been able to play important parts in its evolution. In the 1950s and 1960s it was to be driven more powerfully than before by the decisions – or indecision – of politicians, themselves swayed by social changes and their political prejudices.

For the 1949–50 session the great majority of students were still attending evening or part-time day courses (4,141, excluding the three secondary schools). Only 1,126 were attending full time. Their main subjects were mathematics, the sciences, and engineering. About a quarter of all students were working for degrees but of those taking full time courses a much higher proportion, about two-thirds. All degree courses were for internal University of London degrees. About two-thirds of the students still came from greater London and about a third from Kent with only about 151 from other parts of Britain and 113 from overseas. Their ages (the schools included) were anything from 13 to 30.

These figures show that the Polytechnic was still essentially a local institution, catering for local needs. On the one hand there were students in the

Facing page: *Formal dance in the Great Hall, Avery Hill College, 1951.*

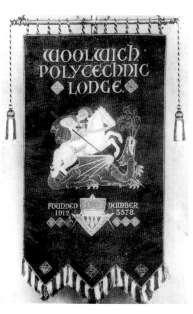

Chemistry Department taking postgraduate courses and doing fundamental research. But on the other there were apprentices learning bricklaying. Keith Reed remembered seeing a member of the Building and Architecture Department teaching plastering. With a fine sweep he would demonstrate how it was done, his plaster adhering perfectly to the wall, then invite the class to try. The result was 20 boys with their faces covered in lime plaster. Courses in practical skills like these were a response to the needs of some local employers who would not release employees or pay their fees unless they believed their courses would teach them something useful.

One result was obvious. The qualifications of the staff varied widely. In 1949–50 there were now 88 teaching full time (as well as 26 at the secondary schools), the largest number in the Department of Mechanical Engineering (20). In addition there were 172 part-time teachers (23 at the schools), the Mechanical Engineering Department again having most (30), closely followed by the Mathematics Department with 25. It was not any growth in total student numbers which had caused these further increases in the five years since the war, but the fact that many more were taking full-time degree courses.

To teach or supervise the work of these there were men like Lowry, head of mathematics, about to become Acting Principal for the first time, and Vogel, head of chemistry, both of whom had written widely used textbooks, did original research, and were 'recognized teachers' for internal degrees at the University of London. But other staff were qualified only to teach crafts. Those in the Building and Architecture Department were soon joined by others in the Business and Commerce Department, launched in 1952 with courses in shorthand and typing.

Whatever their qualifications, teaching and administrative staff either were, or soon became local. Secretary Halliwell was typical. An extrovert Lancastrian from Wigan, he was by now deeply involved in local affairs, a tax commissioner, and a member of the Hospital Board. He in particular was responsible for giving the Poly what staff and students of the time remember as a family atmosphere. He would organize all manner of social events from treasure hunts to the famous Christmas parties, so popular that there had to be several on successive evenings. Tickets would change hands on a black market and those who had been unlucky would wait outside in the hope of getting someone else's exit pass.

The feelings of long-serving staff about their local, part-time students were described by W. G. Spencer when he retired as head of the Electrical Engineering Department in 1951, a position he had held since succeeding Mallett in 1938.

My last word is to express my unbounded admiration for the ordinary evening student. When executive, advisory, ordinary and subcommittees

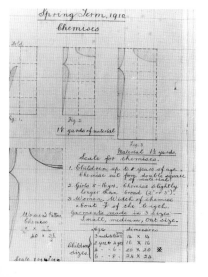

are turning [*sic*] their reports about technical education I find great comfort in thinking of these students working steadily and enjoying it. I feel that in the future students of this class will fill many of our highest positions in the professional class as well as in the technical and artisan classes.

Milton Ashworth, Scoble's successor as head of Mechanical Engineering, an 'old gentleman' by the 1950s, had similar feelings. Joyce Webb (later secretary to three Principals/Directors) remembered that 'his life was his work', his students were 'his lads', and occasionally he would help one to get an award, finding a few extra marks by 'reassessing' his exam paper. Ashworth (who never lost his Geordie accent) had the disconcerting but endearing habit of greatly delaying the banking of his salary cheques, at this time distributed by hand, so causing consternation at the year end. The books would appear not to balance – by the equivalent of Ashworth's recent pay.

Less senior staff were equally committed. Brian Manley remembered how James Poole, 'a superb teacher who could describe physical phenomena in ordinary language', explained to him one day in the nearby Director General public house 'the linking lines of magnetic force in a dynamo' by linking arms.

Important in creating the Polytechnic's family atmosphere was the arrangement of the administrative offices, all set close inside the Thomas Street entrance. Here everyone knew each other and worked with and for each other. Vital in preserving its local character was its status as grant-aided, not maintained. The LCC, later the ILEA, made it a block grant, but it could spend this, within limits, in its own ways. It had its own Clerk of Works, Mr Edney, and maintenance sections, with locally recruited carpenters, electricians, and other tradesmen. Edney was 'a character, a Hampshire carpenter by trade. He would take as long to tell one about his holidays as he took to take them. He was loved by all' (Reed).

Members of staff were responsible for various of the building's services. Ernest Sainsbury, for example, senior lecturer in electrical engineering, was in charge of lighting and other electrical matters (in 1950 the Poly was still lit by DC, power provided by its own three generators) and Arthur Lee, senior lecturer in mechanical engineering, was in charge of heating and water.

The overall statistics fail to reveal just how local its students mostly were, the majority not merely from London but from Woolwich itself or from nearby places like Charlton where great industries still flourished. This was, of course, especially true of the three secondary schools which remained part of the Polytechnic: the Boys' and Girls' Technical Schools, and the Junior Art School. In 1949–50 the Boys' School (which had Engineering and Building Divisions) numbered 376, the Girls' School 212, and the Junior Art School 49.

The Craft Tradition

Facing page: *Pottery, leatherwork, and an embroidered banner, Woolwich School of Arts and Crafts, 1925–6. Needlework notebook, Avery Hill, 1910. Fashion at the Jubilee Exhibition, 1950, by the Secondary (Technical) School for Girls. On the loom, 1950s, Avery Hill.*

This page: *Setting up an exhibition in the Fashion Department of the Polytechnic, 1969. Baking demonstration, 1959. Jointing pipes and bricklaying, Hammersmith School of Arts and Crafts.*

Some Governors and staff were particularly reluctant to see these schools transferred elsewhere.

Others, however, understood that they must go, and their arguments were put strongly to the Governing Body by Hugh Lowry during his first period as Acting Principal after Mallett's death. Firstly, the close connection between the Boys' School and the Polytechnic had already diminished. For example, 20 years earlier it had taken half the teaching time of the staff of the Physics Department. Now it only occupied one and a half teachers' time from a department of 14. Secondly, 'no end of correspondence has now to go through the Principal or the Secretary which would normally be dealt with by the Headmistress or Headmaster' of the schools.

He continued,

> Moreover, from the point of view of the future of the Schools as part of a Comprehensive School, it is probably much better that the links with the Polytechnic should be severed now so that they can form a tradition as separate entities before being absorbed in the Comprehensive School.
>
> There is no reason to think that the Schools would necessarily lose by the separation of control. Is it maintained that Shooters Hill School and King's Warren School have lost during the last 20 years by leaving the Polytechnic?

Finally, strongest argument, 'the advanced work urgently requires more room, and the quickest way of getting some more is the removal of the Schools'.

In response the Governors minuted their recognition that 'the Secondary Technical Schools, must, under the final plan, eventually be transferred from the Polytechnic to schools provided by the London County Council', but resolved that until this happened 'it would be in the interests of the schools for them to continue as part of the Polytechnic'.

An illustration from the Magazine (by R. Singleton), reflecting on the decline of the Arsenal in the 1950s.

Now at last in 1951 the Government published its White Paper on Higher Technological Education which, importantly, recommended 75 per cent government grants for the costs incurred by colleges in running advanced courses. In 1953 Woolwich's Higher National Diploma and Higher National Certificate courses were recognized for these grants. More important, however, from the point of view of Woolwich's secondary schools, was circular 255 which followed the White Paper and specifically required 'colleges which have been selected for development' to transfer their elementary work to other institutions.

There was least difficulty in disposing of the Girls' Technical School; it needed less in the way of workshops or laboratories. And in September 1954 it was successfully transferred to the new Kidbrooke Comprehensive School. But in 1955 James Tait, appointed Principal in 1951, was still having to argue for the transfer of the Boys' Technical School. He told Governors that not only did the Ministry of Education now require this to be carried out, but that while the schools remained at the Polytechnic they gave the LCC a good reason for refusing to give the Polytechnic new accommodation. The LCC could argue that in due course all that was needed would be provided by the removal of the schools. Furthermore, 'the tone of the Polytechnic as a college may be raised when young boys are no longer using the same premises as the adult students.'

Eventually the LCC agreed to take responsibility for the Boys' School from

1 August 1956. But this was by no means the end of the matter. To the irritation of the Governors, it continued to call itself the Woolwich Polytechnic School. It also continued to use the Polytechnic's workshops, refectory, gymnasium, and sports ground. In 1958 the Governors asked it to cease to do this and by 1960 it had relinquished the workshops and refectory, but not the gymnasium and sports ground, and in March that year the Governing Body minuted that it was

> conscious of the necessity to develop the advanced work of the Polytechnic and considers that it is more than ever essential that pupils of the Boys' School should not use the Polytechnic premises, even temporarily, as this gives a false impression of the standards of work at the Woolwich Polytechnic.

Dr James S. Tait, Principal 1951–7.

Only gradually during the 1960s did the School cease to use the gymnasium and sports ground. Meanwhile, in September 1956 the Junior Art School (which had had 41 students the previous year) was also transferred to the LCC.

As Tait had told the Governors, the argument about disposing of the schools formed part of the continuing accommodation saga. For some 15 years after the end of the war the LCC found various reasons for rejecting or delaying the Poly's increasingly desperate applications for more space, one of them that shedding the schools would solve the problem. When the Governors complied, either by shedding the schools or shedding junior work, they did so because they hoped to be able to demonstrate that they still did not have enough.

Silence had followed the Governors' submission in 1944 of its plans for the island site and on 27 November 1947 Mallett had written to the LCC,

> Many years ago it was suggested that for the further development of the Woolwich Polytechnic it would be necessary to acquire the island site, that is the site bounded by Wellington Street, Polytechnic Street, Calderwood Street and Thomas Street, and drawings were actually sent to you in 1944 showing a proposed building on this site. These proposals stand as far as the site and the building are concerned, but not as to the detailed use to which the building would be put.

He attached new plans which showed that the Polytechnic would require the whole site for its classes, and that there would be no room in the island site for the Junior Schools. The Governing Body would like these to be housed in a nearby building.

When, eventually, on 28 May 1949 the LCC's Education Officer replied he not only claimed that the Governors had overestimated the number of students who would be enrolled in coming years, but added,

> It should also be pointed out that when the Building Department and the Secondary (Technical School) have been removed together with ordinary national certificate and City and Guilds courses there will be several thousand feet of space available for other students. In the circumstances I am not in a position to recommend the Council to designate the whole of the island site.

The LCC's plan eventually excluded the public house in Thomas Street, the bank on the corner, and certain shops in Wellington Street. This enabled it to ask the Governors for a new plan, since the old one was out-of-date. The Governing Body complied, now taking account of the space which would be released by the secondary schools and the 'lower part-time day and evening work', sending the relevant extracts to the LCC in February 1951. At the same time it provided statistics which showed that between 1939 and 1951 student hours had risen by 85 per cent. 'The only extra accommodation to offset this increase', it wrote, 'was the lease of MacBean Street School which gave 13 extra rooms. The first consideration for the extensions should be the existing accommodation. This it will be realised from the figures given, is totally inadequate for the present number of students.'

The following May it recorded without comment, 'In the minutes of the London County Council Education Committee dated 12 March 1952 extensions to the Polytechnic are included in the Further Education Building Programmes in 1954–57.'

That July however, the LCC Education Officer wrote to the Governors,

The detailed proposals submitted by the governors in October 1950 and in July 1951 are considered to be a little ambitious and will need modification in the light of the accommodation position when all the junior work is withdrawn. In the present conditions it is unlikely that the whole scheme of development will be found possible within the next ten years.

Of the six proposals only the first three would be considered for the 1954–7 programme.

By 1953 the Governors had learned that the Minister of Education had decided that it was not possible to include even these in the 1954–5 programme. Further delays followed, partly because the Metropolitan Water Board appealed against the requisitioning of its premises in Wellington Street which the plans required, partly because the revised plan submitted in July 1952 did not satisfy the LCC's Town and Country Planning regulations. It was May 1954 before the LCC Education Officer wrote to the Governors, 'As you know, we are still waiting to hear whether the Minister will agree to put the first stage proposals in a building programme and until this consent is received I think that it would be unwise to undertake further work on the plans.'

The following January (1955) the Chairman of the Governors and the Principal, Tait, by this time it would seem in some desperation, met Mrs Cole, Chairman of the LCC's Further Education Subcommittee, who told them that 'she thought the plan . . . would go through the various committees within the next month, and then would be recommended to the Ministry of Education.' In March, however, the Governors became aware of a minute of the LCC Education Committee which read 'the proposed (building) extensions of Woolwich Polytechnic will not be proceeded with for the present (i.e. the 1955–6 programme).'

The Governors noted that since this 'appeared to conflict with the assurance given by the Chairman of the Further Education Subcommittee, the Principal had written to the Assistant Education Officer. . . . He proposed to await a reply

... and if not received shortly or if unsatisfactory he would again seek an interview with Mrs Cole.'

There matters stood at the end of 1955. It was not until June 1956 that Mrs Cole gave this second interview, and the saga was by no means over. But already it was too late to prevent Woolwich's inadequate accommodation being severely criticized by HM Inspectors in 1954 and this being one of the causes of the dismaying news it received in 1956.

Events which led to this news had begun with the reports of the Percy and Barlow Committees in 1945 and 1946, and continued with the LCC's scheme, published in 1949, which had proposed that eight London colleges should concentrate on advanced engineering courses and had required colleges selected for development to dispose of their lower-level teaching.

Though this White Paper had helped persuade the Polytechnic to dispose of its Girls' Technical School, and the other two schools were to go in 1956, there had been no parallel reduction in lower-level work. In 1954–5, to use one form of measurement, postgraduate and other degree work amounted to 32,880 student hours of teaching, lower-level student hours to 61,959.

By then HM Inspectors had come and gone. Their general conclusions were complimentary. 'The work throughout the Polytechnic is of a very high order not withstanding the accommodation difficulties. There is a keen spirit of enthusiasm among the staff and students and the well-organized departments are working harmoniously together.' About the Polytechnic's accommodation however, they were severely critical:

The provision of lavatories is inadequate and there is no separate provision for the Board Room or for the Principal. There is no waiting room; visitors are shown to seats in one of the corridors.

The refectory is in the basement and the ventilating system is quite inadequate. During meals, with large numbers of people present, the temperature reaches too high a value for comfort. The kitchens are too small with only one outside window and conditions are most unsatisfactory. The maintenance staff have to work in the basement workshop under conditions it is difficult to tolerate. The rooms are, in general, too small, lack suitable ventilation and work must invariably be done in artificial light.

The only departmental store in the building is a small room used for issuing chemicals and apparatus to students. An exit door has been boarded up to make an alcove to hold the scrubbing and polishing machines used by the cleaners. Stores have to be kept in the laboratories or in the corridors. There are no students' cloakrooms and lecture rooms and laboratories are cluttered up with students' coats and other belongings, which have to be carried from room to room. The laboratory staff of 44 have nowhere to work, eat and rest and keep their belongings except the laboratories and workshops.

There are two social rooms for the students in the main building and one of these is frequently used for Polytechnic business. The Union has purchased property adjoining the Polytechnic which contains a number of small rooms none of which is really suitable for Union purposes.

A dismal-looking hut serves as a billiard room and lavatory accommodation is in the yard outside.

Their other criticism of was the amount of elementary work still being undertaken. 'The right solution', they wrote, 'may be to provide for much of the elementary technical and craft work in a subsidiary institution leaving the Polytechnic to concentrate on full-time and part-time advanced-level courses.' Under Circular 255 much of Woolwich's work had been recognized, and shedding elementary work would conform with the circular's requirements.

Here was new pressure on the Polytechnic to transform itself into an institution primarily concerned with degree-level teaching. It might seem perverse that its Academic and Technical Boards, meeting together on 10 November 1954 to consider the report, should instead have minuted that the transfer of elementary work 'could only be justified if we could look forward with confidence to the development of advanced work by an increased enrolment of full-time students' and that all which these committees would recommend was that elementary work should not be allowed 'to extend in numbers of groups beyond those existing'. But the truth is that the Polytechnic had no choice. As Tait told the Governors in his Principal's comments on the inspectors' report, 'There is no existing establishment in the vicinity to which we might transfer our less advanced work, and so it is difficult to give the matter the serious consideration recommended by the Inspectors.'

Meanwhile, for the past nine years the Government had failed to act on an important recommendation made by the Percy Committee in 1945: that there should be 'a course for engineers equal in length to a university first-degree course, but made up of alternate periods of full-time study and work practice.' Instead there had followed, in Harold Dent's words, 'Years of sterile controversy about – of all things – whether the award such an engineers' course as the Percy Committee proposed should be a degree or a diploma.' Now at last the Government set up the Hives Council, more often known as the National Council for Technological Awards, for this purpose.

James Tait was a member of this Council. Tait, a Scot, had come to the Poly from Northampton Polytechnic (today's City University) and was, like Mallett, an electrical engineer. 'Although he has had only a few years in his new office,' HM Inspectors wrote in 1954, 'he has a firm grasp of the organisation. The harmonious relationship between members of the staff, and between departments, is a tribute to his leadership and tact.'

One senior member of the Electrical Engineering Department remembered that Tait would give him his examination papers to mark. But the same teacher considered that, 'though perhaps not a leading scholar, he could charm the birds out of the trees', and that he was highly conscientious, claiming correctly that he would be at his desk at 9.30 every morning, dressed and available to anyone who wanted him. His problem was that too many people outside the Polytechnic wanted him, with the result that he sat on innumerable committees. In 1956 he contributed to *Chanticleer* a two-page account of the dinners, lectures and ceremonies in which this outside work had involved him in a single month.'

Distracting as this could be, it also benefited Woolwich, as Tait's appointment to the Hives Council showed. 'I had the honour', he wrote in the same article, 'to be appointed to the Board of Studies in Engineering and subsequently to the National Council for the new award so it is unlikely that Woolwich will lag behind in any new development.'

Tait was right. The Polytechnic took quick advantage of the Diploma of Technology, the name the new award had finally been given. As the Percy Committee had recommended, courses leading to it were to be of sandwich type. They were to last four years, at least one year to consist of 'industrial training'. This could either take the form of a complete year of such work (thick sandwich) or of six-month periods (thin sandwich). With its previous experience of sandwich courses, Woolwich was well qualified to revive them. Its courses for the new award in mechanical and electrical engineering were among the first in the country which the council recognized.

'Recognition' was one of the features of these courses. Unlike university degree courses, their syllabuses were not prescribed by the awarding university, but devised by the college itself and submitted to the National Council for Technological Awards for its approval. This enabled colleges like Woolwich to devise courses which suited their local industries.

It was these industries – GEC, G. A. Harvey & Co., Royal Arsenal, AEI, Standard Telephones, Cable and Wireless, to name some of the larger – which might sponsor employees to take the new courses, continuing to employ them during their 'work practice', and after graduation. It seemed to staff of the time who were teaching technology that the new courses and awards were 'the final solution (the best of all worlds)'. A new golden age had arrived. They were not to know that it would last less than ten years, for it later became more commonly the responsibility of the Polytechnic to find firms to employ students during their work periods. These students were said to be college-based, as opposed to 'industry-based' and were supported by local authority grants.

The Government's new commitment to advanced technological education seemed confirmed during the following year when it published (February 1956) a new White Paper on the subject. Certain colleges, this proposed, were to be nominated as Colleges of Advanced Technology. These would receive £70 million to improve their facilities. They would help to increase the number of students qualified in technology the country produced each year from 9,500 to 15,000. 'The Government', it announced, 'wish to see the proportion of advanced work at these colleges vigorously increased', and listed 24 such colleges, Woolwich Polytechnic among them, with the implication that all of these might hope to be designated Colleges of Advanced Technology.

Woolwich Polytechnic certainly hoped so. When the Education Committee of the Governing Body discussed the matter in March it minuted, with obvious surprise, 'as yet it is not definite that Woolwich will be selected as a College of Advanced Technology'. In case its qualifications were in doubt the Governing Body sent the Ministry of Education a report on its activities during the previous five years. It had already been doing the sort of work which an Advanced College would be required to do, it had suitable staff and equipment, a Governing Body with some independence, and a good record of examination results. In June, however, the Minister chose just eight of the 24 colleges named by the White Paper, including only three in London. Woolwich was *not* one of them.

9

Down but Not Out

1956–1965

❧ ❧ ❧ ❧ ❧

WOOLWICH POLYTECHNIC'S FAILURE TO BE SELECTED as a College of Advanced Technology was deeply discouraging. In Michael Locke's words, it was 'the most traumatic event since the disputes of its infancy' (*Traditions and Controls in the Making of a Polytechnic: Woolwich Polytechnic 1890–1970*). Tait at once wrote to the Ministry of Education. In reply he was told:

> The Minister wishes me to emphasise that he has thought it essential to apply strictly the first condition in the Appendix to Circular 305, namely that the college of advanced technology must concentrate exclusively on work at advanced level. According to the Minister's information more than half the day-time work in the Polytechnic is at present below that level, and although he notes that the negotiations now proceeding will permit removal of some of the lower level work he cannot yet regard the Polytechnic as being within sufficiently close striking distance of the definition of a college of advanced technology to justify him in designating it.

Given that these were the Minister's criteria his decision was no doubt correct. Though the Girls' Technical School had gone, it was not until the end of the 1955–6 session that the other two schools went, and much of the rest of the Polytechnic's work was indeed not of advanced level. Measured in student hours of study, now only about 35,000 hours were devoted to degree or postgraduate work, out of a total of 98,000. In other words there had been little change since 1950 when the figures were 17,000 out of 50,000. Apart from the secondary schools the Polytechnic was still offering many courses leading to awards or qualifications below degree standard, those of the new Commerce and Management Studies Department being typical.

Facing page: *View looking south across Woolwich in 1964, with the power station in the foreground, Churchill House top left, the island site to its right with the spire of the Town Hall above and Riverside House (East) in the centre, behind the power station chimneys.*

On the other hand the Polytechnic could fairly claim that the LCC had still not provided a college to which it could pass less advanced work. This may have suited those who believed it should remain a local institution providing a wide range of courses at all levels, but it did not make it any less true. If the Minister was also influenced by the 1954 Inspectors' comments on the Polytechnic's accommodation (as he must surely have been) the Governors could with equal justice claim that this was not their fault. In spite of their numerous applications, the LCC had allowed no new buildings or improvements since 1939.

The year after Woolwich's great disappointment Tait resigned. Staff considered him to have been a good Principal, even if some in retrospect thought that he had treated his time at Woolwich only as a step in his career. If so it was a successful one. He returned to Northampton Polytechnic, where he was to be appointed the first Vice-Chancellor when it became the City University.

His unsatisfactory relationship with Halliwell was another reason for his leaving. The two had never agreed; Joyce Webb, a member of the Principal's office staff, remembered that they were continually showing ill will towards each other in the most trivial ways. Behind this lay basic differences in what they wanted for the Poly: Halliwell in broad terms conservative, Tait progressive.

Tait was succeeded by Harold Heywood, a mechanical engineer with much experience in industry and teaching, including periods at Regent Street Polytechnic and most recently as Assistant Professor at Imperial College. Though he had as much charm as Tait, he was in contrast 'marvellously laid-back', his regular 20-minute siesta in his office being typical. Like Tait, he had outside distractions, but of another kind. His special interest was solar energy. 'Where the sun shone, there you would find Dr Heywood.' He had already made long visits to California, Arizona, and Egypt. In Joyce Webb's opinion, research was what really interested him and he was not a good administrator, believing, like Napoleon, that much correspondence, if ignored, would answer itself. Instead he would sit, smoking his pipe and thinking. He was extremely well liked, very loyal and supportive to his staff. He introduced a series of public lectures by such distinguished people as Edmund Hillary (within a few years of his conquest of Everest) and Professor Bondi. And, despite his easygoing attitude to life, the Polytechnic continued to change in important ways during his ten years, largely because he was urged forward by Derrick Godfrey, at first as head of the Mathematics Department, then as Vice-Principal. Godfrey, in Keith Reed's words, was 'the not-too-hidden power behind the throne'.

If there was one man who was responsible for pushing Woolwich relentlessly towards becoming an advanced college of one or another kind it was Godfrey. From the start he was determined that it should not again miss a chance of the sort it had missed in 1956, and he had a clear vision of the way to ensure this. 'On occasions', Reed remembered,

he might appear to pursue an objective too relentlessly and to perhaps lack the lighter touch which can so often bridge a difference or smooth over an awkward moment. Such feelings could have been heightened . . . by the extent of detail which he would prepare, and be seen to have prepared, prior to any discussion. . . . This was most evident during early exchanges with senior officers of other colleges when possible merger proposals were to be considered, and at internal meetings where contentious issues had to be resolved. The plain fact is that he would have thought things through to a conclusion . . . whereas others might well be responding on a more emotional level.

His thick glasses added to the impression that he was a private person, seeming to create a barrier between himself and others. Certainly he was 'not given to easy exchanges upon chance meetings, nor ever to displaying inner feelings or emotions'. But once someone interested him he was direct and frank. He was a man of tremendous integrity, never shirking responsibility nor blaming others.

His other problem, Joyce Webb remembered, was that he believed everyone else to be as honest as himself. When there was a problem he would not know which of two people's stories to believe.

Polytechnic Street in the 1960s.

Circular 305 which followed the 1956 White Paper created four kinds of college. After Colleges of Advanced Technology came Regional Colleges, then Area Colleges and Local Colleges. Woolwich was designated a Regional College. Though Regional Colleges were also encouraged to develop advanced work, they were intended to provide more part-time work and to cater more for the needs of their own regions. In short they were intended to have a different rather than an inferior role, but it was an ill-defined role and not one which those with a vision like Godfrey's could accept. To them it seemed that Regional meant second rank. As a result almost all the changes of the next ten years were made by the Polytechnic in the hope that they would improve its chances of promotion to a College of Advanced Technology or the equivalent.

Some of these changes were the result of the so-called rationalizing of the teaching of certain subjects in London. For Woolwich this meant surrendering various departments. The School of Art – from the first an integral part of the Polytechnic, saved before the First World War in spite of suggestions that art teaching was something a place like Woolwich did not need – was one department to suffer. At this time it was offering full-time and part-time courses in painting, fabric design, printing, book illustration, and pottery, and had acquired an excellent reputation largely as a result of the leadership of Heber Mathews. It was not destroyed instantly, nor by a thousand cuts, but by a mortal blow which allowed it to be easily snuffed out a few years later.

First sign of danger had come in Tait's time when, on 24 April 1954, the Assistant Education Officer of the LCC wrote to the Governors suggesting that 'the School of Art should be withdrawn from the Polytechnic and merged with Goldsmiths' or Camberwell School of Art'. Tait protested and for 18 months nothing more was heard of this proposal.

Then (December 1955) Tait told the Governors that he had 'received a copy of a "Report by HM Inspectors on Art Education in Major Establishments of Further Education – Inspected 1952–1954" which had been accompanied by a compliments slip requesting "Opinions forthwith".' The Governing Body agreed with his proposed reply to this 'indifferent method of request'.

"SWARTHY AND FIERCE-LOOKING"

C. GEARY

"MAY I HAVE THE PLEASURE?"

E. MACKLEY

THE POLYGON

Art on Paper in the 1950s–60s.

From left: Polygon *illustrations from early 1950s by C. Geary and E. Mackley,* Avery Hill Reporter *design, late 1950s by L. Jefferies, and front cover of* The Polygon, *1951.*

Facing page: *Christmas card produced by the Garnett College Printing Group, 1959, and 1960s illustrations in the* Avery Hill Reporter *by J. B. Bullen and J. Sillett.*

Mathews now prepared a full comment on the report, pointing out its numerous distortions, and in February 1956 the Chairman, other Governors, and Tait met LCC officials to discuss the matter. At this meeting they were told what underlay the report. As part of a complete reorganization of art schools in and around London, Woolwich was to lose all its full-time art courses. The LCC's arguments apparently persuaded the Governors that further resistance was useless for at the end of the month they accepted a recommendation which read: 'we consider there are no substantial grounds for further opposing the proposed withdrawal of the full-time course. We consider that the matter of extending part-time day classes and of introducing short courses on specialist topics, etc. should be actively pursued.'

The LCC finally ordered the closure of full-time courses from September 1956 and though Mathews asked the Governors to reconsider their decision, telling them that he believed it would lead to the collapse of the whole School of Art, all they would agree to do was to send the Ministry of Education a full history of the life and achievements of the School of Art, and inform it that 'the withdrawal of the full-time course is viewed with deep regret, as in our opinion, an important branch of our Advanced Work is being brought to an end at a time when such work is being encouraged and stimulated as a national policy by the Government.'

Mathews was by no means alone in deploring the closure. On 23 October 1957 all eight heads of department wrote in protest to the Chairman of the Governing Body, 'If the full-time classes are closed the school is likely to degenerate into little more than an evening institute and in this case it is somewhat unfair that the staff, who have been appointed mainly for full-time work for the National Diploma in Design, were not offered alternative employment at other art schools.'

During the following year the Governing Body continued to appeal, ineffectually and with decreasing conviction, against the closure, at the same time asking the LCC whether it would find Mathews an equivalent position if he wished to leave his diminished school. This the LCC would not promise to do, while Mathews could not decide whether or not he wanted it. Finally, on 21 January 1959 he suffered a stroke (or perhaps heart attack) and was taken to University College Hospital where he died ten days later. In a long appreciation the Governors recorded that he had 'received the decision of the Ministry and the Council that the senior full-time school should close with misgivings and distress and there was little doubt that the loss of the school caused him considerable anguish.' In plain English, it had killed him.

Two years later the LCC Education Officer proposed the total closure of the School of Art. In response the Governors noted that 'under ordinary circumstances' they would have resisted this new deprivation and only agreed to it because, even when the 1964 extensions were built, there would still be 'a grave deficiency of classrooms', which would 'seriously endanger the development of Advanced Technological Studies'. Again the LCC had imposed its will by starving the Polytechnic of space.

At the same time the Polytechnic's Building and Architecture Department was 'rationalized'. The LCC's arguments, as with the School of Art, were that, on the one hand too many London Colleges were offering building courses, and on the other hand many of Woolwich's courses were 'not of the calibre the Polytechnic would wish to develop as a Regional College'. Again the lack of adequate accommodation at the Polytechnic gave the Ministry reason for choosing to transfer the existing courses to South-East London Technical College where the accommodation was 'not as fully used as it should be', and for rejecting the Polytechnic's suggestion that it should set up a Diploma of Technology course in building, since, in the opinion of the Ministry's official 'the Department could not satisfy the Hives Council's regulations in relation to accommodation and staff'.

The Education Committee of the Governing Body once more recommended accepting the closure of the Department, as well as the Ministry's rejection of other alternative suggestions (one of these that the higher-grade work should be retained as part of the Civil Engineering Department). In agreeing to this surrender the Governing Body only asked to be assured that the Ministry would 'give every support and encouragement in the development of advanced work'. There had recently been cases in which it believed that it had not received the support it might have expected.

Within a few months it considered that there had been another such case when Kingston College of Technology's B.Sc.(Econ.) course was approved in preference to Woolwich's. On 1 May 1959 Heywood wrote to the Education Officer in protest

Official forms for approval of this course were re-submitted to you on 16th October 1958, and I would ask if these could be referred to the next meeting of the Distribution of Courses Committee of the Regional Advisory Council. When we agreed to relinquish our Building Department we were

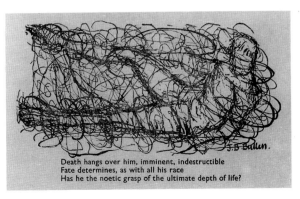

Death hangs over him, imminent, indestructible
Fate determines, as with all his race
Has he the noetic grasp of the ultimate depth of life?

Electrical machines lab in the new extensions of 1965.

Machines for testing creep in metals at high temperatures, Mechanical Engineering Department 1965.

assured by representatives of the LCC and Ministry of Education that they would support the development of advanced work at Woolwich Polytechnic.

The Polytechnic suffered a further loss in 1961, as part of the LCC's revised scheme for further education, when this proposed that it should lose its Department of Domestic Science. Once more the Governors complied. The LCC's 1961 scheme included proposals for a more drastic change: that the Polytechnic should engage in a phased transfer of all its first-, second- and third-year Ordinary National Certificate courses to Woolwich Day College. Along with the closure of the School of Art, the Department of Building and Architecture, and the Department of Domestic Science this meant the loss of 40 per cent of its work.

Nevertheless it did now begin a steady transfer of its lower-level courses. By January 1962 GCE O-level and first year ONC work had gone to Woolwich Day College, and Heywood reported that he was ready to transfer GCE A-level work in economics, commerce, and art subjects to Catford College of Commerce 'when wished'.

Making space by transferring lower-level work was one thing but filling the gap it left with advanced work was another. New advanced courses required the approval of the LCC/ILEA and the Ministry of Education, and this would only be given when a department had staff of the required quality to teach them. To recruit these was no easy matter because staff were only allowed in proportion to the numbers currently taking courses. Since the proposed courses had not begun the only way to acquire the staff they would need was to appoint teachers who were over-qualified for the courses they would at first have to teach.

Even this was not enough to get approval for an advanced course, because it would have to attract a minimum number of students; in 1957, for example, courses in mechanical and electrical engineering could not be started until they had at least ten first-year students and in other subjects unless they had six.

The methods which the Department of Commerce and Management had to adopt in order to begin advanced work were typical. Between its establishment in 1952 and the 1955–6 session it had moved upwards to GCE A-level courses but no higher. It had by then, however, a large number of students and this enabled it to appoint four more staff (making ten in total) with unnecessarily high qualifications. For the following two sessions a total of 24 courses in, for example, shorthand, typing, and GCE O-level were transferred to Woolwich Day College. This, together with the qualified staff whom it had not been required to relinquish, enabled it to start a postgraduate course in industrial management in 1958, and an external degree course for a University of London B.Sc.(Econ.) in 1960. In 1963 the Department's GCE A-level courses were transferred to Catford College of Commerce and that year a course for a degree-level Diploma in Management Studies was launched.

The Engineering Departments, central to the Polytechnic from its earliest days, were others which found it easier to shed lower-level courses than to start new higher-level ones. They had an additional problem. The local industries which for 60 years had supplied students for their evening, apprentice, and sandwich courses were moving away or closing down.

Important stages in the Engineering Department's shedding process began in 1955–6. That year the last of the Ordinary National Certificate courses in mechanical engineering were dropped. The following year machine-shop engineering courses were transferred to Woolwich Day College. In 1963 the motor-vehicle course also went there, and that year the welding course went to the North-West Kent College of Technology at Dartford.

Important stages in the expansion of full-time degree-level work began in 1956 when the revived sandwich courses were launched, leading to the NCTA's Diploma of Technology. But it was only in the later years of the 1960s that there was a virtually complete transformation of these departments to full-time students

The beginning of the 1960s saw the introduction of computers to the Polytechnic. This Stantec-Zebra Digital Computer was installed in the Mathematics Department in 1960 and is now in the Science Museum. It had less processing power than a programmable calculator in the 1990s.

working for degrees or the equivalent, and to part-time students working for Higher National Certificates or above.

This was a result of the Robbins Report of 1963 and the adoption of one of its most important recommendations: that the National Council for Technological Awards should be replaced by the Council for National Academic Awards. There were key differences between these two bodies, one of the most obvious that the CNAA could make awards which were degrees in name as well as nature. More significant, however, for its effect on institutions like Woolwich was that the scope of courses under the CNAA extended beyond science and engineering into the social sciences and the arts. Furthermore the CNAA would receive applications for a variety of full-time courses, whereas the NCTA was devoted to the sandwich-course concept, involving programmes specifically connected to industry.

For the Engineering Departments the transition from NCTA courses to CNAA courses was smooth, with course approvals continuing. But as time passed there was increasing difficulty in securing industrial placements, as a result of the increasing reluctance of firms to sponsor students for sandwich courses, and Woolwich, like other colleges, not only switched to mainly college-based students but also to full-time courses. Over the same period the concept of the 'modular' course gained ground, students selecting, within limits, their subjects from a 'menu' on offer. Thus progressively the flexibility allowed by the CNAA greatly outstripped that which the NCTA had allowed, and eventually the same courses could be offered to part-time students under a two-year-for-one scheme.

There was no doubt about the popularity of the new degrees, many students choosing them rather than courses leading to internal degrees at the University of London, which in consequence either began to have a higher proportion of overseas students, or to have so few students that they had to be abandoned. This move away from the University of London was fiercely opposed by members of staff like Vogel, head of Chemistry, and Smith, head of Physics who had long-standing connections with the university which they were reluctant to relinquish.

A major consequence for Woolwich of the wider range of courses which the CNAA would accept was the founding or expansion of departments like Humanities, Management, and Economics, and the most dramatic expansion of advanced work occurred in these subjects.

There were other developments in Heywood's years, including the creation of a Civil Engineering Department from the Mechanical Engineering Department, the establishing of electronics as a subject in its own right, and the introduction by Godfrey, while head of Mathematics, of computers and computing on a grand scale. And though much of the expansion of advanced work was still a few years ahead – the CNAA only met for the first time in 1964 – by the end of that year all Woolwich's full-time and sandwich work was for degrees or the equivalent, it was carrying out as much of this as some colleges of the University of London, it had more advanced students than some of the Colleges of Advanced Technology, and lower-level work had been entirely transferred to other institutions.

All this, together with the Robbins Report's elevation of the Colleges of Advanced Technology to degree-granting universities and the suggestion that other institutions could hope to be similarly rewarded, gave the Governors the confidence to issue at the end on 1964 a statement of its ambitions and their justification:

Dr Derrick Godfrey, Principal of Woolwich Polytechnic, 1967–70, and Director, Thames Polytechnic, 1970–8.

In view of the long experience of the Polytechnic in conducting internal degrees courses as an 'Institution with Recognized Teachers' of the University of London . . . it would be appropriate for the Polytechnic to attain either independent technological university status or to become a school of the University . . .

During the period prior to independent status being attained, the present links with the University of London should be strengthened by development and extension of degree courses in the Polytechnic and as soon as the Council for National Academic Awards is established the Polytechnic should submit courses for their approval on a wide front.

By 1964–5 the number of full-time teaching staff had risen to 151 (88 in 1949–50). Since those of the Building Department, Domestic Science Department, and School of Art had gone, the increase was more significant. It was a direct result of the increase in advanced work, not of total numbers. Interestingly, it was no longer the Mechanical Engineering Department with 30 which had most, but the Economics and Management Department with 36. There had been two other significant developments. Many fewer part-time staff were now being used. And staff were being allowed an increased amount of time for research in lieu of teaching.

Notable members of the staff to retire in this period included D. H. Smith, who had succeeded Vinycomb as head of Physics. Smith was

a man of great method, who ran a tight department. He was rightly proud of the physics workshop which he established. Of those who worked there, Arthur Rawdon, was a precision instrument maker and turned out work of the highest order. Smith was chief examiner for the practical physics examination at the University of London and would devote much of the summer term to the preparation and conduct of these examinations at the University itself. (Reed)

Another who left (1964) was George Freeman, who had succeeded Spencer as head of Electrical Engineering. His parting gift from the Poly was a splendid leather-seated chair, which he referred to as his electric chair. Known to students as Guff, he was said to be able to solve any electrical problem by the use of circle diagrams. He was a recognized teacher of the University of London, and served on the examination board there for many years, some as its Chairman.

On 22 June 1959 the Principal gave a retiring tea-party for two senior lecturers, E. L. Sainsbury (electrical engineering) and N. Gross (mathematics) who had taught at the Poly for 40 and 39 years respectively. It was Sainsbury who had been in charge of the Poly's electrical supply and equipment. Gross was 'an excellent and much liked teacher, very short, barely reaching the blackboard, but with a voice like a fog-horn'.

There had also, by 1965, been marked changes in the Polytechnic's student body. Most significant had been the fall in the numbers taking evening and part-time day courses from 4,141 to 1,908. There had been a corresponding rise in full-time day or sandwich course students from 1,126 to 1,395. The places students came from had also changed. Now 2,645 were from Greater London (2,947 in 1949) and 365 from Kent (1,532 in 1949). More significantly, 734 now came from other places in the UK (151 in 1949). These figures included 170 from overseas, Indian students (30) and Nigerian (32) the most numerous. But whereas in 1949 there had been 33 Poles there were none in 1965.

Already by 1950 some overseas groups had begun to form their own clubs. First in 1946–7 came the Indian Students' Association. If mutual support was one of its aims, it claimed that the most important was to acquaint Poly students with 'Indian literature, art, and above all Indian philosophy'. While the British were generally acquainted with classical Greek, Roman, and Egyptian civilizations, about Indian they knew very little, though it had been 'just as great . . . and far more ancient'.

By 1957 there were five more such clubs: Arab, Chinese, Pakistani, Polish, and West African. The Chinese Student Association had been particularly active, holding a Chinese New Year's party the previous February at the sports pavilion attended by more than 100 guests including the Vice-Principal, Lowry.

In 1963 there was a symbolic change in another, increasingly influential, area of Poly life. Then the students finally acquired in name what they had already had in practice for several years, a Students' Union.

Its evolution from the Union of Clubs and Societies started by Mallett in 1934 had been complicated. Little had happened during the war years, but then, with the influx of ex-servicemen as students, many of them taking full-time degree courses, events moved quickly and sometimes dramatically. C. A. (Corky) Prior was the student chiefly responsible for starting the change.

He and fellow students of the mid-1940s found a situation similar to that of the early 1930s, when the Athletic Club had been dominated by members who had no other connection with the Poly. As a result Polytechnic students had taken little interest in it. By 1943 the members of the old Athletic Club were now in turn dominating the new Union of Clubs and Societies although it had been founded specifically to reduce their influence. They had run the Union well, raising a trust fund for equipping the Union House and the Den, staging dances throughout the War, but as in the 1930s, many 'had never had any connection with the Poly whatsoever apart from membership of the Athletic Club' (*Chanticleer*, May 1948). It was not surprising that students were again taking little interest in the Union.

'As an active student', *Chanticleer* continued,

Corky has been variously described as headstrong but steadfast, tactless, a bully, hard-hitting but far-sighted in student matters. He arrived at a time when there was a complete lack of leadership among students and a marked disinterest in running Union affairs. And with his arrival came his supporters in large numbers.

Corky started a semi-secret society of

hand-picked members with a common purpose, whose ideal was the Polytechnic as a University, and whose medium to the public was the

Students and 'Cock' the mascot marching down Harwood Street.

mascot – 'Cock', as he was then called ... Cock Club discussed the realization of their ideal which was to take place in three stages; first the establishment of a student majority on the Polytechnic Union Council; second the securing of an adequate support from the mass of students ... third the formation of an Undergraduates Guild to carry out the affiliation of the Poly to the University of London Union.

To gain a student majority on the Union Council he took advantage of its constitution which required it to include 'a delegate from each club and society'. He therefore started 'a whole lot of new House Clubs', and got them recognized. In 1945 students at last formed a majority.

The first test of mass student support came in the Autumn Term of 1946 when hundreds of University College students arrived *en masse* one morning to avenge the theft by Cock Club of the U.C. mascot 'Phineas'. Corky's men spread the word to departments, ran out the hose, climbed on the Refectory tables and made speeches: practically the entire Polytechnic took part in the battle royal which ensued. So it seemed fairly obvious that the time had come for the final stage – the establishment of the Undergraduates Guild.

This came about during 1947 and by May 1948 its officers were settling the final details of affiliation to the University of London Union. *Chanticleer* was in no doubt about the importance of this affiliation. It meant that 'Woolwich Polytechnic Undergraduates will have attained to University Status as a body, and will be considered on a par with the University College, or King's College of London University. . . . In the words of our Principal, we students 'Have consolidated our position'.

But if Mallett approved, there was a difference between these changes and those of 1934. They had not been imposed on students from above but brought about by the students themselves, in particular by their leaders, Corky Prior and 'his staunch henchman, Johnny Edwards'.

On 2 March 1949 members of the Union carried out a more daring raid when they captured the Regent Street Polytechnic's mascot, Quinnie, 'a rather corpulent pig made in plaster', although a meeting was in progress in the room in which the pig was housed. 'The meeting seemed too astonished to interfere.' A message was left reading 'This little piggy went to Woolwich' and that was where he was taken, to be painted in Woolwich Poly colours with WP on his buttocks before being set on the Quintin Hogg statue in Portland Place. The exploit had received 'an excellent write-up in Regent Street Poly's Mag,' *Chanticleer* reported, and had included the promise " 'We will remember", but it seems that so far they have forgotten what it is that they remember for life still progresses peacefully at Woolwich and Cock continues to gather dust.'

During the next 20 years, when rags continued to form a picturesque part of Polytechnic life, Woolwich was not always so successful and its mascot suffered various indignities. In 1951, he was stolen by Chelsea Poly during a dance, and in 1953 by Goldsmiths'. The most spectacular battle for his recovery took place in 1958 when Enfield Tech. had taken him, the weapons flour bags and fire extinguishers. 'When all the fighting had subsided the rag organisers agreed that the Presidents of the two Colleges would compete for Chanticleer by having a race across Southwark Bridge on children's scooters. The race was well supported by hundreds of students and nearly as many policemen and several press cameramen. Mr Ian Baldwin our reigning President, put up a magnificent performance and won the race.'

In 1960 Chanticleer was taken by Northern Polytechnic, but successfully rescued. His year-long abduction by Wye College in 1967, however, was only ended by the payment of a ransom of 80 pints of blood to the Blood Transfusion Service. He was then put on permanent display at Woolwich, and although he remained 'the centre of devious plots and schemes', was protected by what the *Students' Handbook* claimed to be a raid-proof system.

In early years it was the ex-service students who inspired the more adventurous of such rags, organizing them 'like military operations'. Mallett tolerated them, pleased perhaps that Woolwich should distinguish itself in any way. Some staff were less enthusiastic, Vogel observing that he could 'tolerate student pranks but not chemical warfare'.

Meanwhile, after only two years it had become clear that the Undergraduate Guild, so hopefully founded in 1948, was failing to satisfy Polytechnic students, whose complaints remained much the same as before. A letter to *Chanticleer* in May 1950 explained these:

> I think it was our worthy principal who first realised that the students weren't getting a fair deal; and it was he who conceived the idea of a Union of Clubs and Societies, wherein the students could take an active and equal part within the older members of the union who constituted the Athletic Society [Club]. But the opposition which he was met with

on this issue was astonishing! And this opposition, strange as it may seem, came from certain members of the Union who are now known as, and who publicly proclaim themselves to be, the most active supporters and, indeed, the progenitors of the present Union. Yet these noble gentlemen actually threatened resignation from the Union when they thought their ship was sinking. It is these same worthies who today object so strongly to the rising status of the student in the Union.

H. T. Sisley, President of the Union of Clubs and Societies from 1953.

The result was the formation of a new body, the Student Board. This represented all full-time students, not merely undergraduates; part-time students would also benefit and, in the editor's view, it was 'reasonable that they should have some say in its foundation and work'. The Governors approved of the Board for a trial period of three years but did not give it independence; it became merely one of four committees of the Union of Clubs and Societies, the others being finance, athletic clubs, and house clubs/entertainment.

This was one reason why students were not satisfied. The Student Board was not, they claimed, a fully independent students' union as long as *ex-officio* members (i.e. members of the Union of Clubs and Societies, who were not necessarily students) could attend its meetings and influence its decisions. They had another complaint. It had absorbed the old University Guild and many of its competitive activities were now against other universities, but since it was merely a committee of the Union of Clubs and Societies the clubs and societies taking part in such competitions were the responsibility of different committees.

In 1953 Herbert Sisley became the President of the Union of Clubs and Societies. Sisley had been connected with the Polytechnic for no less than 53 years. He had joined the office staff in 1899 and would say that his first duty had been going round the Poly rooms at dusk lighting its gas and oil lamps. Two years later he became a member of the Athletic Club; football was his game, and as centre-half he was 'able to use his height and weight with much advantage'.

From then onwards he was only away from the Polytechnic during the First World War when he served in the Royal Artillery. Until 1922 he was a student for various periods as well as part of the administrative staff, and he eventually became Chief Clerk and Accountant. When the Union of Clubs and Societies was formed in 1934 he was its first financial secretary and it was largely he who had managed its finances so successfully. 'If at times at Union Council meetings he . . . expressed his views in a forthright manner it was never because he was a "party" man, but always because his sole motive was the good of the union as a whole' (*Chanticleer*).

The same year (1953) the Student Board was judged by the Union Council to have worked 'very satisfactorily', and was renamed the Students' Union Society. All full-time students were required to join. The subscription was £2, but this included membership of the University of London Union and of the National Union of Students. Now the Students' Union Society began to organize its own sporting clubs and its own house clubs, for example a debating society; and its sporting clubs began to arrange fixtures with the clubs of various universities. The new clubs became known as the Wednesday clubs, the old ones as the Saturday clubs because those were the days on which they played.

For a time the Students' Union Society remained part of the Union of Clubs and Societies. Even in 1959 when it had become the most important part of the older Union there was strong opposition to granting it independence and it was not given this until 1963. It was then that the old Union became the Polytechnic Union and the Students' Union Society became simply the Students' Union.

In the following years the clubs and societies run by the Polytechnic Union dwindled while those managed by the Students' Union multiplied, soon numbering 16 clubs and 26 societies, the latter including Anglican, Darts and Dominoes, Folk Song, Natural History, and Winks societies. Its numbers also multiplied. By the time it changed its name these had already reached 1,000 and in 1966 part-time students were allowed to join if they wished. Two years later its aims were redefined. It was to:

Occupy itself with the student activities of its members and the organization and furtherance of such activities

Occupy itself with the student opinions of its members and the representation of such opinions.

Occupy itself with the welfare of its students and the improvement of facilities to further their welfare.

Occupy itself with the academic and intellectual interests of its members and the representation of such interests.

By now the Department of Education and Science had recognized the importance of the Students' Union by proposing that the union fee should be added by local authorities to a student's grant.

Facing page: View along Polytechnic Street, Woolwich (above), *and* (below), *the former Woolwich swimming baths, now the Students' Union, in Bathway, Woolwich.*

Building at Woolwich, early 1960s

The Wellington Street site, 1962. The present Wellington Street entrance is on the right of the development. Beyond the building site are shops and Barclays Bank, at the corner of General Gordon Square. They are now owned by the University, and the former bank houses various administrative offices.

The two Unions at first retained a link in an organization known as the Association of Unions which had overall responsibility for their financial affairs, but by 1969 they had drifted so far apart that they were entirely separated, the Students' Union retaining responsibility for the affairs of current students, the Polytechnic Union becoming in effect an old students' club under the name, Woolwich Polytechnic Association. As such it remained active, and in 1969 had 1,200 members.

It was during the 1956–7 session that the Students' Union Society first published a *Students' Handbook*. 'The booklet does not clash in any way with the production of our magazine,' *Chanticleer* assured its readers. Certainly early editions of the handbook were strictly practical, and its paragraphs on the different sports clubs and house societies were recruiting notes rather than reports of matches played. In 1960–1 it said about the Poly Hoboes (YHA), 'This club was originally founded to satisfy the escapist tendencies of students; unfortunately its members all appear to have escaped.' In 1960, when there were 17 clubs and 13 societies, the President advised new students, perhaps over solicitously, 'not to try to take part in every activity mentioned in this handbook'. Two years later there was a Weightlifting Club.

In 1966–7 the *Handbook* acquired official approval, containing introductions by the Principal, Heywood, and the new Secretary, P. C. Oxlade. It was also more in the nature of a magazine, with news of recent Poly events and general articles, one beginning, 'It's not really that there are insufficient girls at Woolwich as that there are just too many men.'

It was only in the 1970s, however, that it began to give frank advice about previously unmentionable student problems. The 1976–7 issue carried two pages on

Facing page: Architectural features. From top left: Cupola, Manresa Chapel; ceiling, Manresa Chapel; lighting in the Library, Avery Hill; fireplace in the entrance hall of Colonel North's mansion at Avery Hill; supporting dragons, Ward Room, Chatham; detail of plasterwork, Manresa House.

Exterior and interior of Thomas Spencer Hall of Residence, Woolwich.

drugs, explaining in detail the three categories into which the 1971 Act had divided them (hard, soft, and amphetamine/barbiturates) and telling students to call Release if in drug trouble. Equally frank pages followed on contraception, abortion, and VD, on the law and what to do if arrested, and on bugs and scabies.

Alongside the *Students' Handbook* a succession of Poly newspapers came and went. Earliest was *Poly News*, at first a weekly, then a fortnightly. In 1973–4 the editor of a new fortnightly, *Handjob*, explained that it didn't belong to the Union, or indeed to its own editorial board or editor, but 'to each and every student', its great merit that it would be uncensored. But by 1976–7 *Handjob* had gone and a new newspaper, *Links*, was appearing, under the auspices of the Union but with 'an editor who was not a member of the executive so that the paper presents an independent view within the Union'. In 1990 came *The Buzz*, advertising itself as a new student magazine. Issues of all these, even the early *Students' Handbooks*, are collectors' items.

In the early 1960s the Polytechnic finally got the new accommodation for which it had been waiting since 1944. During 1956 the LCC had found further reasons for delaying approval of the Polytechnic's plans. It now required 'a schedule showing the courses to be run, the number of students – under headings, full-time, part-time day, and evening – likely to attend [the] courses, and the accommodation required to meet these needs, showing how this accommodation is subdivided between what already exists and the proposed extension.'

When the Chairman and Principal had their second meeting with Mrs Cole and other LCC representatives on 6 June, they explained that 'plans for extensions had been discussed for well over 10 years and on several occasions when something definite appeared to have been achieved a change in conditions, e.g. financial stringency, Recoupment Regulations, the White Paper on Technical Education etc., had deferred a decision and in the present instance further delay had occurred by a request to prepare schedules of accommodation in accordance with the Ministry's Building Bulletin N.5.'

At this time the Ministry had not chosen the proposed Colleges of Advanced Technology and the LCC made it clear that until it did so no decision could be taken on the future sphere of activity of the Polytechnic – this clearly involving the accommodation it would need.

Two years later (December 1958) the unresolved question of whether or not the Building and Architecture would be shed by the Polytechnic was another reason for delay, and next March the Chairman of the Governors wrote to the Leader of the Council about reports of still more delays. In answer he was told 'I have read your very disturbing letter of 16 March and referred it to the Chairman of the Education Committee . . . the architect hopes to start building work on the site in 1960 (not 1964 or 1965 as suggested in your letter).'

Now at last the LCC began to co-operate actively with the Polytechnic, lending its architects to help in the drawing of final plans. These were approved by the Governors in October 1959. The building of the Wellington Street and Polytechnic Street blocks was to start in September 1960 and take about 18 months, of the Thomas Street block to start thereafter and take 12 months.

This timetable proved optimistic; building in fact began in March 1961. And protests continued to the end about the inadequacy of accommodation. In 1960, 1962, and again in 1963 Vogel complained to the Governors in his report on the Chemistry Department. In 1963 he commented:

> The Department is again full to overflowing. Adequate bench space for all members of staff conducting research cannot be given; many are obliged to work in the students' laboratory and even to share a limited amount of bench space. At least 6 Ph.D. students are working in the undergraduate laboratories. Our research students (18 full-time) have nowhere to consult journals and reference books nor have they adequate facilities for discussion of their work with their supervisors; a room . . . is desperately required for them. Several requests for such a room have not, so far, led to a definite decision; in the meantime our . . . research students are working under, what are in my opinion, unnecessarily difficult conditions. Admission of several research students has been refused.
>
> Modern apparatus . . . for advanced teaching and research cannot be adequately housed in the laboratories. Whilst grants are usually available for the purchase of modern apparatus, the more urgent problem is the provision of room to enable existing apparatus to be used by students and staff in moderate comfort.

During 1963, however, the Polytechnic was finally able to start to use the first two of its new blocks. During 1964 the Thomas Street block became available, and in 1965 it rented part of the entirely new and separate Riverside House.

1960s Building Outside Woolwich

Extensive building took place during the 1960s in the other institutions which were to become part of the University.

Facing page: *New buildings at Avery Hill (from top right): Dining hall and Bursar's office, 1963; Art and Craft department; new library; Consitt Hall accommodation block.*

Below left: *Catering and staff residential accommodation at Garnett College, adjacent to Mount Clare, Roehampton, 1966.*

10

From Woolwich Speech to Thames Polytechnic

1965–1970

❖——❖❖❖——❖❖❖——❖❖❖——❖❖❖——❖❖❖——❖

IT WAS NO WONDER that the Polytechnic expected 1965 to be a year in which to celebrate. Not only would it be able, after 20 years of frustrating delay, at last formally to open its new buildings, but this would also be its 75th anniversary. True, the Governors were sorry not to secure 'a Royal Person' to be a guest of honour at the celebration banquet scheduled for 27 April, but they hoped instead for the Secretary of State for Education, Michael Stewart. In the event they got his successor, Anthony Crosland. What they did not expect was Crosland's speech. In this, to become known as the Woolwich Speech, he was to describe the Labour Government's plans for a transformation of the country's higher education system.

During the previous year it had become clear that the Robbins Report had made a serious miscalculation. It had forecast that by 1973–4 there would be 51,000 students in full-time advanced technical education, but this number had been reached by 1965–6. The report had taken the traditional view that the country's universities should expand to cope with the additional students. Given its estimate of numbers there seemed no reason why they should not do so. Its proposal that the Colleges of Advanced Technology should become universities was part of its plan to make this possible.

Crosland not only faced different circumstances, since it had become clear that the universities could not cope, but also had a different view of the whole hierarchical pattern of higher education which placed them at the top of a pyramid based on elitism. If perpetuated, he said, 'such a system would be characterised by a continuous rat-race to reach the First or University Division, a constant pressure on those below to ape the Universities above, and a certain inevitable failure to achieve the diversity in higher education which contemporary society needs.'

We would not survive in today's competitive world if Britain alone downgraded the non-university professional and technical sector. No other

Facing page: Shell Production Shop, shortly before the Royal Ordnance Factory at Woolwich Arsenal was closed in 1966. The institution had sent students to the Polytechnic since the latter was founded.

country in the Western World does so – consider the Grandes Ecoles in France, the Technische Hochscule in Germany and Zurich, Leningrad Poly in the Soviet Union. Why should we not aim at this kind of development? At a vocationally oriented non-University sector which is degree-giving and with an appropriate amount of postgraduate work with opportunities for learning comparable with those of the Universities, and giving a first-class professional training. Let us now move away from our snobbish caste-ridden hierarchical obsession with University status.

He gave three other reasons for proposing a new binary pattern for further education, in which technical colleges would be equal in status to universities but different in nature. Firstly, the 'ever-increasing demand for vocational, professional and industrially-based courses in higher education', needed 'a separate sector with a separate tradition and outlook'. Secondly,

> a system based on the ladder concept must inevitably depress and degrade both morale and standards in the non-University sector. If the Universities have a 'class' monopoly of degree-giving, and if every College which achieves high standards moves automatically into the University Club, then the residual sector becomes a permanent poor relation perpetually deprived of its brightest ornaments, and with a permanently and openly inferior status. This must be bad for morale, bad for standards.

Thirdly, he considered (as a socialist) 'that a substantial part of the higher education system should be under social control, and directly responsive to social needs'.

For all these reasons, he continued,

> We believe in the dual pattern. The University sector will continue to make its own unique and marvellous contribution. We want the public sector to make its own equally distinguished but separate contribution. And between them we want – and I believe we shall get – mutual understanding and healthy rivalry where their work overlaps.

Not everyone welcomed Crosland's binary proposals. Some years later Valerie Pitt, future head of Humanities, spoke about

> the so-called Woolwich Speech delivered here at a grand dinner, stiff with aldermen and other local worthies, in best soup and fish, with a chaplain to say grace. Very proper. The Minister arrived late and in a lounge suit and caused great offence. His real offence however was not the breach of manners but the content and manner of his speech . . . what we got . . . was clearly a Ministry brief coming out of the appalling Whitehall assumption that while some people might be educated along the lines of their own talents and potentialities at the universities, the rest were to be trained in other places to serve the economy. It was a long-standing assumption. As long ago as the 1890s R. B. Haldane had argued in the House of

Commons that the London Polytechnics were . . . capable of delivering 'a cheap and efficient university education to workmen' so as to keep us level with the artisans of Germany and France. You will note the word 'cheap' and the obsession both with the skill base and the need to see off foreign competition. To do Crosland justice, costs don't seem to have been at the forefront of his mind: what was, was the government's need for numbers, and more numbers of students which the Polytechnics could supply and the Universities, the Minister thought, could not. He wanted literate, technologically literate, helots though of course that's not what he said.

If Pitt was right about Crosland's unspoken purpose, he has been proved right in that what he was aiming to prevent has occurred and the consequences are what he feared. Now that his binary plan for higher education has been abandoned and all but one or two of his new polytechnics have become universities, they have turned increasingly (in pursuit of numbers) to the teaching of the social sciences, so providing the country with an excessive number of social science graduates and leaving it with the same shortage of first-class technologists from which it has suffered for a hundred years.

Crosland listed the policy decisions which must follow from his general principles. For Woolwich the one which most obviously affected it was that for at least the next ten years there would be no new universities. Superficially this seemed like the extinction of an ambition which it had had, in one form or another, for at least 60 of its 75 years, and which had been encouraged by the Robbins Report.

Nevertheless Governors and staff were on the whole pleased by Crosland's proposals. If university status could no longer for the moment be the Polytechnic's goal the prospect of reaching another goal had been improved and the road there could be much the same. Indeed, Heywood told the Academic Council and Board of University Studies that 'no change was . . . necessary in

Churchill House on the corner of Green's End and Thomas Street, 1960s.

our statement of aims . . . we should do everything possible to make our standard of work comparable to that of a university.' In other words university status need only be temporarily postponed in favour of another promotion.

What this other might be became clearer in 1966 when a new White Paper first named Crosland's proposed new colleges as polytechnics, and became still more precise in April 1967 when the Secretary of State proposed that, by various mergers, 30 new polytechnics would be created.

The way to qualify as one of these was to continue to expand advanced courses, in particular by making full use of the new degrees which the CNAA was prepared to approve – degrees which, far from narrowing work to technology and science, could include a far wider range of subjects. At the same time the Polytechnic hoped to continue to run courses for internal University of London degrees and it was now that the debate between those who favoured a change to the former and those who favoured staying with the latter became fiercest. There was so much passion and anxiety that, after one meeting of the Academic Board at which dropping the University of London connection was raised, a supporter of the University snipped the item off the bottom of all the agenda papers in case the University discovered that it had even been discussed (Michael Locke).

Part of the problem was that the university three-year courses in engineering were largely filled by overseas students while CNAA four-year courses were filled with UK students, a development which some staff considered unfortunate. The issue became more complicated in 1966 when the Pilkington Report greatly increased the minimum number of students which a course had to attract before it would be approved, raising this to 24 for full-time and sandwich courses and to 20 or 15 for different sorts of part-time courses. Students now became involved in the argument, submitting a memorandum to the Governing Body which drew attention to their anxiety that courses which were not adequately filled would be cancelled at such short notice that students would be forced to change college or lose a year.

The case for retaining University of London degree courses was not improved when the University refused to recognize Polytechnic teachers in new subjects. But ultimately, in one sense, it was the students themselves who made the decision in favour of CNAA courses inevitable by supporting these and not supporting University of London courses. This was hardly surprising since many of the CNAA courses were of sandwich type and thus a student could be industry-sponsored. With one of the better sponsorships he or she was paid a salary (to which his parents had to make no contribution) and far better off than a student with a local authority grant. At the end of the 1967–8 session Godfrey reported that the Governing Body and the Academic Council had decided 'gradually to reduce our University of London courses and to expand our CNAA courses'. The change was not immediate and two years later he could still only say that 'further progress' had been made in 'the replacement of all the University of London degrees by new courses leading to degrees of the CNAA'.

Meanwhile the Academic Council, in a detailed development plan submitted to the Governing Body in January 1968, had proposed a total of 32 new full-time first-degree or master's-degree courses, and 15 part-time ones, along with the discontinuing of recruitment to eight University of London undergraduate courses.

Language laboratory, late 1960s. Languages subsequently became part of the Business School.

Commenting on this plan, the University of London suggested 1974 as the date by which all University of London courses would have ceased.

Later in 1968 a plan for entirely restructuring the Polytechnic's teaching arrangements was adopted. The various departments were to become parts of three faculties: Science; Engineering; and Business Studies, Management, and Humanities. Thus, within a few years of being compelled by the LCC and Ministry to narrow its teaching to the sciences and engineering, it was able to redevelop or start the teaching of a range of other subjects.

The three faculties were established for the 1969–70 session, with Charles Wheble as head of the new faculty (subsequently to be more simply renamed the Faculty of Social Sciences and Humanities). 'Charlie', Valerie Pitt remembered,

> had no pretensions to be an academic but he managed to acquire highly skilled and talented colleagues to supplement the rag bag of managerial oddments of his original department – and it worked. It's a universal view that the man was like someone out of an H. G. Wells novel – a friend perhaps of Mr Polly – rotund, always formally dressed, a bit of a vulgarian. There was however more to him than all that suggests. For instance he was supposed to be a Rosicrucian – and certainly was liable to express naïvely 'mystical' opinions.

Wheble must be given much credit for expanding the new faculty so successfully. By 1970, 36 per cent of students were working in its courses, only just less than the 38 per cent in mathematics and science courses and substantially more than the 24 per cent in engineering courses.

It was now that Valerie Pitt, a fine academic scholar herself, was made head of Humanities. In this position she created a unique body of teachers of her own choosing who gave her department a reputation extending beyond the Polytechnic. She became one of its most memorable characters, with strong views of her own, as her judgement of Crosland's binary policy demonstrated, and was much admired and loved by students and staff, though both groups also found her formidable.

The prospectus for the 1969–70 session explained that the CNAA, since its establishment, had required all syllabuses for its degrees, not least those in science and engineering, to include 'liberal studies' and it was such courses which the General Studies division had provided. For the following session, as part of the new faculty it was also able to offer a CNAA full-time course leading to a BA Hons. Humanities, the first of its kind in the country.

The Government's plans for its new Polytechnics were not as simple as they at first sounded. It did not mean them merely to become state-sector technological universities, catering exclusively for full-time or sandwich students taking degree courses. Crosland wanted them in particular to give many young boys and girls 'the second chance'. In a speech in January 1967 he described the sort of students he was thinking about:

> Perhaps they left school early, perhaps they were late developers, perhaps they were first generation aspirants to higher education who were too modest at the right moment to apply to a university, perhaps they had started on a career and thought that a technical college course would more directly improve their qualifications for doing it. The important thing is that the leading technical colleges, by their capacity to provide for students at different levels of ability and attainment (and that is why I call them comprehensive) provide a chance for students of these kinds not only to

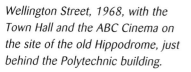

Wellington Street, 1968, with the Town Hall and the ABC Cinema on the site of the old Hippodrome, just behind the Polytechnic building.

tackle degree level work part-time or full-time, but also to develop their latent capacity to do so.

In other words the new Polytechnics were to be encouraged to continue some less advanced courses. The 1966 White Paper had said much the same thing. The new polytechnics, besides catering for degree students, should cater for those 'seeking a qualification that requires a course of higher education which is below degree standard; [and for] the many thousands of students who, being already in employment, can find time only for part-time and/or evening courses, whether they lead to a degree or to a qualification below that standard.'

Woolwich's Education Committee resolved (March 1966) that 'further thought should be given to sub-degree work and that the Polytechnic should retain some, if it was in accordance with national policy'. And in its 1968 development plan the Academic Council included four new diploma courses. But there was to be no general halting or reversal of the trend towards degree work.

To become incorporated as a new Polytechnic Woolwich, besides expanding its advanced teaching, had to fulfil other conditions, one of the most important requiring it to reshape its Governing Body so that it would have greater independence from its local authority. Another was that staff and students had to be given more power, either within the Governing Body or as part of academic boards, or both.

Between 1912, when the Polytechnic's Trust Deed had last been revised, and 1956 the make-up of the Governing Body had not changed. Of its 23 members, ten were appointed by the LCC, an arrangement which seemed fair since the LCC continued to make by far the largest grant for its support. Other organizations which still gave it grants nominated twelve of the remaining members, leaving just one member to be chosen by the University of London.

In 1956, however, the White Paper on Technical Education commented approvingly on local authorities which arranged for representatives of industry to have places on the Governing Bodies of their technical colleges. It approved, too, of those which gave Governing Bodies power to spend as they chose the sums which the authorities granted them. Three years later a Ministry of Education circular repeated the first message. 'The vigorous participation of representatives of industry and commerce in the life of the establishments is a matter of the utmost importance.' It dismissed the idea that funding bodies were required to have direct control of their colleges. 'It is not legally necessary that representatives of the authority maintaining the establishment should be in the majority. Indeed, in a number of cases representatives of the authority do not account for more than one-quarter of the total.'

The Polytechnic could fairly claim that it already had the sort of independence which the White Paper and Ministry circular favoured. If the LCC representatives on its Governing Body were more than a quarter of the total, they were less than a half. However, in the late 1950s it began to discuss with the Ministry and the LCC a new Trust Deed which would further reduce the number of LCC members, partly as a result of government pressure, partly because greater independence was generally considered to be a feature of a college of advanced study. The 1956 White Paper had actually used the phrase 'independence appropriate to the level of their work'. Eventually in 1962 the Governors, the Ministry, and the LCC approved a much changed Governing Body. The LCC's representatives were halved to five, the Woolwich Borough Council and the City Parochial Foundation each lost one representative, on the other hand Kent County Council was given one (36 per cent of full-time students now came from Kent), the University of London was given a second, and there were to be more co-opted members, this to allow existing Governors who would lose their sponsors to be retained, but also to allow the co-option of the sort of representatives of industry whom the Ministry favoured. The new Governing Body now consisted of the following members: LCC 5, City Parochial Foundation 3, Woolwich Borough Council 2, War Department 2, University of London 2, Kent County Council 1, co-opted 8.

In this form it had a short life. The following year (1963) the Robbins Report claimed that the staff of colleges, both technical and teacher training, remained frustrated at the control exercised over them by their local authorities, and the small part which they were able to play, as a result, in the management of their own affairs. Here again the staff at Woolwich had less to complain about than staffs of some colleges. Since 1932 it had had an Academic Board, responsible for all work leading to university degrees. In 1949 the Governing Body had explained to the University of London: 'The Academic Board in effect controls the university work of the Polytechnic.' For work at lower levels there had been a Technical Board, consisting of all heads of departments and three other elected members of the staff.

In 1964, the Academic Board was more appropriately renamed the Board of University Studies. At the same time the Technical Board became the Board of Technical Studies, the new name intended to mark its improved status. It was now responsible for work leading to the new degrees awarded by the Council for National Academic Awards, established the same year.

The CNAA was another body which began to press for greater staff participation in the running of colleges. Next year it wrote: 'The teaching staff of a college which proposes to offer a range of courses leading to the Council's degrees will be expected to play a responsible part in deciding the academic policy of the college. . . . It is hoped also that representatives of the staff will serve on the Governing Body of the College.'

The Inner London Education Authority (which now funded the Poly in place of the LCC) had also written to its colleges, Woolwich included, asking whether they agreed that there should be academic representatives on their Governing Bodies. And in 1965 it made specific proposals: the Principal and two members of staff should be Governors.

Woolwich did better. In October 1965, its Governors agreed a new Governing Body which was to include the Principal and three members of staff. The City Parochial Foundation was left with only one representative and Woolwich Borough Council (absorbed by Greenwich in 1964) with none. The three members of staff were to include the Vice-Principal, one head of department elected by the Academic Council, and one less senior teacher elected by the whole staff.

This new Governing Body also had a short life, but for a different reason: government reaction to student discontent. Drawing up proposals for the

Woolwich Polytechnic students outside the former Young Men's Christian Institute building, c. 1970.

126

Polytechnic's government took so long (more than six drafts for the composition of the Court of Governors and the new Academic Board were in turn rejected) that the later ones were affected by the riots, sit-ins, and other student protests of 1968. One result at Woolwich had been the Joint Advisory Committee with its membership of Governors, staff, and students, but this was insufficient for the Department of Education which now positively required Governing Bodies to include student members.

The Students' Union had already had its importance recognized by the granting to its president from 1967–8 of a sabbatical year to allow him or her to attend full-time to Union affairs. In Godfrey's annual report of that year (his first as Principal) he congratulated the Union on its choice of Dave Yorath for the position. There had been 'many productive discussions' between himself, the staff, and Yorath, representing the Union.

The following year's *Students' Handbook* gave a more colourful picture of Dave Yorath,

Avery Hill students at the Houses of Parliament after a debate on teachers' salaries, 1967. Student protest towards the end of the 1960s led to their representation on the Governing Body of the Polytechnic.

the Union's hardest drinking, quickest thinking, worst-dressing Sabbatical President. . . . Notwithstanding his weakness for the more human joys of life, Dave's expert knowledge of student affairs is widely sought – usually by his mother or the porters. He has promised to go on the wagon next year (having often been told he should have been on the stage), but look out for his slouching figure in the Bar.

Nevertheless co-operation between Godfrey and Yorath enabled Godfrey to report that, 'Amid the unfavourable publicity which has been given to student affairs, it is pleasant to report that relationships at Woolwich have been good.' About the same session Yorath wrote, 'The helpful attitude of Polytechnic officers and staff did much to assist us in our arguments in favour of student participation in college affairs.' Another form which this participation took was the admission by the Governing Body of students to its meetings, first as observers, then in September 1970, by which time Woolwich Polytechnic had become Thames Polytechnic, of two student representatives as full members of the new Court of Governors.

Woolwich had a further problem in making itself acceptable as a new polytechnic. It had to agree to the sort of enlargement which the Ministry, believing that bigger must be better, now began to propose to most of the new Polytechnics. For Woolwich this was an amalgamation with the 'main professional courses' of the Hammersmith College of Art and Building. The Governing Body first heard of the proposal on 28 November 1966 and called an urgent meeting a fortnight later to learn more from E. Walker of the ILEA.

Walker explained that the courses which it was proposed should be transferred to the Polytechnic were those in architecture, surveying, town planning and structural engineering, and would include a Higher National Diploma course in construction. Heywood told the meeting that the Academic Council welcomed the proposal. Adding a new group of specialist courses in a new area of study would, Woolwich believed, improve its chance of being chosen as one of the new polytechnics. The Hammersmith departments were not only likely to get CNAA approval for their courses, so in themselves increasing the

The Hammersmith School of Art and Building, 1910.

Hammersmith School building students at work, 1954.

Polytechnic's range of approved courses, but would help it to obtain approval for courses in its traditional subjects, since the CNAA required all its courses to be offered in an academic environment which provided opportunities for the study of a wide range of subjects.

From Hammersmith's point of view amalgamation with the Polytechnic would have similar advantages. Its courses, both full-time and part-time, led mainly to the professional examinations of the Royal Institution of Chartered Surveyors or of the Royal Institute of British Architects. As part of the Polytechnic it would be able to submit redesigned degree courses which would have a better chance of getting CNAA approval.

Hammersmith College of Art and Building had been founded in 1881 as a small evening class which met at the house of Frances Hawkes in Brook Green, Hammersmith. Here students learned the practical techniques of art which would fit them for careers as craftsmen. In 1885, now known as the Brook Green School of Art, it moved to Brook Green Studios, but 13 years later, with 300 students, it was too large for these and local residents launched an appeal for a new institute. This would have an expanded curriculum which, when it was eventually opened in Lime Grove just west of Shepherd's Bush in 1907, still included such practical crafts as cabinet-making, house-decorating, embroidery, and plastering, but to which architecture had significantly been added.

By then the school had been taken over by the LCC, but it was not until 1930 that its general nature was recognized when it was renamed the Hammersmith School of Building, Arts and Crafts. Now its Lime Grove premises were expanded to accommodate a new Technical School of Building. During the 1930s the Building School expanded to include surveying, engineering, and the administrative aspects of building.

128

Left: *1930s exhibition display of students' work.*

Below: *Wig-making classes at Hammersmith.*

Wartime evacuation to Bath and nearby Calne, was followed in the late 1940s by another renaming, the school now becoming the Hammersmith College of Art and Building. At the same time it began to offer evening classes in architecture, which was made a separate department. Soon afterwards two full-time tutors came to Hammersmith from the architecture department of Wimbledon College of Art, one of them, Paul Nightingale, becoming head of the Hammersmith department, and full-time courses were started. These continued, however, to be largely conducted by visiting practitioners, who included such well-known architects and artists as Denys Lasdun and Russel Spear. From 1959 the RIBA had recognized its intermediate diploma course.

There were two important developments in 1968: the addition of landscape architecture to the college's portfolio, and the transfer of all three departments to Vencourt House, half a mile west of Hammersmith Bridge.

Working parties now set about devising ways in which Woolwich Polytechnic and the Hammersmith departments could be made into a single organization. By the autumn of 1968 they had a draft scheme ready for approval when the Department of Education decided that it was necessary for legal reasons that each new polytechnic should draft its new constitution in a form appropriate to a limited company. At first it seemed that this would require the entire rewriting of the scheme, but in the end the draft was satisfactorily amended and duly approved.

As part of the scheme certain of Hammersmith's Governors joined the new Polytechnic's Court of Governors. This brought to the Polytechnic two Governors with new expertise: Norman Harris, a professional surveyor, one-time President of the Royal Institution of Surveyors, and Ingwald Kraft. Both men were able to give valuable advice on future Polytechnic building projects, and in their turn, became Chairmen of the Court of Governors.

E. Norman Harris, Chairman of the Court of Governors 1976–9, was originally on Hammersmith College Board of Governors.

Facing page: *Riverside House (East), the five storey block in the centre, occupied by the University since the 1960s, with the river beyond.*

Ingwald Kraft, Chairman of the Court of Governors 1979–82, also came from Hammersmith College.

The new Polytechnic already had a name: Thames Polytechnic. This was a decision which Godfrey came to regret; certainly today it seems to have been a desperate answer to the question: 'What on earth do the two colleges have in common?' Answer, 'they are more or less connected by the Thames.' But at the time the choice seemed to have slightly more justification. By now there was a proposal to move the Polytechnic to an entirely new site in the Thamesmead development being constructed on derelict marshland beside the Thames north of Plumstead.

As it stood, the departments were not only some 15 miles away at Hammersmith, so causing great difficulty in creating a genuinely merged organization, but their premises at Hammersmith were a nine-storey tower block, entirely unsuitable for a college in which students must change classrooms, and often floors, once an hour. Bringing the two parts of the new Polytechnic together at Thamesmead would solve both these problems.

In the event, after years of frustrating delay, another solution had to be found. First, in 1978, the Polytechnic rented Churchill House, a building at Woolwich on the corner of Thomas Street and Green's End, into which it moved the Architecture and Surveying Schools. At the same time the Landscape work went to the newly acquired but then under-used Dartford College site. There the Architecture work followed in 1981, so reuniting the School. These moves were fiercely opposed by those who were moved. As one senior member of staff who was responsible for organizing them said, 'When asking a teacher to change his classroom can produce a nervous breakdown, you can imagine what it was like asking two whole departments to move some 15 miles, then a further 10 from an urban setting to a rural one.' The architects in particular claimed that many of them had professional contacts (or indeed businesses) which depended on living and working in south-west London where much of the profession practised. And all staff had either to make long daily journeys or move house. Once forced to move, however, the architects were reasonably content at Woolwich and (after even fiercer resistance) positively delighted by their new Dartford premises. These, apart from having a charming rural setting, were redesigned to provide excellent specialist features, including studios in the converted gymnasia.

Early in these years the Polytechnic lost two of its most notable characters. First to go, in October 1965, was Halliwell who retired after 33 years as Secretary and Clerk to the Governors. It was little wonder that, to many staff and students, he had seemed 'the man who really ran the place'. Seventeen staff, students, secretaries, and other members of the administration contributed appreciations to a commemorative booklet that also listed the astonishing number of changes of his time, some of which he had personally initiated, virtually all of which he had organized.

Many wrote of his astonishing knowledge of Polytechnic matters, his ability to deal quickly and sensibly with a huge variety of questions, and his remarkable energy. A few gave less expected details. One contributer remembered Halliwell describing the long hours he had spent at the College of Heralds devising a coat of arms for the Poly as 'one of the most interesting jobs I have undertaken . . . with the Polytechnic'. Another remembered that Halliwell had been much concerned with the impression the Poly's porters made on visitors, once suggesting that the head porter should wear a frock-coat. About his annual staff treasure-

hunts, A. Weaver, Organizer of Physical Education, remembered how he would devise 'a new route, interesting places, a decent meal, prizes', and would check on every detail to make sure that the evening was enjoyable for everybody. 'I am now an authority on the Kent countryside, Kent road signs, Kent history, Kent pubs and brewers.'

Halliwell was keen on almost every sort of sport especially hockey – though not tennis ('a daft game!'). He also found time to become a member of the Air Training Corps. 'I can see him now, in just trousers and shirt, marching up and down in the Hall having a refresher course under the watchful eye of Sergeant Gage.'

Organizing with meticulous care celebration dinners was one of his specialities and it was a lucky chance that the final one which he stage-managed was the setting for such a significant event as Anthony Crosland's Woolwich Speech. The MBE he was awarded when he retired was deserved.

The following year the death of Arthur Israel Vogel, head of Chemistry, while still in office aged only 61, was a sad loss to the Polytechnic. Vogel had come to the Poly 36 years earlier, in 1930, and within four years been promoted to head of his department. In this position he expected his staff to work as hard as he did himself, his first concern always for his students. Dr Jeffery, his deputy for many years, remembered that he was 'particularly solicitous for the progress of junior members of his laboratory staff, and nothing gave him greater pleasure than to witness the careers of "lab. boys" who subsequently achieved the status of qualified chemists.'

Facing page: Churchill House, from General Gordon Square, Woolwich.

Besides teaching he vigorously encouraged research in his department and himself undertook widely respected research, his special interest the refractive indices and surface tensions of different chemical compounds. The essential feature of this research was the purity of the compounds and just before he died he had prepared a paper on the 1,000th pure compound to be investigated in his laboratories. During the war when fire-watching he would sneak away in quiet periods to work in his lab.

When wartime evening classes were transferred to the weekends there was a problem: as a Jew Vogel could not teach on Saturdays and Jeffery, the only other whole-time member of the department still in London, found himself teaching classes in organic, inorganic, and physical chemistry on a single day.

Vogel's other achievement was the writing of a range of textbooks used throughout the country, and indeed abroad. The revised 5th edition of one of these (*Quantitative Inorganic Chemical Analysis*) was published in 1989, just fifty years after the first edition had appeared.

Halliwell was succeeded as Secretary to the Governors by Peter Oxlade, a man of very different character, cool and precise, but someone who was to make an equally valuable contribution to the Polytechnic and was probably more suited to the problems it faced between 1966 and 1970. He could work, colleagues remember, 23 hours a day and be as meticulously accurate in the twenty-third hour as in the first. It would be hard to exaggerate his part in devising the complicated arrangements for the transformation of Woolwich Polytechnic into Thames Polytechnic. When this eventually occurred in 1970 he was appointed Secretary to the new Court of Governors.

In the years of transformation Oxlade worked closely with one Governor in particular: G. Ainsworth Wates (Chairman 1965–8; his father, G. Leslie Wates had

Construction of Thomas Spencer Hall, 1968. Rooftop view across Wellington Street.

Sir Thomas Spencer, Chairman of the Governing Board, 1949-52, after whom the Polytechnic's first hall of residence was named.

been Chairman in 1945–7). Wates the younger, a lawyer by profession, had the legal expertise required for the long negotiations and drafting of the many consequent documents.

In thanking him the Governing Body wrote of his 'powers of leadership', 'professional knowledge', and 'incisive style'. It picked out in particular 'the marathon series of meetings and discussions' which had followed the proposed amalgamation with departments of Hammersmith College of Art and Building, when Wates was Chairman of the Steering Committee, Chairman of the Co-ordination Committee, and a prominent member of the Constitutional Working Party. 'Imperturbably', it concluded, 'he led the Governing Body and its various committees through an extremely difficult and important period to the threshold of an exciting future.'

The services of another Governor, Sir Thomas Spencer (Chairman 1949–52), were recognized when the Polytechnic's first hall of residence was named after him. Spencer had been a pre-First World War Poly student, since then rising to become the Chairman of the Standard Telephone Company. Each year he would make a personal inspection tour of the Poly.

The architects had shown the Governors their plan for what was to be Thomas Spencer Hall in November 1966. It would accommodate 250 students in study-bedrooms in a five-storey block to be built on part of the Grand Depot site, and would include a sick bay, dining-room, kitchen, common rooms, and flats for wardens and other staff. If the Ministry of Housing and Local Government, and various other bodies agreed to the plan the building could be completed in June 1969.

It was the London Borough of Greenwich which caused difficulties by reducing the size of the site it would allow the Poly and objecting to the amount of amenity space in the architect's plan. As a result it was not until November 1967 that the Governors were able to approve a revised plan. Now the block was to be ten storeys in height but provide more or less the same accommodation for students and staff. The rooms on the first and second floors were to be specifically designed for female students. Close by there were to be three squash courts. But the proposed completion date was set back a year.

After further modifications, including the redesigning of the fittings in the students' rooms to give them 'pale-yellow sun-blinds' and 'colourful bed-spreads and chair coverings' so that they would have 'a warm appearance', a contractor's tender was agreed early in 1969 and the building was partly ready for the start of the 1971–2 session. Spencer himself formally opened the hall on 29 November 1971.

The vital roles Wates, Spencer, other Governors and the Secretary played in the transformation of the Polytechnic during these five years should not obscure the central role – often not clear from official records – of the Principal, Godfrey. It was characteristic that, when the position of Director of the new Thames Polytechnic was to be filled, he should have insisted on applying for it like anyone else, and only appropriate that he should have been chosen. The staff would have been dismayed by any other choice.

11

Growing Pains

1970–1978

I T MUST HAVE SEEMED LIKELY, once the amalgamation between Woolwich and Hammersmith had been properly arranged, that Thames Polytechnic would emerge from a thicket of negotiations into gentler country. This was not to be, and it was to face a succession of different but no less difficult problems, the most potentially traumatic the move to Thamesmead.

In 1970 – to the dismay of many staff but official enthusiasm of the Court of Governors and Principal – this still seemed inevitable. It had first been proposed in 1964, and complicated discussions had followed. These by 1972 had reached a stage at which the Polytechnic had been allocated a $12\frac{1}{2}$-acre site as part of the new complex. On 13 March that year a group of Governors went to Thamesmead where they were distressed to be told that the site had in effect been reduced by $1\frac{1}{2}$ acres. (By way of comparison, in 1995 the University completed the purchase of 135 acres of land at Dartford with planning cases for 1,000,000 sq. ft. of development and Dartford was to be merely one of six locations for the University.)

The Polytechnic's reduced allocation led to more negotiations, and by April 1973 it had been given a new 18-acre site in a better position. The same month the Chairman reported that the Court of Governors had approved an Academic Development Plan which the Department of Education had requested, 'for the time when the Thamesmead site would be occupied and when we might expect to have some 6,000 students'. To those who favoured the move all looked hopeful. The most obvious gain would be that Thames Polytechnic's two parts would be physically as well as organizationally united; the plan was that when the initial stage of construction was complete the Faculty of Architecture and Surveying, as the Hammersmith departments had been named, would move there first, to be followed by the Woolwich Faculty of Social Sciences and Humanities.

Now, however, the whole scheme began to collapse as a result of the country's

Facing page: Students marching through London, campaigning for higher grants; in the foreground, Thames Polytechnic students.

135

economic problems. Godfrey had to tell the Governors that Stage 1 was not included in 1974–5 'starts list'. It would be reconsidered for the following year but he was 'not optimistic . . . given that many 1973–4 cancelled projects would presumably be given priority', and therefore advised the Governors to consider moving the Hammersmith faculty to rented accommodation somewhere else in South-East London. He added that if no further information became available during the year the Court 'should ask itself whether Thamesmead was any longer a political reality and should look at alternative ways in which the Polytechnic might develop.'

This was the beginning of the end. By April 1975 the Chairman was having to report his disappointment that there was still an 'absence of any firm information on a starting date for the Thamesmead project'. The Polytechnic was still 'planning towards' the move to Thamesmead, but 'the scheduling of the development plan is now in some disarray.'

Next year the Chairman admitted that, because of the unfortunate economic climate, the Court had been 'hardly surprised at not receiving any firm news of the Thamesmead project'. Reporting on the following session the Director wrote, '1975–6 will be remembered as the year that the Thamesmead plan disappeared for the foreseeable future.' Thus the great move was never officially declared abandoned but allowed quietly to fade away.

What remained was a memory of an enormous amount of wasted planning. This had been largely undertaken by Gordon Hunting. Hunting had worked at the NCTA and CNAA before joining the Polytechnic in 1968 as Godfrey's Vice-Principal. His plans for the Polytechnic at Thamesmead were generally considered by the ILEA and the Department of Education to have been a model of their kind.

Planning of another kind blighted the new Polytechnic's early years as a result of an attempt to restructure it on the fashionable matrix system. The underlying idea of this, largely pioneered at Hatfield Polytechnic, first put into practice at Thames Polytechnic in 1971–2, was to subdivide the activities of the different faculties and departments, with the aim of leaving those who actually taught free to develop their subject, teach and engage in research, relieved of such practical preoccupations as administering the resources they needed and other peripheral duties. So-called Divisions, of which there were 40, were to undertake what could be roughly called teaching duties; Schools were to undertake what could be called resource allocation and course administration.

To clarify this division Godfrey wrote in 1973 that the Schools were 'responsible for the organization and academic development of courses', and the Divisions for 'development of courses, and the teaching and research in subject areas', a definition which well suggests the demarcation disputes which might result. Those who had devised the new structure had not, unfortunately, foreseen some of these difficulties. It was, for example, only teaching staff and in particular heads of the old-style departments who knew what resources were needed and could argue for them. As for the less senior teaching staff, some of whom were assigned to both a School and a Division, they no longer knew for whom they were working. A problem of the time, which it was hoped the new structure would solve (though how is unclear) concerned 'service teaching' (the provision by one department of teaching required by students who were on courses administered by a different department). There was a general belief – though few supporting facts – that the department supplying the service was inclined to treat such courses as second best.

Furthermore, a large number of committees had been built into the new structure. Six years earlier Anthony Sampson had memorably described a camel as a horse devised by a committee, but the lesson had not been learned and staff at the Polytechnic spent hundreds – probably thousands – of hours devising what some considered to be the sort of camels which only a gathering of inventive academics could have devised. Apart from the time and effort this wasted, the reorganization, by introducing formalized appointments of, for example, senior course tutors and heads of divisions, produced too rigid a structure which made it difficult to reassign staff when this was necessary, an impediment which even Godfrey, who was at first enthusiastic about the new arrangements, eventually recognized. It was left to a new Director, Norbert Singer, who arrived in September 1978, to sweep away much of this paraphernalia, a process which his successor has continued. In spite of the new structure Keith Reed, Godfrey's Deputy Director from 1973, believed that the Polytechnic's teaching did not suffer, something he described as 'a bit of a miracle'.

With two, later three, student members of the new Court of Governors, student relationships with the Polytechnic authorities should have remained as satisfactory as they had been at the high point of student protest in 1968. But here, too, well-meant reform aimed at satisfying students by giving them a greater say

Student demonstration outside the Royal Festival Hall, November 1971.

in the running of the Polytechnic was followed by almost ten years of rumbling dissatisfaction. In the opinion of some staff the granting of sabbatical years to a handful of office-holders of the Students' Union was a contributory cause; free from academic work some, though not all, had nothing better to do than cause trouble.

There was an early hint of difficulty in 1970–1 when the Students' Union asked the Court of Governors to abandon its right to authorize the Union's constitution, so allowing it to become totally independent, a request which the Court refused. More disruptive trouble began in March 1972 when students staged an occupation as part of a campaign for better grants. It lasted two weeks and was reported self-approvingly in the 1973–4 *Students' Handbook*:

> The occupation was run by five committees – security, catering, publicity, alternative education and cleaning/maintenance.... There were about 200 students occupying the college and a meeting was called twice daily to make decisions on the running of the occupation.... Publicity was one of the hardest things to achieve, especially favourable articles, however, we were visited by reporters from the local newspapers *Mercury*, *Globe*, *Kentish Independent* and *Erith Observer*, and nationally by the *Guardian*, *Morning Star*, *Observer* and *Workers' Press*. On Friday 2nd March after one week of occupation, a motion was proposed to continue and was carried by a large majority. The second week carried on much the same as the first, with many students [allegedly] changing committees (to gain experience). However, arrangements were made for pre-exam students to have lectures – but Dr Godfrey the Director directed lecturers not to attend as he feared clashes between students and staff.... On Friday 9th March at a packed Union meeting the occupation ended, but even then only by a small margin. Since

then the NUS grants campaign was an anti-climax. Wednesday March 14th was the day when students were to stay at home – not much different from any Wednesday.

In October 1975 and May 1976 there were one-day occupations of the Polytechnic's administrative offices, both carried out without warning immediately after votes at Students' Union meetings. Again the students behaved properly, apart from reading some of the Director's and Secretary's files. More alarming to the Governors was the head porter's report that students had keys to all those administrative offices which did not have mortice locks, but this was denied by a student Governor. These occupations were also against the size of government grants, a matter over which the Governors had no control.

In February 1977 there was a week's occupation in support of demands some of which in this sense were more reasonable: (a) no tuition fee increases; (b) an end to all quota systems for overseas students; (c) no discriminating fees; (d) no policing of overseas students; and (e) a public statement from Dr Godfrey endorsing the above demands.

Godfrey, expecting a vote for the occupation, had already, as in previous occupations, closed the whole Polytechnic. He had also told the Students' Union that although he was 'sympathetic' to some of their demands and would be willing to discuss them, he would not do so while any occupation continued.

In November 1977 there was a further 24-hour occupation, this time in protest against government cuts in the funding of education. And in February 1978 there was a 19-day occupation in protest against cuts which would mean that the Polytechnic would have to axe 126 of its places open to overseas students. Apart from considering this racist, the Students' Union believed that it seriously threatened the survival of six courses.

Student Protests of the 1970s

These pages, left to right:
Student demonstrator in Trafalgar Square.

Students and police, Powis Street.

March across Waterloo Bridge demanding bigger grants.

Rally at Hyde Park Corner.

Demonstration by Avery Hill Students.

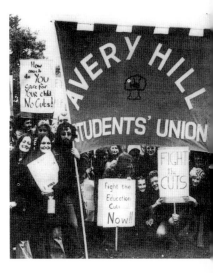

The *Students' Handbook* again gave a sympathetic account of this occupation:

> Eventually at the beginning of February when negotiations were at an end Thames Polytechnic Students' Union organised a disruption of the Finance and General Purposes committee in an attempt to obtain a reversal of policy from the Court of Governors. They once again ignored us.
>
> An Emergency General Meeting was immediately called and 1,000 students attended. A motion calling for an occupation of the Woolwich Site of the Polytechnic to pressurise the Court of Governors to reverse their decision was carried.
>
> A long campaign then began against the racist quota system. The Director's response was to close all three sites of the Polytechnic and halt all teaching. He agreed quotas were racist but instead of fighting the ILEA policy he attacked students.
>
> During the course of the 3 weeks in occupation TPSU regularly picketed the Director's home in Dartford to pressurise him into recommencing teaching, but he went to Wales for a holiday! We appeared on the ITV London Programme. We led the National Union of Students' demonstration against quotas through London and we were supported by sympathy action in other colleges.
>
> The occupation was reaffirmed at two subsequent Emergency General Meetings at Woolwich and Dartford sites. But the chief stumbling block was the political unwillingness of the Stalinist NUS leadership to co-ordinate a national campaign against quotas. Indeed it took the NUS executive 8 days to send us a three line telegram of support. . . . Once again an initiative against attacks on students taken up by colleges at a local level was betrayed by the NUS executive.
>
> Finally in the last days of February an Emergency General Meeting at Woolwich of some 1,500 students voted unanimously against quotas but a majority vote ended an occupation which was consciously isolated by the NUS Executive.

This report leaves much out of account, for example Godfrey's responsibility for protecting the many millions of pounds' worth of Polytechnic equipment which the occupiers might have damaged. It does, however, suggest that his strictly correct behaviour made it easy for them to turn him, personally, into the object of their hostility. In Valerie Pitt's words, 'Those diabolical children picked on him because he was "management" though in fact he was very liberal, even left wing in his attitudes. It upset him because, I think, he hadn't a clue about what was happening – or its essential triviality – and couldn't ride it.'

His replacement in September 1978 by Norbert Singer was indeed followed by better relationships between students and the Polytechnic authorities. In June 1978 a full staff discussion of occupations had broadly supported Godfrey, but one of its 12 comments had been that there was 'a communication gap between the college authorities and the students'. And that October – by which time Singer had arrived – the Court reconsidered the way in which it should respond. One alternative was to continue the policy of totally closing the Polytechnic, another,

still more confrontational, was to take action through the courts to have the occupiers removed. The other two suggestions were to impose a cooling-off period.

The Court finally resolved that 'In the event of a partial or total occupation of the Polytechnic there shall be an initial "cooling-off" or "lead-in" period to enable intensive discussions to be held with the decision on further action resting with the Director according to circumstances.'

Student occupations at Thames Polytechnic now ceased. It should be remembered, however, that they were not only a Thames Polytechnic phenomenon, indeed Thames was by no means the most severely affected, and that by then a different climate existed in the student world at large which resulted in them also ceasing elsewhere.

Disruptive as they had been, no fundamental damage had been done and it could be argued that they were an educational experience, teaching students how to organize themselves, negotiate, and act in ways likely to get results in real-life situations. Many staff, however, would not agree with this, seeing them as not only politically motivated but often engineered by a minority in meetings which had no quorums.

These early troubles should not obscure the fact that Thames Polytechnic emerged in the 1970s as an entirely transformed, far more professional, national rather than local institution, concentrating on the teaching of a wide range of subjects at advanced level, thus in practice the equivalent of a university and distinguished from a university in only a few remaining ways.

The most obvious of these was that it was still not able to grant its own degrees, which were now being entirely granted by the CNAA for success in courses which required the CNAA's approval. These courses were 'reviewed' by a peer group drawn from industry, other polytechnics, and universities, a feature which did much to improve standards and which also differentiated them from courses which an individual university might devise.

Another important difference was that many Thames students were taking sandwich courses, which were thus more obviously connected with the careers they planned than the courses of a normal university student. This was, in the CNAA's opinion, as it should be, and some of the courses it approved were intentionally vocational. A consequence of this, and of the need to find places

Student Life under the GLC

Clockwise from left: *Cover of an Avery Hill prospectus. Study bedrooms at Garnett College and Thomas Spencer Hall. Prospectus cover showing the Thames Barrier.*

141

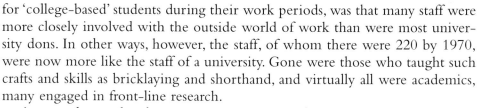

New computers for the 1970s: installation (above) and (below) innards of 'The Prince'.

for 'college-based' students during their work periods, was that many staff were more closely involved with the outside world of work than were most university dons. In other ways, however, the staff, of whom there were 220 by 1970, were now more like the staff of a university. Gone were those who taught such crafts and skills as bricklaying and shorthand, and virtually all were academics, many engaged in front-line research.

Among those who deserve mention was Stanley Mason, who came from Liverpool Polytechnic to be head of Mechanical Engineering. Mason had started his working life as a coalminer, and while a student would continue to work in the pits during vacations to earn his keep. At the Poly,

> within a matter of months he had reinvigorated a somewhat demoralised staff with his infectious enthusiasm. He built up a research group on bulk-solid-handling techniques which quickly gained an international reputation. He had an extraordinary talent for leadership by example and invariably managed to achieve what, at the outset, seemed unattainable. He was a splendid colleague, greatly admired by staff at all levels, and a great loss when he left in the 1980s to go to Glasgow, subsequently becoming Principal and Vice-Chancellor of the Glasgow Caledonian University. (Reed)

Another was Jack Sonn. Appointed to the Physics Department after the War, he later became a senior and finally principal lecturer in the Mathematics Department.

> Over more than three decades Sonn was a much trusted spokesman for the teaching staff through the teachers union. He was a first class teacher, as good as any other over the same period. He was also capable of making lengthy spoken contributions to meetings without notes which could be recorded verbatim and require no subsequent editing. (Reed)

To Valerie Pitt, Sonn was an example of the Polytechnic's characteristic humanity.

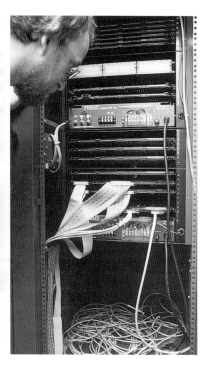

> Jack's Marxism was rooted in the experience of the thirties and was, one might say, entirely unpolemical. He took a stand certainly on certain issues but was always courteous, rational and where he could be, helpful. It was very interesting to watch the contrast between his approach and that of the sixties Marxists who arrived in the Polytechnic at a time when it was expanding.
>
> There were other characters [She continued] who had played an earlier part in developing the Polytechnic ethos . . . there was Betty Jones for instance, who was the Librarian when I first went there. She was a misfit really – she thought the place below her and was an exceedingly difficult colleague even before she became ill. Even so – she had a view of what a Library ought to be in Higher Education diametrically opposed to the instrumentalist attitude of the governors and some of the older teaching staff, which finally permeated the place.

Among the administrative staff to make important contributions to the Polytechnic's smooth running in these years was Barry Bleach, who came from Bristol to be the first Academic Registrar and set up the unit. A keen cricketer, he eventually collapsed and died on the cricket field. Before that he had left to become secretary to the CNAA, to be succeeded at Thames by Brian Betham, described by colleagues as 'a real gentleman'. Betham's special interest was Arabian affairs. He spoke Arabic fluently and had a notable library of Arabic books. Before his appointment as Registrar he was principal lecturer in the School of Humanities, teaching history and assisting Miss Pitt to administer the school. He died in service, his loss mourned by the entire college.

The years 1956 to 1970 saw the second great transformation in the nature of the Polytechnic. The first had occurred when it changed from the sort of young men's Christian institute that Hogg and Didden had founded into what was primarily a further education college. Certainly it retained sports clubs and societies, but they became no more important to it than, say, the games and societies of a public school. Like the later transformation, the first had been imposed on it by the body or bodies which financed it and had taken place over a number of years.

The second great change was from being a college which provided education of many sorts, evening, part-time, full-time, for students who might be schoolboys or university graduates, of the sort which the people of Woolwich and its neighbourhood needed, to a college largely providing full-time courses leading to degrees for students who came from all over the country and from abroad. As part of this transformation into a national institution, it ceased to specialize in science, mathematics, and engineering and instead taught as wide a range of subjects as a university.

Electrical engineering, early 1970s.

If there were new problems as Godfrey's ten-year regime drew to a close he was not responsible for them. One was the limit which the Government admitted for the first time in January 1977 that it wished to put on overseas student numbers. 'Notwithstanding fundamental objections to the Government policy,' Godfrey wrote, 'the Court decided to accept the restrictions implied by the DES circular.' For Thames Polytechnic the target the following year was set at 323 overseas students.

More generally, Godfrey reported that 'During this session, as in a few previous sessions, the development of the Polytechnic was strictly limited by the standstill in finance.' Nevertheless he was able to say that the CNAA had made its five-yearly inspection and that there had been 'a substantial measure of satisfaction with the Polytechnic and its work'.

For this, he personally should again be given much of the credit. His contribution to the Polytechnic was immense. He guided it through the most critical ten years of its life, and with tremendous work and vision transformed it into an institution of higher education at national level. It could easily have had a different future.

12

Madame Österberg
and the Dartford Legacy

1885–1976

Facing page: *Kingsfield House, Dartford, in 1935.*

IN THE 1970s, 1980s AND 1990s Thames Polytechnic (and the University of Greenwich as it became) amalgamated with a succession of other colleges or parts of colleges – seven in total – the two earliest and most significant being the teacher training colleges of Dartford and Avery Hill. The underlying cause of these two forced marriages was government policy, which aimed at reducing the excessive number of teachers being trained in the country, in the belief that school numbers would fall. They were suggested to the Polytechnic simultaneously in 1972. Though not the Polytechnic's initiative, it had no objection to expanding into teacher training and the negotiations which followed were a major preoccupation for Godfrey and the Polytechnic staff during his later years.

Dartford College, one of the smaller, more specialist, and therefore more vulnerable colleges, had an even longer history than Woolwich Polytechnic, having opened five years earlier in 1885. Its founder was a Swedish lady, Martina Bergman. This, the central event in her life, led to a transformation in the physical education of British schoolchildren and in particular of British girls, by the introduction of what was known, somewhat misleadingly, as Swedish drill.

Miss Bergman had been born in 1849, favourite daughter of a Swedish wheat farmer, her country background no doubt contributing to her belief in a healthy outdoor life. She had first worked as a teacher, but it was after she became a librarian that she met the Stockholm schoolmaster, Edvin Österberg, later to become her husband, who changed her life by persuading her to return to teaching. To train for this she began, aged 30, a two-year course in gymnastics at the Royal Central Gymnasium Institute in Stockholm.

By then the founder of the Institute, Per Henrik Ling, had died and it was being run by his two children, Hilder and Hjalman Ling. Under their influence Miss Bergman became a lifelong advocate of the Ling system. Ling, the father,

Martina Bergman, later Madame Österberg, as a student at the Central Institute, Stockholm. She is wearing Swedish national costume.

145

had claimed that his exercises fell into four categories: educational, aesthetic, military, and medical. True, the Institute had been founded with Royal support to improve the physique of Swedish soldiers, but it was the exercises which had a medical purpose that came to interest him most. They included his 'free-standing' exercises, so-called because they needed no apparatus, in contrast to those of a contemporary system invented by a German, Guts Muths, which needed the trapeze, parallel bars, dumb-bells, and various other contraptions. Ling's exercises were intended to improve health and bodily development by improving posture, and because of their medical purpose they led him to study anatomy and physiology. In her passing-out exams Miss Bergman was awarded all A grades apart from one B grade.

Now she travelled to study gymnastics in other European countries and it was while in Britain in 1881 that the London School Board offered her the position of Superintendent of Physical Education in Girls' and Infants' Schools.

The appointment of a foreign lady to teach the poor schoolgirls of London Scandinavian exercises was not such a strange event as it sounds. For many years Sweden had had a reputation for its teaching of gymnastics, and from 1850 Dr Mathias Roth, Hungarian by birth, had been publicizing Ling's system in England, writing a succession of pamphlets, speaking at meetings, and pestering educationalists. In particular he had drawn attention to the large number of army recruits who had to be rejected because of their poor physique. Though this had made Swedish drill well known it had had few practical results. The year after the Education Act of 1870 boys at board schools were allowed two hours of military drill a week, but nothing of the sort was suggested for girls.

Facing page: *Kingsfield House, Dartford, 1995* (see also page 150).

Only with the London School Board, composed since its establishment in 1870 of elected members, did he have any success, eventually finding a supporter in Mrs Alice Westlake. Girls, Mrs Westlake discovered, were almost totally deprived of any sort of physical activity in the Board's schools. She called Roth before her committee to explain the Ling system. He brought with him Miss Froken Löfving, a gymnast form Stockholm, and in 1879 Miss Löfving was appointed Superintendent of Physical Education in Girls' Schools, at a salary of £300 a year.

Miss Löfving was only a failure by comparison with her successor. After a year she was able to organize a successful, hour-and-a-half display by girls from London schools, not one of whom, *The Times* commented, 'stepped off with the wrong foot'. But she left soon afterwards, and because the Board was short of money this led to an interval of a year before Mrs Westlake could persuade it to appoint Miss Bergman to a similar position and even then at the reduced salary of £200.

The Ling system, which it was Miss Bergman's duty to introduce into the Board's girls' schools, was ideal for the purpose, since it needed not even a playground. Often the exercises were done with half the girls standing between the rows of desks, the other half on the desks' seats. To spread its introduction, she organized courses which one teacher from each school had to attend. They were held in the evenings on three nights a week from 7 to 8.30 at Saffron Hill School, Clifton Road School, and Haverstock Hill School. Those who passed the end-of-course examination were given a certificate by the School Board. When Miss Bergman was appointed there were 80 certificated physical education teachers in Board schools, six years later there were 700.

To publicize her work she would hold 'open-practices', to which teachers and parents could come. Grander than these was the display she gave in June 1883 at Knighton Park, home of Edward Buxton, Chairman of the London Schools Board. Guests of honour were the Prince of Wales, future Edward VII, and his princess. A hundred girls aged four to seven from Islington, Limehouse, the Borough, Bermondsey, Poplar, and Ratcliff demonstrated movements 'by which the neck, and spine, the joints and every muscle were brought into active and harmonious exercise, the lungs being exercised by singing and counting'. All wore white hats with red ribbons. Afterwards the Prince said that it had been 'a remarkable sight . . . considering the localities from which those children had come'.

Satisfactory as all this was, Miss Bergman began to regret that she was exclusively working with poor girls. 'Is it not rather funny', she wrote, 'that you here in England think that what is good for the poor cannot be good for the rich?' It was to spread her teaching to the upper and upper-middle classes that she founded her private teacher-training establishment in Hampstead, later to become Dartford College.

Aside from her wish to be free from the School Board, with which she had had difficulties, the most obvious (and acceptable) reason for her new venture was that she wished to convert English upper-middle-class girls to a healthier lifestyle and in the process to develop for them a career as physical education teachers

Facing page: Cricket at Dartford campus.

'Converting the English upper-middle class to a healthier life style'; natural dance movement, 1935.

which, for girls of their class, had not previously existed. She had another reason, today somewhat less fashionable. Many of the poor girls she worked with were such bad specimens, as a result of poverty and poor nourishment, that they could never become the fine physical specimens she admired. Later she was to say about them, 'The physique of this class was so lowered and impaired by neglect and by bad conditions of housing, food and clothing, that unless the conditions could be changed, no radical improvement could be effected.' 'If they are starving I think it is better for them not to have any exercises.' Such girls could never be the basis for her freely admitted aim of 'individual and race perfection'. She wanted a better 'balance between the physical, intellectual and moral faculties. These qualities, transmitted by inheritance, would perfect the race', enabling her to train her 'beautiful English flowers'.

The college she founded, to which the first four young ladies came in the summer of 1885, was at 1 Broadhurst Gardens, Hampstead. Officially it was named the Hampstead College of Physical Training, but often called the Hampstead Gymnasium. The following year, when she gave evidence to the Cross Commission (established to enquire into the working of the Elementary Education Acts) her college was the only one out of 73 teacher training colleges in England and Wales (and probably the only one in the world apart from Stockholm's) to have a full-time course in physical education.

The Hampstead fees were high, confirming its aim of introducing Swedish practice to the country's upper and upper-middle classes. In compensation it guaranteed that it would find successful students positions with salaries of no less than £100 a year. Teacher training was its central activity, and again it taught its students to teach Ling's variety of Swedish drill, which put emphasis on its medical usefulness. As a result the students studied anatomy, physiology, and hygiene (all of which Miss Bergman taught herself) besides massage and exercises specifically designed to be remedial. Periods of so-called 'clinic' were included in the timetable. In 1909 the clothes list for students (who were all boarders) ended, 'The student, if she has in her possession, is required to bring, a microscope, a half skeleton, disarticulated. Otherwise bones may be hired in college for a small fee.'

The sort of teachers she aimed to produce would 'guard the children's development, prevent deformities and keep an eye on the whole hygiene of the school.' In other words they would act as a school's officer of health. They would also give their 'whole time and interest' to their schools and be 'leaders in the games field as well as in the gymnasium'.

The sports and games she referred to were swimming, lawn tennis, and (surprisingly) fives, but there were soon also instructors in fencing and cricket. Swimming was taught at first over a bench in the gymnasium. From 1888, however, when the Hampstead swimming baths opened across the road from the College and Madame Österberg (as she had become after her marriage to her old Stockholm friend) was appointed superintendent, the girls swam there. For cricket and tennis they had to go by public transport to Neasden where there were courts and a pitch.

We play in our gym-suits [one girl remembered], which is a very comfortable arrangement, but we have to resign ourselves to being called 'those

148

Eating gooseberries for dessert, 1903. A healthy diet was an essential part of the regime.

dreadful girls' by the passers by, and to overhearing discussions of our character in the train by men who don't know how troublesome skirts are and
by women who don't know how delightful it is to be free of them.

Games and sports were to become a principal activity of the College, though
Madame Österberg herself is said never to have understood the subtleties of
English games; one student remembered that during her whole two-year course
Madame never visited the Neasden grounds.

Facing page: Outdoor gym, 1900s.

As well as training teachers, the College treated private patients, some of
whom became residents. First of these was the future Duchess of Hamilton.
Madame Österberg claimed that she had successfully treated cases of neuralgia,
paralysis, and spinal curvature. When a second house, 5 Broadhurst Gardens, was
bought, it provided space for a medical gymnasium and rooms for in-patients.

The year after its foundation the College began to give the sort of open
practices her London school girls had given. By now her gymnasium was
becoming well known and people in the educational world, the Principal of
Holloway College among them, wrote to congratulate her.

Even the pets appeared to go through rigorous physical training (photograph from 1910s).

The students' day was an exacting one by modern standards. It began at 7.15
a.m. with a cold bath, followed by an early lecture, before breakfast at 8.30. In the
morning there were more lectures between 9.00 and 1.30 and in the afternoon
from 3.00 to 6.00 (in winter), then tea and private study until supper at 9.00. In
summer tea was at 4.30 followed by games. On some evenings there were debates,
plays, or musical entertainments instead of private study. Bed was at 10 p.m.

Madame Österberg was proud of her College and her healthy, English girls,
and they found her an inspiring leader, but they were also alarmed by her. She
was rarely complimentary, often critical and would expel any student who
showed such inadequacies as nervousness, a weak voice, or a physical deformity.
She had little sympathy for those who were ill, telling them that they had 'mis-
managed themselves'.

Soon local and national papers and magazines began to notice the Hampstead
Gymnasium. In 1888 the *Hampstead and Highgate Express* wrote that it offered
the best system of physical training for boys and girls yet devised by science, and
that by training competent teachers it would spread the system throughout the
country. Looking back on the College's first six years, the *Woman's Herald* wrote,

Kingsfield House, standing in 14 acres of wooded parkland, bought by Madame Österberg in 1895.

Mr Mauritzi, the vaulting teacher, catches 'a short fly'.

'Totally undisturbed by committee resolutions, untrammelled by inspection, and never interfered with by inexperienced advice, she had the great advantage of being left alone to her own devices.' Such praise was the more remarkable since the College still had only just over twice as many students as when it opened.

Ten years after opening her Hampstead college, Madame Österberg bought Kingsfield, a large country house on Dartford Heath in northern Kent and moved her students there. She made the move partly because of a rumour that her Hampstead houses would be demolished to allow a new railway line from Manchester to central London to be built, but she must also have been tempted by the many features which Kingsfield had and Hampstead lacked. Apart from being in the healthier countryside, it stood in 14 acres of wooded parkland which could be used for sports and games. Here on 17 September 1895, 27 students arrived, 14 new recruits, 13 who had already taken the first year of the course.

At Dartford work continued much as it had in Hampstead. Practising the Ling free-standing exercises and learning how to teach them remained at the core of the course, supplemented by lessons in anatomy, physiology, hygiene, and massage. Madame Österberg still did much of the teaching, though she now had a staff of six. Increasingly she used young ladies she had trained herself, the only outsiders now being the cricket and tennis coach, Mr Ballad of Neasden, the vaulting teacher Mr Mauritzi, and the physiology teacher, Miss Martin.

There were, however, changes, one of the most important that much of the work could now be done out of doors. Often the exercises were performed on the lawn, and during the first term at Dartford outdoor jumping and vaulting continued until November. At first the house's ballroom was used as a gymnasium, but soon an outdoor gymnasium was built in the woods.

150

Another change for the better at Dartford was that the Wilmington Board Schools with 200 children were near by and more convenient for practice with real classes. Students would go there up to four times a week and on Saturday mornings the children would come to the College. When the College expanded, students also went for practice to Dartford schools.

The really important contrast between Hampstead and Dartford, however, was in the opportunity the new house's grounds provided for games, which began to play an even more important part in the girls' lives. Only swimming was at first less easily available, but even this was arranged in the River Darenth, from a 'secluded garden'.

Other sporting activities began with a track, laid out by Dr Toles, a visiting American. This was used for running, marching, and cycling – all students had to bring bicycles. Even Edvin Österberg during his visits would use the track. With the square red beard he always grew, he was a notable sight, doing his twelve circuits 'poised on an extremely upright machine', wearing 'tail coat and top hat' (though the surviving photograph of him with his mount shows him in knee-breeches and hunting cap). No wonder he became 'a father figure to many of Madame's girls' (Jonathan May, *Madame Bergman-Österberg*, 1969).

Within the track a cricket field was created, and during the first season the college began to play matches against other elevens, one of the earliest Oxford High School. By 1898 the College team was notable for its overarm bowling. It was not until 40 years later in 1925 that the national Women's Cricket Association was founded. In summer, tennis was also played, and in 1899 three asphalt courts were laid.

During the winter the cricket field became a hockey field and at hockey, too, the College began to play other schools and colleges. And the same American who had laid out the track successfully introduced basketball. In America an essential feature of this was the bouncing of the ball on a hard surface. It was at Dartford that it was first adapted for soft surfaces and given the name netball, with its own rules. By 1904 another new game, lacrosse, had been introduced, again well before the national Ladies' Lacrosse Association was founded in 1912.

Much of this took place in defiance of contemporary convention. In 1910 when a student played hockey for Kent in her college tunic instead of a regulation skirt (which had to descend to less than six inches from the ground) a correspondent wrote to the *Hockey Field*:

Miss Alma Wikner, the most trusted assistant of Madame Österberg.

Oakfield Lane, Dartford, before 1920. The curiously wrought post on the left is still at the entrance to the Dartford campus.

That costume is without doubt, ideal in that it cannot hamper the movement of the bearer; but, at the same time, does not suit itself to public grounds. To show the adoption of this dress for public matches may prove detrimental to hockey. I quote an extract from a letter received by a county player from her fiancé. 'Please look at the Sporting and Dramatic, and see the awful apparition who plays for Kent.'

The College tunic was another of Madame Österberg's introductions, so short that it would just brush the ground when the student knelt. In 1913 it so impressed a Japanese student, Tokuyo Nikaido, that when she went home to found the Japanese College of Physical Education, it was made the college's academic dress.

For the people of Dartford, still then a small town, the College was something of which they were proud – though *they* also noticed the girls' dress:

The students wore very short skirts (their tunics) and some of them were very well built!!! The children of Dartford benefited greatly from the remedial work done by students at the College clinic. (Mrs G. Pile)

As a young schoolgirl I can remember going from Wilmington School to Madame Österberg's College twice a week when we were taught netball, cricket and rounders. They were smashing ladies. We went round the village at Christmas with them singing carols, and each Christmas we had a lovely party. (Mrs R. Williams)

One of my most vivid memories is of a young girl of about four years of age. She was brought into the clinic tied to a board. She too was given exercises and manipulations and after a few years she walked. (Miss Peggy Freegard)

The students wore navy gym-slips with sash, pin striped blouses, black stockings and shoes. They were very strong and were rich people's daughters. (Mrs H. Newell)

Numbers steadily increased at Dartford, not as a result of Madame Österberg's encouragement, but despite her belief that a small college was better. She selected

Dr Edvin Österberg, a notable sight on the cycling track.

Below: *Demonstrating a hockey strike. The game was developed at Dartford.*

Below right: *National dancing practice.*

new students with the greatest care. Parents, she wrote, needed to be 'dispossessed of the idea that those with feeble intellects – those, in fact, who are unfit for other callings – can take up the work of physical training. . . . My girls are destined to become pioneers in all that relates to hygiene and a more rational method of life for the sex. To carry out this great work effectively they must possess not less but more than average intelligence.'

She would take only half those who applied for admission and soon dismiss a third of those taken. Parents had to sign a form agreeing not to object if this happened to their daughters. In 1905, by which time a new block had been built, total numbers reached about 60, but for the next ten years they stayed at this level.

Madame Österberg remained a disciplinarian, called Napoleon by her girls. Students remembered her arrival in the dining-room, when every back would straighten, and even the misuse of a hairpin would be noticed. They had the impression that, if they did anything wrong, Madame Österberg would know. To say they were well trained is an understatement. Indoctrinated would be more accurate. When one student, applying for a job, was told she would need to 'put her best foot forward', she answered, 'Sir, my feet are equally strong.'

Another student remembered her first morning when 'we were all lined up in our tights and jerseys, for our tunics were still to be made, and Madame came down the line looking at each girl in turn and criticizing in what seemed to be at the time a very cruel way, causing several girls to break down completely.' Her biographer lists typical comments. 'If you cannot control your legs, how can you control your class?' 'No student of mine ever says "I cannot". The day may come when you feel nervous. Remember that you are one of Madame Österberg's students.'

Possibly she knew from 1913 that she was ill. Certainly she began to plan for the survival of her life's work, trying at first to give the College to the nation. This suggestion was too unusual for the Board of Education, and indeed for the Cabinet, to which the President of the Board referred it. The Board did, however, help her to form a trust to continue the running of the College. Full details of this were settled by 6 July 1915. She died on the 29th.

Essentially the trust deed required the trustees together with a Committee of Management to continue to run the College as Madame Österberg had run it,

Lacrosse on the front lawn.

Photographs from girls' albums in the 1920s. The two outermost pictures show the short tunics introduced by Madame Österberg which later became commonplace in colleges and schools.

153

Natural dance practice, 1932.

Madame in her prime.

with the same aims: to promote young women's health through Swedish gymnastics. There was one curious change. Though she had often used male teachers the trust deed required female teachers to be given preference, and 'every instructor for the actual physical training of the pupils' was to be a woman. No doubt she considered that the many she had trained would now make this possible but it probably also reflected the agitation for women's rights, then at its height.

Her own place as Principal proved difficult to fill. Miss Meade, the first to be chosen (she was offered the job when already on board a liner about to sail to become a Rajah's daughter's tutor) lasted only a year, and so did her successor. In total during the 60 years between Madame Österberg's death and the merger with Thames Polytechnic there were 11 Principals or Acting Principals – the last of them a man.

The most important change in the form of the College's course came quickly when, in 1919, a third year was added. It was another 41 years before all teacher training colleges had to run three-year courses. With an added year it became possible for students to specialize. In 1922, for example, among the students in the third year 24 were specializing in games, ten in dancing, and ten in massage and medical gymnastics.

An equally important change was foreshadowed in 1928 when the country's teacher training colleges were divided into eleven groups, each group centred on a university, though it was only in 1936 that specialist colleges became part of this scheme. Dartford then began an association with the University of London, its students able to work for the University's Diploma in Theory and Practice of Physical Education.

A third year meant half again as many students, and this made more accommodation essential. In 1929 it built Oakfield Hall and hostel. By this time it had acquired another 28 acres of land for more playing-fields, and in 1930 a swimming-pool was built. Despite such changes it remained

154

during the 1930s very much the college Madame Österberg had founded, its students intensely proud of its reputation and of belonging to it. In 1939 when Meg Lewis arrived from a Welsh grammar school the Principal was Miss McLaren, a strict but fair Scottish lady with a strong Scottish accent. Meg remembered that girls from Yorkshire, Tyne Tees, Wales, and even Cornwall had to attend Speech Training classes, but never those from Scotland. Her co-educational background made her astonished at the 'all women' nature of the establishment. 'No Dartford student left the grounds without permission, and even with, we had to be back in college by 4.30 p.m.'

She also remembered that 'our integrity and character were never in question.' When she took her first examination at Dartford 'the lecturer gave out the papers, then looked at her watch and said she would be back to collect them in two hours. Not one of us moved from our seats, no one glanced at anyone else for fear of misinterpretation.'

When the Second World War began the College did not at once leave the London area, but only in 1940, when France fell, decided it was uncomfortably close to Germany's invasion armies. Then Miss Bird, an old Dartford student, a Dartford Trustee, for many years Chairman of its Committee of Management, and one of the founders of Benenden School where she taught divinity and PE, discovered three hotels at Newquay on the north Cornish coast to which Benenden and Dartford could both move. At once the College changed its name to 'Dartford College of Physical Education', afraid that 'Bergman-Österberg Physical Training College' would sound Germanic to the bucolic Cornish.

Dartford's girls, like many London students evacuated during the war, retained nostalgic memories of the experience:

So fierce were the SW gales at times that games were impossible. But the surf breaking on the shore with rising clouds of spray was magnificent to

Medical gym for remedials, 1935. Madame Österberg had treated cases of neuralgia, paralysis, and spinal curvature.

watch. Food was rather scarce . . . but we walked over the Gannel River in search of lovely cream teas or dived into the Oyster Bar in Newquay to supplement College suppers. Teaching practice was formidable. Up before dawn to travel halfway round Cornwall before eventually reaching our destination, but made so very welcome on arrival. Occasionally a whole day free! Then off on bicycles to the middle of the moors or another sea coast.

The decision to leave Dartford proved wise. Kingsfield was hit by a bomb. On the other hand much damage was also done by British and American troops billeted in the students' rooms.

After the war Dartford's experience was curiously similar to Woolwich Polytechnic's. It fell increasingly under the influence of the Ministry of Education and the LCC, money being their weapon. Since the College had no funds for the sort of improvements which were now considered essential, its trustees decided that it must surrender full independence, and become grant-aided, a status it eventually achieved in 1950 after an earlier failure.

Though this allowed such important additions as a new, covered swimming-pool, opened in 1957 by Princess Alexandra, it was only a temporary solution. Its contribution to the new pool again left it penniless and now a new hostel was needed to allow it to expand in numbers and become financially viable. The Ministry of Education agreed that the hostel was needed, but refused to contribute unless the College was transferred to a local authority. In 1960 the trustees were forced to agree to this condition but were allowed by the Ministry to transfer to the LCC, the choice of the majority of its Committee of Management, not to Kent.

At once the LCC began to impose changes which would give Dartford the features common to its other teacher training colleges, in particular replacing its Committee of Management with a Governing Body with 12 out of the 15 members appointed by the LCC. Among other changes during Dartford's period as a maintained college, three were important. It took the fashionable view, encouraged by the Ministry of Education, that the College was too small, and in 1968 began to make provision for an increase in its numbers from the current 165 to 750, a development which led to new halls of residence, a new sick bay, new staff flats, and new lecture and tutor rooms.

The same year it ceased to be exclusively a PE teacher training college by introducing a three-year course to train teachers for general teaching in primary and middle schools. And, while Woolwich Poly, after the 1963 Robbins Report, gradually abandoned its long connection with the University of London, Dartford did the opposite. An optional fourth year was added to the course in which students could study for a University of London B. Ed. Hons. degree. In 1969 its first five candidates were all awarded degrees.

Despite these changes Dartford struggled to retain its traditional nature, as the small, specialized physical education college which Madame Österberg had founded in the nineteenth century. It also retained its tradition of games playing and training teachers of games – one result being a number of sportswomen with national reputations. Of these the best known was Rachel Heyhoe Flint who left Dartford in 1960 and subsequently played both cricket and hockey for

Exterior of the new gymnasium of 1964. This building subsequently became a studio for Architecture and Landscape students. In the hurricane of 1987, the roof blew off, shortly after major internal alterations.

Gymnastics in the 1960s' gym.

England. Her score of 179 against Australia in 1976 was still (in 1995) a record for a woman in a test match in this country.

Mary Duggan (1943–6) also played many times for England. About her final match against the Australians in 1963 *The Times* wrote, 'The peak of the day's pleasure came from a not-out century of grace, distinction and considerable power by Miss Duggan, England's captain.' She returned to become Dartford's Vice-Principal, but sadly died young, aged 48. Colleagues believed that it was for her teaching rather than her cricket that she would have wanted to be remembered.

Others were Elizabeth Constantine (1955) who played regularly for England at lacrosse; and Sue Mappin (1969), who played tennis for England four times in Wightman Cup teams. Like Rachel Heyhoe Flint, she became known as a TV and radio commentator. Many more could be mentioned, but even a larger selection should not distract attention from the thousands of others who never became well known but served in schools and colleges throughout the world, contributing to the health, confidence, and well-being of many communities.

In the early 1970s, when Angela John, future Professor of History at the University of Greenwich, went to Dartford as a young lecturer she remembered that:

> people still spoke rather reverentially of 'Madame'. The PE staff were a group of dedicated professionals and the college was run on rather formal lines. It was overwhelmingly female though there were some young men doing Primary Education. Because of the PE emphasis there was apparently an extra food allowance (presumably from ILEA which funded us).

158

The meals were therefore very good and reasonable and I used to feel quite soporific after eating a mammoth cooked meal all for 26p.

The end was near. It was now that the Department of Education and Science set about reforming the country's teacher training arrangements. The basic aim of its new policy was set out in 1972 in a White Paper entitled (ironically from Dartford's point of view) 'Education: A Framework for Expansion'. In practice it wanted on the one hand to reduce by 40 per cent (50 per cent in London) the number of students being trained to become teachers, on the other to force the smaller or more specialized teacher training colleges to enlarge the range of their courses or form closer associations with other further or higher educational institutions. The Labour Government which replaced the Conservative Government in 1974 retained these aims. Dr Eric Briault, the Education Officer of the ILEA, as part of the Authority's response, had already asked Dartford to consider linking itself to Thames Polytechnic. He also suggested a link of Thames with Avery Hill, and there were preliminary discussions between Godfrey and Avery Hill's Principal, Mrs Jones, but, partly because of Mrs Jones's defiant determination to remain independent, partly because Avery Hill was a much larger college, with more broadly based teaching, nothing was to follow for another ten years.

At first Dartford also resisted a merger, preferring independence and the expansion which it was currently attempting, but when the Education Officer

Sixth form course in Architecture and Landscape, 1980-1, after the amalgamation with Thames Polytechnic.

Final practice teaching at a nursery school, late 1950s. With the Department of Education encouraging all teachers to have degrees, the general primary schoolteachers training courses at Dartford were redesigned after its amalgamation with Thames Polytechnic.

ruled this out, it agreed to form a working party of members of both colleges to devise a detailed plan. This first met in February 1974, and after long and complicated negotiations the amalgamation officially took place on 1 August 1976.

Now a serious and in the end fatal problem occurred. From the first meeting between Dartford's principal, Mrs Chamberlain, and Thames Polytechnic's Director, Godfrey (March 1973), it had been clear that Dartford was reluctant to abandon its connection with the University of London in favour of working with the CNAA; but it had been persuaded by Thames Polytechnic that retaining the two authenticating bodies was undesirable. Thames had argued that, with 20 degree courses approved by the CNAA, it had the experience which would help Dartford to revise and obtain CNAA approval for its courses. This was now important since the Department of Education was strongly encouraging all teachers including those specializing in PE to have degrees, rather than, for example, the Teacher's Certificate from the University of London's Institute of Education for which most Dartford courses were designed. Part of the Government's aim was to diversify the work of teacher training colleges so that, as the demand for teachers continued to fall, some would be qualified for other careers, and it was this diversification which made it necessary to plan additional courses to propose to the CNAA.

But obtaining CNAA approval proved far more difficult than had been expected. The Dartford course for women teachers of sports and gymnastics had been directed largely towards teaching physical skills. The CNAA required its courses to be more academic and theoretical. Several attempts to transform it were rejected, and by the time the CNAA finally approved a Movement Studies degree course the Government had progressively reduced teacher training quotas for Dartford, eventually ordering the Polytechnic to discontinue altogether the sporting-gymnastic activities on which the College had been based.

Dartford's other course, for the general training of primary schoolteachers, was, however, successfully redesigned, and highly regarded by the inspectorate and the CNAA, which gave it approval in 1979. But the loss of the PE course and the Government's reduced quotas had caused a dramatic fall in numbers of students at Dartford. In 1974, 215 new students were admitted, four years later only a hundred. 1974 was in fact the year when it had most students – 630 – and it never reached the 750 for which accommodation was still being created. From 1977 onwards permanent staff were being made redundant, and after a brief life, this course was also abolished.

Thames Polytechnic should not be held responsible for the transformation of what had been designed as a merger into a closure, and the destruction of a college with long traditions, unique skills, and dedicated teachers. A number of these were coaches or referees at a national level in their particular sports, and most had assumed, not unreasonably, that they had secure careers. Thames, on the contrary, had made great efforts to save Dartford and the decision to close was a government one. Keith Reed, who, as Deputy Director, was closely involved with each phase of the so-called merger considered the outcome 'a very sad and sorry state of affairs, difficult indeed to see the wisdom, or the justice of the decision', a judgement which he thinks 'no less true today, indeed quite the reverse'.

On the other hand there were some at Woolwich who considered that Dartford's intrinsic academic weakness made the closure of its teacher training courses inevitable. Norbert Singer, Thames's Director from September 1978, remembered that on his first visit there he was shown gymnasia, swimming-pools, sports grounds – but where, he asked, were the classrooms?

The Polytechnic's one gain was a fine new campus with a large amount of residential accommodation and 38 acres of grounds. Short of space as ever, nothing could have been more useful, and it progressively took advantage of this turn of events. During the 1978–9 session Thames Polytechnic students lived in Dartford's halls of residence, each day being bussed to Woolwich. But it was the way in which the gymnasia, drama and dance halls would convert to studios that decided the Polytechnic to move, first Landscape Architecture there from Hammersmith, then two years later to move Architecture there after its short stay in Churchill House, Woolwich. The Civil Engineering School went next, in the summer of 1985, and the following summer, after more conversion work at Dartford, the School of Surveying, so reuniting the old Hammersmith departments and at the same time creating a Faculty of the Built Environment.

Following the merger the teacher training staff from Dartford were restructured to form the Faculty of Education and Movement Studies. This comprised the Schools of Movement and Recreation Studies and of Education and Teaching Studies. Individual teachers were assigned to these schools, or to associated divisions, or, if they taught such subjects as geography, history, mathematics, and English, to the appropriate divisions at Woolwich. When it was decided to close a course, this took four years from halting recruitment, and staff thus had a longish time in which to consider their future. Nevertheless many found it both an unhappy and uncertain time. Those who had been exclusively concerned with physical education courses were in the greatest difficulty. Some were give posts in other ILEA colleges, some succeeded in obtaining appointments elsewhere, others chose to retire early.

Shortly before the amalgamation Kenneth Challinor had been appointed Dartford's first male Principal. As part of the Polytechnic he became Assistant Director, with responsibility for co-ordinating the unifying of the two colleges. In this he was much helped by Dartford's Secretary, Fred Smith. Following the amalgamation Smith became the Polytechnic's Senior Assistant Secretary.

Both Challinor and Smith, despite the circumstances, made invaluable contributions to the Polytechnic during the ten years which followed the merger. Smith master-minded the many physical changes at Dartford including the upheavals caused by successive waves of Schools from Woolwich. He had had a lifetime's experience as an LCC/ILEA administrator and nothing seemed beyond his scope to discharge in a quiet efficient manner. In all this he was ably assisted by a newly appointed bursar, Lyn Pitcher. (Reed)

Meanwhile the Students' Union organized its own amalgamation, setting up a Dartford executive with a Vice-President and an office. The *Students'*

Handbook (1976–7) explained that

> The social frivolity of Dartford is naturally situated around the bar, where numerous spontaneous activities occur. Discos, bands, folk evenings and films are held every week on site and transport will be available between Woolwich and Dartford for mutual participation and enjoyment (all the men are at Woolwich!!).

Facing page: *Oakfield, built 1929.*

Madame Österberg's College has gone, but the Bergman-Österberg Union survives, set up in 1902 for old students in rivalry to the Ling Association (1899) of which Madame disapproved because it was open to those she had not trained. By 1995 the Union had a full archive at the College, meticulously attended by Mrs Sheila Cutler, its keeper. Each year members of the Union return to Dartford for a reunion, and in 1995 it celebrated the 100th anniversary of the College's move to Dartford.

The Bergman-Österberg Union for old students still survives, and members return to Dartford each year for a reunion. The picture above shows former students waiting at the station in the 1920s.

13

Norbert Singer –
A New Broom

1978–1985

'WE WERE FREQUENTLY AT OUR DESKS BY 8 A.M. (he was often still at his at 8 p.m.).' So wrote Keith Reed about Norbert Singer, who succeeded Godfrey as Director in September 1978. For the next eight years Singer and Reed, as Director and Deputy Director formed one of the Polytechnic's most effective partnerships. 'At such times,' Reed continued, 'I learnt that if you need something badly then each and every opportunity, emphasis and nuance has to be directed to that end – it has to be willed to come about.'

What Singer willed was 'to put Thames Polytechnic on the map'. At the time there were five London polytechnics and a general feeling that this was one too many. Singer himself, during a previous job (he had been at the Polytechnic of Central London, then Deputy Director of North London Polytechnic) had prepared a private paper which identified Thames as the obvious one to go. It had good staff and did high-quality work, but it was by some way the smallest and – at Woolwich and Dartford – was geographically on London's periphery. Everything he did during the next 18 years had as its aim expanding Thames so that the scale and quality of its activities put it on a level with or above the other four and ensured its survival.

About Singer, Reed wrote,

His arrival set up all sorts of waves . . . . Why was this? An answer must include the way he went about his task. He was overtly ambitious for the Polytechnic to succeed and expand, his powers of persuasion were immense, and his door was always open – perhaps because he was so often out and about the college, seeking to know why this or that was being done. . . . He seemed to welcome discussion, sometimes rather heated discussion if not downright opposition. . . . He lived and breathed Polytechnic business. . . . The upshot was that, after the initial shock, he got on good terms with all . . . the Governors, the academic and administrative staff, the house staff, the teachers' union and, as important as any, with the student body.

Dr Norbert Singer, Director of the Polytechnic 1978–93, and first Vice-Chancellor of the University.

His secretary, Joyce Webb, described him as essentially 'a shirt sleeve person'. She would sometimes feel that others were taking advantage of his lack of formality, turning it into familiarity, but he never in fact allowed this to happen. On the contrary, he 'did not suffer fools gladly' and could 'tear them off a strip', but they would 'always come out smiling'. As Robert Allen (future Dean of the Faculty of Human Sciences) wrote when Singer retired, 'Even when Norbert was less than charming, rarely has he been felt to be capricious or vindictive; it probably meant that someone was not doing their job.'

John Parsonage, Dean of Science, considered that Singer's success was a result of his running the Poly like a family. 'Outside you couldn't bad mouth it. Inside, by God there could be some family rows.' At meetings Joyce Webb believed that he would intentionally provoke argument. It cleared the air. In his office he would sometimes sit chuckling as he leafed through the minute books of Governors' meetings. Singer's view of minutes was that they bore little relation to what had actually happened. How could they record an exasperated committee member telling Professor Valerie Pitt to put away her embroidery – this was not a meeting of the Women's Institute?

About Reed, Singer said,

Keith Reid, Deputy Director 1973–86.

[He] was one of the wonders of this world. He knew every screw in every room of every building of the Polytechnic. Above all he stood for quality – that is why the reconstructions he supervised have lasted so well. But what surprised me was that in addition he was a man of great imagination. It was his idea for example to move Architecture and Civil Engineering to Dartford, so creating the Faculty of the Built Environment. Only his essential modesty prevented him applying for a Directorship at Thames or elsewhere, a position for which he was fully qualified.

Singer had once noticed on Reed's CV that the only job or promotion for which he ever applied was his first at Woolwich Polytechnic.

In another way they were well-suited partners. Reed's essential caution balanced Singer's continual testing of new ideas. Mark Cross, who arrived in 1982 in his early thirties to be head of Mathematics, remembered how they worked. If he went to Singer with an idea, Singer would listen, then send him down the passage to Reed. 'I think he has a reasonable case. See what you can do for him.'

Reed's first reaction would often be 'You can't do that.' But this was not the end. He would ask for the next question: 'Well, what can I do?' Solutions were what interested Reed. 'He was like a father to me,' Cross remembered. 'He and Norbert were a really good team.'

Even these tributes to Reed do not do full justice to his contribution to the Polytechnic. First appointed a full-time teacher in 1950, he became in succession Senior Lecturer, Principal Lecturer and head of the Department of Electrical and Electronic Engineering at Woolwich, then Assistant Director and finally in 1973 Deputy Director of Thames. From 1967 he was a member of their Governing bodies until he retired in 1986. That year, when awarding him an Honorary Fellowship, the Chairman of the Governors said that Reed had almost entirely originated the ways in which the Polytechnic's space, resources and staff were allocated. It was appropriate that in the same year the new Civil Engineering laboratories at Dartford were named the 'Keith Reed Buildings' and equally deserved that the following year he was awarded an honorary Doctorate (of Technology) by the CNAA, the only member of the Polytechnic past or present to be given this award. More difficult to suggest is the way in which, over 36 years, he became a father figure not just to young teachers like Mark Cross but to the whole Polytechnic.

The amalgamation with other institutions during Singer's years was an integral part of his plans for expanding the Polytechnic. About these he would sometimes be asked, 'wouldn't that change the nature of the institution?' to which he would reply, 'Yes, but why not?' Each of them gave Thames more strength and influence. For clarity, however, it is best to describe first the reforms he undertook at Thames as he inherited it, with its Woolwich and Dartford campuses.

One of the most important was his modification of the so-called matrix system of Schools and Divisions. It was, he considered, a crazy system, in which a teacher did not know for whom he was working. When told to do something by his head of School he could say, 'My head of Division would not let me', and vice versa. Singer's reforms were intended to make each member of staff responsible for a comprehensive (and comprehensible) sector of work. Put another way, he gave greater responsibility to the Faculties, and hence to the Schools to carry out the decisions of the Academic Council.

Parallel with this went an overhaul of the Polytechnic's many committees. In 1980–1, a report on the functions of the Academic Council, on the Faculty Boards, and on various other committees produced fewer committees with a better idea of their functions. Already, thinking clearly about committees and their functions, which included those that devised courses, was leading to every course submitted to the CNAA being approved.

Equally important was the gradual introduction of a modular scheme replacing courses with pathways each consisting of units of study. Increased flexibility and limited choice of units became possible within the structured content of pathways leading to named awards. This approach was in contrast to that of some other British institutions which in the 1980s began to adopt a wholly modular system, allowing a pick and mix approach reminiscent of the American pattern of University education.

The library at Riverside House, mid-1970s. Library services were hugely expanded under Singer.

Though Thames under Singer's influence moved in this direction, he did not favour such extreme dilettantism, but required non-core courses to be related to the core subject thus covering a coherent body of work leading to a degree. The system was eventually to be described as credit accumulation, but what could count as credit was restricted.

At the same time the separation of full-time, part-time, and sandwich students was abandoned. If a particular module formed part of a student's main course the student was able to take it, whatever the shape or length of his course as a whole. By the end of the 1983–4 session Singer was able to report that 'nearly every course in the Polytechnic is now able to admit students attending on the part-time mode.'

In his first annual report (on Godfrey's last year and his own first) Singer identified other problems which the Polytechnic faced and described ways in which they were being solved. The first was that it 'had not totally absorbed the implications of the fact that the move to Thamesmead would not now occur.' It was also clear that there was going to be little money available for new buildings or the refurbishing of old ones. To cope with these connected problems the Academic Council and the Court had agreed a Development Plan, a key element of which was the appointment of Trevor Dannatt & Partners, a firm of specialist consultant architects, to survey the Woolwich site and recommend ways in which its buildings could be best maintained and most effectively used. During the next two decades this firm, and in particular Colin Dollimore and David Johnson, made vital contributions to the upgrading of Thames's buildings, not only at Woolwich but also at Dartford, Avery Hill, and the other campuses which it acquired.

Next in importance came a change which the ILEA was making in the basis on which it funded its colleges. For 'teaching needs' – an imprecise criterion – it was substituting student numbers and the staff required to teach them at approved student–staff ratios. These were initially fixed at 8.9 : 1 for laboratory-based studies (e.g. engineering and science) and 10.5 : 1 for library-based studies (e.g. social sciences). Since Thames had considerably lower student–staff ratios one way to respond to the new basis of assessment would have been to reduce its staff. Thames had chosen the other alternative: to increase students. In Singer's words, 'a vigorous recruitment campaign was mounted, which, anticipating the report for next session, did indeed result in the enrolment of students whose quality was no less than in previous years and was adequate to cover the staffing base at the Polytechnic.'

To arrange such matters in detail he set up a Resources Subcommittee of the Academic Council, which as part of its responsibilities made decisions about student–staff ratios. The Committee was chaired by Keith Reed who considered it an example of the way in which Singer took a keen interest in all that happened but was willing 'to delegate the taking of decisions within agreed limits'.

In his next report (1979–80) Singer commented on what he considered two of the Polytechnic's most important but least satisfactory support services: the library and the computer system. Soon after he arrived he remembered telling the head of Library Services that he was giving him £50,000 and would like a proposal for spending the money. When, four weeks later, he asked for the proposal the librarian replied, 'I thought you were joking.'

In 1937 the library had still been housed in the old Board Room of the original William Street building, where the books were kept in glass-fronted cases. In 1939 however, it moved into part of the extension completed that year and throughout the war, despite bomb damage, grew slowly until in 1948 it had almost 5,000 books and 1,000 bound volumes of periodicals.

During Betty Jones's long post-war regime slow progress continued, but in 1964 when its area was more than doubled by the addition of a second floor during the rebuilding of that year, the emptiness of the elegant new shelves showed up the lack of actual books. At the same time there was an adverse report on the library which still only had a staff of three and a half. As a result two new professional librarians were appointed, but the totally inadequate budget of £3,000 made expansion difficult and though in the next year a new library was opened in Riverside House and 2,500 books moved there, both libraries remained chronically short of actual reading matter.

Mechanical engineering project, late 1970s.

The formation of Thames Polytechnic in 1970 and the acquisition of the library of the newly incorporated Hammersmith departments began a period of expansion. Jean Allford came from Leeds University to take charge, books increased to over 51,000 and the staff to 16, but her regime ended in disagreement with the authorities, and she resigned in 1975.

Though the Dartford merger brought the Polytechnic another new library it continued to be ill-supported, and only in 1981 could Singer report on some improvements. Despite these he considered in 1983 that library accommodation was still the Polytechnic's 'most serious and intractable problem'. He believed that it was one which, in the years ahead, would become even more important. Now that the National Advisory Board was proposing a further reduction in the ratio of staff to students, it would become essential to provide students with space and books to enable them to do more of their work on their own. The CNAA visiting party had confirmed that library space was inadequate. The Polytechnic had again sent plans to the ILEA for improvements, but the Department of Education and Science had not supported them. The Polytechnic therefore planned to act on its own, creating an extra floor of library space in the Woolwich library block and thereafter proposing a general refurbishment of its libraries – provided it was given the funds. This plan went ahead and by the summer of 1985 three and a half floors of the library block had been put to library use, with a further half floor to follow.

The University's libraries of 1995 would have amazed students of a decade or two earlier. There were still books, journals and study places, but they would have seen more and more personal computers, providing access to catalogues, university services, and the Internet. That year the University of Greenwich had twelve separate libraries, spread from its Roehampton to its Medway towns campuses, with a total of half a million volumes, and was spending £2.5m a year or more. Much credit for organizing this huge expansion must be given to Denis Heathcote, who became head of Library Services in 1983.

About the computer system Singer wrote that for some years the existing one (ICL1902A) had been totally inadequate and that after much discussion the

ILEA had agreed to pay £660,000 for a new terminal-based system. The Inspectorate accepted that more staff would be needed to enable good use to be made of this, and the Polytechnic had provided three or four for the purpose. It would not, however, be able to do so permanently without financial support and this was still being discussed with the ILEA.

Next year he thanked David Perkins, head of Computer Services and his staff for 'working flat out' to bring the new system on stream for the beginning of the 1980–1 session. Throughout the session the whole Polytechnic had benefited. The ILEA now admitted the Polytechnic's case for additional staff to run the service but had still not provided the funding.

The Development Plan and effective recruitment continued to be the key features of Singer's policy. About the 1979–80 session he reported that the Plan had been 'central to most of the decisions taken by the Polytechnic'. Importantly, it was a constant reminder to the Polytechnic that the education and training of students was its main purpose. This was the underlying theme of Singer's personal view; though he regarded research as important, he believed that it should never take precedence over teaching.

About recruitment he reported that

The Registry and Schools co-operated wholeheartedly to streamline procedures and to ensure that offers were made as quickly as possible to prospective, eligible students. This proved particularly useful during the summer of 1979. As a result the first-year recruitment of full-time and

School of Architecture and Landscape studio in 1981, in the former dance studio at Dartford. After fire damage, it was extended and transformed into a new campus library in 1993–4.

sandwich students to the Polytechnic reached its highest ever total of over 1,000 at the beginning of the 1979–80 session.

Recruitment for evening and short-course students had also been good and the final effect had been that 'the target student population envisaged in the Development Plan was thus achieved in one year rather than the expected two.' Equally satisfactory was the fact that, against national trends, recruitment for engineering, mathematics, and science courses had been high, giving the Polytechnic a total of almost 1,500 sandwich students.

There had been two significant consequences of these results. Firstly, the general increase in numbers had put even more pressure than before on space, and to provide more the Polytechnic had had to consider making better use of the underused Dartford campus. As a result of long discussions a working party had chosen, from four possibilities, the transfer there of the School of Architecture. Secondly, the growth in the number of sandwich students, most of them now college-based, had meant that staff had had to spend much more time finding placements with industrial companies, which, because of the harsher economic conditions, were less willing to take them.

At the end of the next (1980–1) session Singer reported the successful move of Architecture to Dartford. Had it not been made a further increase in enrolment would have meant the most serious overcrowding at Woolwich so far. The space which architecture vacated had made possible a succession of moves of Schools and Faculties: the School of Surveying to the top three floors of Churchill House, the School of Social Sciences and Humanities to its lower floors. This had left space at Riverside House for the School of Business Studies and the School of Electrical and Electronic Engineering to expand there, and for the Schools of Civil and Mechanical Engineering to expand in the main building. Thus Dartford proved of far greater importance to Thames than merely providing a campus for the old Hammersmith departments, since their transfer there was the removal of the 'trunk' which had been causing a general log jam.

This might have reduced the overcrowding at Woolwich had not student numbers continued to increase. Fifteen years earlier at the time of the foundation of Thames Polytechnic and the merger with Hammersmith there had been 2,000 full-time-equivalent students. Now there were 4,000. In these years, even with Dartford's accommodation added, the Polytechnic's space had only increased by a third (from 31,000 sq. m. to 43,000 sq. m.). It was now some 16,000 sq. m. short of the norms which the Department of Education considered sufficient for the courses it was running. No wonder shortage of accommodation was a recurring theme, year after year, in Singer's annual reports.

Not unconnected were his equally regular protests at the steady reduction of the Polytechnic's funding. For some six years he and the Resources Subcommittee were able, with ingenuity, to avoid reducing staff, but eventually this was no longer possible. Reporting on 1984–5 and the latest reduction, in the form of new Block Grant regulations, he wrote,

It became obvious . . . that existing staff levels could not be maintained in the 1985–6 session. . . . After difficult and lengthy, though always helpful

Facing page: *Lynn Chadwick statues in front of Downshire teaching block, Roehampton* (above), *and* (below) *the leafy entrance to Downshire House.*

negotiations with staff unions, a formula was worked out, as a result of which . . . staffing levels could be agreed. Voluntary severance procedures were put in place in the hope that sufficient people would leave the Polytechnic to enable these agreed lower staffing levels to be attained.

It must be said, [he went on] that the continuing process of reducing both the total amount of money . . . made available to the Polytechnic and the accompanying reduction in unit cost per student . . . has reached a stage where further cuts in cost are difficult to imagine. If these reductions . . . continue they must lead to a reduction in the educational opportunities that the Polytechnic can offer. This seems more than a little strange at a time of increasing high unemployment and when the need for qualified manpower is stressed . . . on all sides. The essential wrongness of what is happening in our institution has been stressed again and again by the Polytechnic, its Court of Governors and the Authority. The need to explain the situation to the Government increases year by year. The hope can only be expressed that as the Polytechnic increases the efficiency of its operations and vigorously points out the worthiness of the policies being pursued, government will eventually be made to see the light of reason.

If by September 1985 the Polytechnic was feeling more and more deprived of the government support it believed it deserved, the same month marked the successful culmination, after long negotiations, of its largest and most successful expansion.

Rugby at Woolwich, late 1970s.

14

Avery Hill

1906–1985

✦ ⊠◊⊠ ✦ ⊠◊⊠ ✦ ⊠◊⊠ ✦ ⊠◊⊠ ✦ ⊠◊⊠ ✦ ⊠◊⊠ ✦

I N OCTOBER 1983 the Inner London Education Authority, as part of a general review of Advanced Further Education, revived the proposal that Avery Hill should amalgamate with Thames Polytechnic. Mrs Jones had gone, but there were many at Avery Hill College who were just as strongly opposed to the idea, arguing on the one hand that it would save no money, on the other that medium-sized colleges were preferred by many students and could develop a better corporate spirit than large ones.

Thames was keener on the proposal. Times had changed and most of the circumstances which had turned the merger with Dartford into a closure had gone. In particular nearly all of Avery Hill's courses already had CNAA approval, and further government cuts in the number of teachers being trained seemed unlikely. Thames also believed that merging with a prestigious teacher training college would improve the Polytechnic's chances (again being discussed in the 1980s) of becoming a university.

From the start there had been something special about Avery Hill, if only that it was the LCC's first residential training college. Two sequences of events had come together in 1906 to produce its foundation. One had led to the Education Act of 1902 which gave local authorities the power to found teacher training colleges, the other had led to the purchase the same year by the LCC of the empty but grandiose mansion of Avery Hill near Eltham, once the property of Colonel North, the Nitrate King.

By the beginning of the century there were over 70 teacher training colleges in England and Wales, but virtually all of them were under the influence of the Church of England or some other religious denomination. Though a higher proportion of the teachers these colleges trained subsequently taught in London schools than its population justified (29 per cent to teach 9 per cent of the country's children) other local authorities were unlikely to allow this to

Facing page: *View of the Winter Gardens and the Mansion, Avery Hill, from the rose garden.*

Pictures from Colonel North's personal album showing (from left) *blasting nitrate, transporting the lump nitrate by mule wagon, breaking and bagging it, and the train taking it to the port for export to Britain.*

continue, and London's population was still growing rapidly. There was, therefore, a fundamental reason for the LCC Education Committee – when it was formed in 1904 – using the new powers the 1902 Act had given it to create its own source of teachers.

Meanwhile in 1883 John Thomas North, a coal merchant's son from Yorkshire, had rented the 'pleasant mansion' of Avery Hill near Eltham, ten miles from the City of London. Aged only 41, North had become so rich by exploiting Chilean nitrate deposits that it was said that if you put his name on a costermonger's cart and turned it into a limited liability company, the shares would be selling at 300 per cent premium within an hour. Five years later North bought Avery Hill, and in 1890 had it transformed into a magnificent mansion in which he could entertain and impress his City friends.

North enjoyed his great house for only six years before dying suddenly in his London office, presumably of a stroke or heart attack. His photograph, in top hat and great coat, with side whiskers and heavy jowls, suggests the consumption of much good food and drink. His family at once offered the house for sale. Together with the land which he had bought it was generally believed (*The Times* gave the figure) to have cost him £200,000. His architect had taken him to court, successfully obtaining payments to which North claimed he had not agreed. But two years passed before it was sold to a Dr Alonzo Stocker, a specialist in lunacy. Perhaps the doctor planned to turn it into an asylum, but he never did so nor did he ever live there, and after three years he too offered it for sale. The following July (1902) the LCC bought it for £25,000.

In May 1903 the Chairman opened the house at a ceremony in the Great Hall. The house and park had nominally been acquired 'for the purpose of open space or for such other purposes as the Council may legally determine on', but in practice the Council had little idea what to do with it. In his speech the Chairman's main defence of the purchase was that, if it had been delayed, London would have engulfed Eltham and it would have cost much more. At first the Parks Committee suggested using it as a convalescent home, but this idea was abandoned and the following year, in the absence of a better one, it agreed with no apparent reluctance to hand over the house to the Education Committee.

Meanwhile, there had been wide anxiety about the country's supply of teachers, this explaining the parts of the 1902 Act which concerned teacher training. The School Boards established by the 1870 Act had had no power to set up teacher training colleges. They could set up so-called pupil-teacher centres and the London School Board had opened 19 of these in just over ten years after the first in 1885, but they were far from satisfactory. The students had to teach for up to 30 hours a week, only being taught how to teach in the evenings and on Saturdays.

The independent teacher training colleges were unsatisfactory for another reason, as a delegation from 23 School Boards headed by the Chairman of the London Board told the Department of Education in 1899. Because most were denominational, many of the best candidates were being rejected for failing the religious entrance tests. This, the delegation claimed, was particularly true of women candidates.

At about the same time the LCC's Technical Education Board (so closely involved with Woolwich Polytechnic in its early years) also became concerned about the supply of teachers, especially those able to teach scientific or technical subjects. But it was not empowered to found residential teacher training colleges and for most of its existence did no more than run in-service courses for teachers. In 1902, however, with the support of the London School Board, it started a day training college, on the London School of Economics' Clare Market site. This offered a three-year course leading to a BA or B.Sc., together with teacher training. But the course was so demanding that, of 62 students who enrolled the first year, only 20 graduated and the college had to provide an alternative two-year course leading to a Teacher's Certificate. Even so it could only make a small contribution to the 600 additional teachers a year which it was estimated that London needed beyond those the existing colleges were likely to supply.

The LCC had good reasons for choosing Avery Hill as its first residential teacher training college. A college in the suburbs would be cheaper to establish, and Avery Hill especially so, since it would only need converting. In the suburbs it could also have land for playing-fields. Avery Hill was, indeed, such an obvious choice that when in December 1903 a subcommittee of the Technical

Colonel John Thomas North, the 'Nitrate King', who bought Avery Hill and transformed it into a palatial residence in 1890. He also owned the famous greyhound Fullerton.

Avery Hill in the 1890s

Above: *The Great Hall hung as a picture gallery.* Below: *Floral tributes in the Marble Hall at the time of the funeral of Colonel North.*

Education Board proposed five or six residential teacher training colleges for London, it took Avery Hill as an example of a suitable site. There was an equally good reason for establishing residential colleges. Students would not have to travel to them each day, nor travel from them to lectures, as the day college students had to travel to different colleges of the University of London for their lectures. There was just as good a reason for establishing a college for women teachers only: the greater need for them. In 1903 the London School Board had recognized this by setting up a subcommittee to consider the problem. The shortage was the result of many more women teachers leaving the profession in their early twenties to marry and have children. Creating a two-sex college in an existing building was considered too difficult.

So it was that for the autumn term of 1906 Avery Hill College opened with 45 resident and 115 day students. As Principal the LCC had chosen Miss Mary Bentinck Smith, a lecturer in mediaeval and modern languages from Girton, Cambridge, who was already widely known as a Chaucer scholar.

All did not go well. Miss Bentinck Smith had staff trouble. During her first term she dismissed the male caretaker for negligence and had to ask a member of the academic staff to leave. She and her successors lost four 'uncooperative' matrons during the college's first year. And either she lacked the skill to delegate or was not given sufficient domestic staff, for one student found her in her flat weighing potatoes to discover the total required by a sitting of 160. Among her other duties was the vetting of the landladies for the many students for

The Front Hall.

The Master Bedroom.

whom there was no space in the Avery Hill mansion. Most seriously, she was disappointed by her students' work. At the end of her first term she believed that 20 of the 160 students would fail their two-year course. The fact that she was proved wrong and only two failed suggests that she was applying Oxbridge standards to girls who at best had London secondary school backgrounds. Nevertheless her disappointment probably helps to explain why, in January 1907, she took to her bed and never returned to her Principal's desk.

More misfortune followed. In February Miss D. A. C. Marshall, the College's first science lecturer, took charge as Acting Principal. Like Miss Bentinck Smith, she came from Girton. After a month she too retired to bed and was not seen again. That July the LCC appointed Miss A. B. Collier as Principal, but after two weeks of the autumn term she was forced by illness to resign.

Now came Avery Hill's first important (Acting) Principal, Miss Philippa Fawcett. Her appointment was not meant to be permanent. She took control to restore morale after such an unfortunate start, temporarily leaving her position as Principal Assistant in the LCC's Education Department. Before that she had distinguished herself as a mathematician at Cambridge by being placed above the Senior Wrangler of her year (though as a woman she could not be given the title), and in South Africa by reorganizing elementary education in the Transvaal after the Boer War.

At Avery Hill, during the autumn term of 1907 and the winter term of 1908

Miss Mary Bentinck Smith, first Principal of Avery Hill College, 1906–7.

Avery Hill College in 1910

Facing page: *The Lecturer's common room and the Front Hall.*

Below: *A first floor corridor with stained glass windows. This part of the building was destroyed by bombing during the Second World War.*

A dormitory at Avery Hill College, c. 1910.

The lounge, Avery Hill, c. 1910.

she restored order and confidence, before returning to the LCC where she worked for the rest of her life. In 1949 the LCC recognized her service by naming one of its training colleges after her. It was probably she who influenced the Education Committee at the end of her two terms to vote as it did by 12 to 11 in favour of appointing another woman Principal, not a man.

The great majority of Avery Hill's first students were Londoners but a few came from as far away as Northumberland, Lancashire, Devon, Norfolk, and South Wales. They were aged 18 to 21 and had mostly served already as pupil-teachers in London schools. None was of the poorest class – the £25 entrance fee made this impossible. Most would now be called lower-middle class, their parents artisans, shopkeepers, clerks, or themselves teachers.

Among other items of clothes they had to bring was a white-straw sailor hat, to which they were required to attach a ribbon supplied by matron for 6*d*. This all students including those in lodgings, had to wear at all times except on Sundays. Students also had to bring a gym dress, and the pattern for making this was included with the clothes list. As described it was in the style of one of Madame Österberg's Dartford gym tunics, ending at mid-thigh, though, surprisingly, a 1909 photograph of Avery Hill students doing PE shows them in skirts ending well below the knee. If they lost any garment they were fined, as were those in lodgings if they arrived late in the morning.

Residents at first slept in dormitories on the mansion's upper floors or in its towers, their beds separated by washstands. For the second term, however, two houses in Glenshiel Road were bought, interconnected and converted into dormitories for 24 more. During each term residents and those in lodgings were allowed only one weekend of leave and two tea permits.

The college day started with assembly in Colonel North's great hall, now a magnificent library, then still hung with crimson tapestries. This was followed by four morning periods, held either in five classrooms in the main building, in

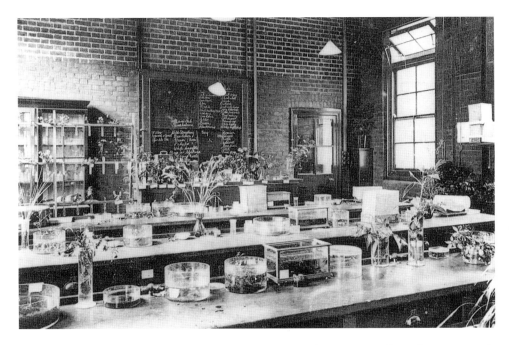

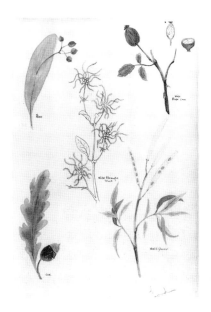

Nature study laboratory, Avery Hill, 1910 (left), and (below) botanical illustrations made by a student in 1907.

six classrooms and three laboratories which had been created in the mansion's stables and coach house, or in the mansion's large conservatory which was used for art. These were broken by a 15-minute interval for milk and refreshments served in the students' common room. For dinner they returned to the great hall where they sat at tables for eight and ate, typically, those staples of the time, boiled fish, suet pudding, prunes, and rice. The two hours after lunch were free before more lectures from 4.15 to 5.45. Next came supper followed by private study until bed at 9.45.

Streaming was the fashion and the girls were divided into seven classes according to their ability. The syllabus was wide, including, besides the usual subjects, nature study, drawing, music, and theory of education. Modern languages were the only omission. At this time they were not taught in elementary schools and just nine of the first girls took voluntary classes in French.

The LCC had spent generously on the house's conversion (£12,500 – half the purchase price), its only meanness the four acres of land which were all the Parks Committee would hand over to the College. Though the surrounding park provided the students with tennis courts and a hockey pitch, it was in other ways unfortunate, allowing the public at all times to wander close by, peer curiously at the students, and call the College the nunnery.

To teach the girls the LCC appointed six full-time staff. At first one was also to be Vice-Principal, but it presently abolished this position as an economy. Most of the six had university degrees. In contrast to her students, Miss Bentinck Smith was well satisfied with her staff, describing them as 'singularly disinterested and devoted in the discharge of their duties'. There was also a part-time teacher for music and singing, and another for drill and hygiene.

If the living conditions, daily routine, and costume regulations suggest that Avery Hill resembled a typical boys' boarding school of the time, in other ways it was democratic. From the start it had an elected Senior Student and prefects, together

Students at dinner in the Great Hall, Avery Hill.

May Queen, 1900s.

with committees which organized all forms of social life from games to dances. Soon these were establishing societies (rambling, cycling, debating, dramatic), running a fiction library and newspaper club, and producing the *Avery Hill Reporter.*

As well as tennis and hockey, games soon included cricket and basketball (probably in fact netball) and teams from the College began to play against other colleges and schools. Dances were for women only, cycling and rambling were in the unspoiled Kent countryside, an early play was *She Stoops to Conquer.* Most debates were on the sort of motions commonly chosen by school and college debating societies of the time (e.g. 'That the British Race is not Degenerate'), but at Avery Hill others concerned female liberation. The students were generally feminist, though there was a short period when the militant tactics of the suffragettes led to the carrying of a motion against votes for women.

Though the students organized so much for themselves, the staff were far from aloof. Miss Ethel Henley, the lecturer in nature study, led rambling and cycling expeditions or visits to the zoo, and on two evenings a week Miss Florence Exton, lecturer in mathematics, would read to the girls in her sitting-room from the Book of the Month. As a whole during its first two years Avery Hill, despite its four different Principals or Acting Principals and modest academic standards, was a happy institution.

When Philippa Fawcett returned to her LCC desk after the winter term of 1908 she was succeeded by Miss Emily Julian. The LCC chose her because of her record as a capable headmistress of Tunbridge Wells High School. Miss Julian was to hold her position for 14 years, including those of the First World War, and to prove herself a stabilizing and successful Principal. She was a tall woman with an impressive presence, remembered for her habit, when displeased, of folding her arms across her large bosom and looking scornfully down her nose at the offender.

By the time she arrived Avery Hill had increased its space for residents by acquiring an unused school building in Deansfield Road (now Rochester Way) and converting it into a hostel for 75. It had also made its most important addition to the College so far by buying the nearby Southwood House with its 13 acres of much needed grounds. When this was opened as a hostel for a further 38 students in the autumn of 1908 it brought the total of residential places to 160. Many more girls than this, however, continued to apply, and from 1908 onwards the LCC began to discuss plans for building halls of residence in Southwood House's grounds so that the total could rise to 200 or 250. Eventually four were built, the last being opened in 1916. They were remarkable at the time because of their central kitchen. 'At Avery Hill Training College', the *Eltham and District Times* reported, 'the pupils merely sit down at dining tables in their separate houses while the cook from her central palace sends out meals to every point of the compass.' They arrived along tube-like passages. The underground students' bar – the Dive Bar – now occupies the kitchen site.

Meanwhile in pre-war years there had been changes to the curriculum, some by design, some by default. Most important of the latter was the College's failure, despite its laboratories and good intentions, to teach science. This was found to be impossible to girls who at their secondary schools had not been given even the most elementary knowledge of the subject. There was to be little improvement in the 1920s and 1930s, and it was then that the few students who wished for science would be sent to Woolwich Polytechnic. For 30 years science teaching at Avery Hill was confined to nature study.

The suggestion that the students also did little PE seems less probable, and based on the fact that there was no gymnasium until 1912. But the PE mistress, Miss Muriel Spalding, had been taught by a pupil of Madame Österberg (and later became Dartford's Vice-Principal). The lack of a gym would not have prevented her teaching Madame Österberg's Swedish system, which required no apparatus.

A view from the gardens, Avery Hill.

Emily Julian, Principal 1908–22, guided the College through the First World War.

More significant was the increasing importance in the curriculum of teaching practice with real classes in a real school. To provide the amount of this which Avery Hill's many students needed was not easy. The only LCC elementary school within reasonable distance was Pope Street School (later renamed Wyborne School), but it was too small and its children mainly from rustic rather than London homes. Just the same it was designated Avery Hill's 'demonstration school' and put 'under the control or predominant influence of the college authorities'. The school's staff were instructed to consider the College's students 'their primary concern'.

Thereafter, as a result of protests from Woolwich Borough Council at one of its schools being used in this way, Gordon School, Eltham, was designated instead. Despite the teaching experience which many of the students had had as pupil-teachers it was an LCC regulation that a member of the College staff should supervise all practice lessons. From 1908 to 1911 they would be taken to teaching practice by a four-wheel horse-drawn van known as the Black Maria, in which they sat on wooden benches facing each other (though a photograph shows 11 of them plus a lecturer sitting on its roof).

In many ways the College grew and prospered in its eight pre-First World War years, but it suffered one disappointment. The LCC had seriously overestimated the demand for teachers and from as early as 1908 when the first intake of students qualified they found difficulty in getting work. The phenomenon was not only a London one. According to the *Times Educational Supplement* over 30 per cent of the teachers who qualified in July 1910 had not found a job by October. One from Avery Hill, having searched for four months in civilized parts of the country, applied for a position in the Shetlands.

There were various explanations: fewer schoolchildren than expected, fewer young women abandoning teaching, and the employment by local authorities of uncertified teachers at lower salaries. Things improved only in 1914 when many

The Black Maria, which took students to teaching practice, 1908–11.

Southwood House, bought by Avery Hill College in 1908, and used as a hospital during the First World War. Halls of residence were subsequently built in the 13 acres of grounds. Southwood House is now the centre of the University's administration.

young male teachers joined Kitchener's New Army and their places had to be filled by women.

In every other way the war was disturbing and distressing. Food became even more basic than before (potato cakes and barley bread), and almost all the domestic servants, of whom there had been a large number, left the College to replace men and make munitions at the Arsenal. After dark the College had to be blacked out and nearby anti-aircraft guns fired at Zeppelins. In October 1915 Roper Hall, an extension to Southwood House was commandeered by the War Office for the wounded, who from then onwards would be seen limping around the grounds in their sky-blue uniforms. A year later students were displaced from two of the halls of residence so that female gardeners could use them while taking a training course in the park.

The students gardened too, in 1917 planting an acre of ground for vegetables. The following summer a group went to Dorset to harvest flax. In many other ways they helped the war effort, staging plays to raise funds for parcels for British prisoners in Germany and sending the proceeds of their May Revels to a home for the disabled. Sometimes they also entertained the wounded at Roper Hall (to tea). A few leavers abandoned teaching and became nurses. Though the only casualty was the death of the caretaker, Mr Gordon, in the navy, most suffered the distress of knowing that close relatives might be killed, as many were.

On Armistice Day, 11 November 1918, the students left their classes and went to Eltham village to celebrate, but finding nothing in particular happening there marched home four abreast, arms linked, led by a policeman, singing all the way. In Colonel North's great hall Miss Julian announced the hymn 'Now thank we all our God', and cancelled the afternoon's lessons.

Avery Hill now recovered its halls of residence and by 1920 had become almost entirely residential with 300 students. The grounds were overgrown –

Aerial view of the four halls of residence built adjacent to Southwood House from 1913 to 1916, photographed before the alterations of 1937. Somerville and the central kitchem block were destroyed by a flying bomb in 1944, but the kitchen basement is now the underground students' bar. Grey, Fry and Brontë Halls are currently used for teaching and staff offices, but are expected to be demolished to make way for the final stages of the 2,000 bed student village.

since 1916 there had been no gardener – and, as often happens with colleges or schools, the once-adequate living conditions began to seem primitive. They were an important cause of a reduction in numbers by almost a quarter.

Before this occurred a new Principal, Miss Freda Hawtrey, had been appointed. She had previously been Principal of the British and Foreign School Society's College at Darlington and was thus experienced in teacher training. She was to stay until 1938, struggling throughout these 16 years to put things right.

'She had no love for the detail of administration', David Shorney noted (*Teachers in Training* 1906–1985). It was not this, however, but the parsimony of the Government and the LCC which made her struggle so difficult. True, she soon persuaded the Governors to complain to the LCC about the College's inadequate and often repulsive food, and by the summer term of 1924 the LCC's inspecting medical officer was able to report that the diet had become good and varied. The LCC also, at her request, restored the sports grounds, providing two new hockey pitches and nine tennis courts. But it was the basic living conditions in the halls of residence and in Roper Hall that most needed to be improved.

Here even the second-year students had only cubicles separated by head high partitions for private study, while first-year students had to use communal studies. Everywhere the heating was so inadequate that in winter they would sit with their feet on stone hot-water bottles, their knees wrapped in blankets. In Roper Hall four or five girls shared a single wardrobe, in each of the four halls of residence there were just five bathrooms for 52 girls.

After years of procrastination the LCC, in June 1931, at last agreed to a refurbishing programme which would improve the heating and convert most of the cubicles into study bedrooms, but by the time this was due to begin the country was in the middle of a financial crisis, teachers pay had been cut by 10

Miss Freda Hawtrey, Principal 1922-38.

per cent, and the number of teachers in training had been reduced first by 2½ per cent then by a further 10 per cent.

Avery Hill was lucky. Instead of making cuts to each of its teacher' training colleges, the LCC closed Greystoke Place, with the result that the others suffered less, and Avery Hill (where, despite the conditions, numbers had risen again to about 320) was allowed to retain 312 students.

It was the Labour Party's capture of the LCC in the 1934 election which transformed the prospects for London education. In 1935 a range of improvements for Avery Hill was agreed and carried out, including the creation of more toilets, changing-rooms and showers, and the introduction of mains electricity. In 1936 a three-year plan was agreed for basic changes which would include the creation of study bedrooms in each of the five halls for up to 27 students and the provision of adequate heating. By January 1938 Roper Hall had been converted, but before work on the others could begin the Second World War had begun.

Fighting for such improvements was by no means Miss Hawtrey's only concern, most important among her others being nursery education. She came to this because of her interest in the McMillan Sisters' nursery school at Deptford. In 1935 the LCC allowed her two months leave to study nursery schools in France, where they were already common, and her published report was many years ahead of its time in arguing for similar widespread nursery education in England. She made training for nursery school work an important part of Avery Hill courses. More generally she was interested in teaching for the underprivileged and in teaching outside the classroom.

At the same time during the years between the wars there was a significant change in the nature of the teaching at all teacher training colleges, Avery Hill among them. Until then it had largely consisted of general secondary education, of which it was assumed that most of the students had had little. By the 1920s this was no longer true and training *how* to teach had become more important. Colleges therefore began to claim that their courses were a special branch of higher education.

Miss Hawtrey was a member of Lord Burnham's 1923 committee which considered this question and recommended closer connections between training

Photographs from a student's album, 1930. Left: crab race, and (right) obstacle race.

 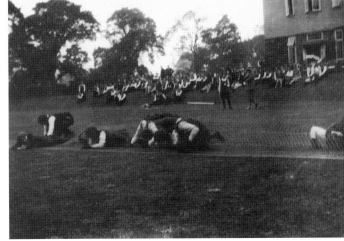

Above: *Flower pot race* (left), *and (right) hockey dribbling.*

Facing page: *Exotic plants in the Winter Gardens, created by Colonel North as part of his mansion in the early 1890s.*

colleges and universities. As a result the Board of Education proposed that universities should in future conduct examinations for Teacher's Certificates. This was eventually arranged in 1928, when the country's teacher training colleges were divided into groups, each group attached to a university. The University of London's group of 22 colleges was so large that it distributed them among its colleges, Avery Hill being allocated to the London School of Economics then handed on to Bedford College. But the University itself validated the certificates, doing so for Avery Hill from 1930 to the late 1970s.

Miss Hawtrey announced her retirement early in 1938, too late for the LCC (after one failure) to appoint a successor for that September, so there was an interlude before, in January 1939, Dr Frances Consitt, Principal of Bingley Training College, became Avery Hill's new Principal. War now seemed close and the Home Office, as part of its evacuation plans for London, suggested that Avery Hill should go to St John's College, York. The plan, however, did not work out. As a result in September 1939 Avery Hill had found no place to which to be evacuated, and twice – for the autumn term after the declaration of war in 1939 and for the autumn term of 1940 following the Battle of Britain – simply closed, its students continuing their courses as far as possible by post. In January 1941, however, it went north where it occupied a newly built block of Huddersfield Technical College.

Though this was more or less adequate for lectures and even had laboratories, it provided no living accommodation and for the next five years some 20 students lived in two rented houses, while the remaining 275 took lodgings. In these they had little chance to study privately. Their training was more seriously curtailed by Huddersfield's lack of sufficient schools for teaching practice. Despite these and many other difficulties, the years at Huddersfield were good ones for the College, during which, unlike virtually every other evacuated school or college, it grew in numbers and took on more staff. Much of the credit for this must go to Dr Consitt, who was helped by her previous experience of Yorkshire.

Not even her local knowledge, however, could solve the lodgings problem in Huddersfield once the war ended and, as a result, Avery Hill was driven back to Eltham in 1946, despite the devastation of its buildings. This had begun on

17 April 1941 with a fire at the mansion started by incendiary bombs, and culminated in the virtual destruction of Somerville, one of the four halls of residence, by a flying bomb on 17 June 1944. In total there were eight incidents, during which, the LCC's architect reported, all the College buildings had 'suffered more or less seriously. As the result of the fire-fighting operations the College was flooded with water which ruined many of the ceilings and left others unsafe. It also induced an attack of the fungus *Merulius Lachromans* often erroneously called dry rot, which commenced its ravages behind the oak panelling on the ground floor. . . . The parquet floors and other elaborate finishings suffered equally and most of the features which gave the College a certain character have now disappeared.' Eventually the greater part of the original mansion had to be demolished.

For three years Avery Hill struggled to recover from the devastation, starting with the summer term of 1946. By then only Fry Hall had been repaired. Here Dr Consitt set up her office and managed to accommodate 74 students. Twenty-three more lived in the unrepaired Roper Hall, while 177 went once more into lodgings. Without the mansion the College was even more handicapped by lack of lecture rooms, and forced to use its two demonstration schools, Deansfield and Gordon. These were two miles away, a distance which resident students had to walk each day, and to walk there and back again for lunch, until 1947 when the LCC provided buses.

Eventually (1948) the LCC erected three prefabricated, unheated residential buildings in the grounds of Southwood House, and the following year it opened three houses in Chislehurst in which 60 students could live. By this time, however, much other restoration had been done enabling the College to be officially reopened by Princess Margaret on 11 July 1949.

Just as Woolwich Polytechnic in post-war years began to attract many students from beyond its traditional catchment area, so did Avery Hill, but to a far greater extent. In the late 1940s 30 per cent of its students regularly came from the north of England, compared to 25 per cent or less from Greater London. They were still mainly from lower-middle class families, virtually none having

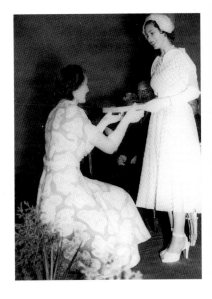

Reopening of the College after damage from the blitz, 1949. Princess Margaret accepts a head scarf presented by the Secretary of the College Union.

Facing page (above): The Honeycomb Block, and (below) the entrance foyer of the Avery Hill Mansion.

The 1957 Jubilee. Arrivals at the college for the celebrations (left), and (right) past students from the 1900s make their way across the park.

Avery Hill in the 1950s

Drama in the Great Hall (above), and (below) *swimming gala.*

professional parents. At the College they continued to take a two-year course, leading to a Teacher's Certificate validated by the University of London.

In the 1950s Avery Hill, again like Woolwich Polytechnic, was in continual conflict with the LCC about its buildings which, despite the repairs of the 1940s, began once more to seem inadequate for its steadily increasing numbers and primitive by the standards of the time. For 15 years Somerville Hall remained a symbolic ruin. At last in 1960 work began on an elaborate plan (agreed five years earlier) to provide it with many new features, including a new educational block, an administrative block, a music block, a craft section, and a second gymnasium.

By then, however, Avery Hill had been caught up in the roller-coaster ride which the Ministry of Education provided for teacher training colleges between the late 1950s and the 1980s, first discovering that it was going to need many more teachers than it had realized for the flush of post-war children, then realizing too late that it was training far too many. Complicating this was another change in government policy when in 1960 the Ministry of Education required all teacher training colleges to give students three-year courses, thus cutting for one year by many hundreds the output of new teachers.

Avery Hill was in one way lucky. Its excellent reputation and already largish size (it was one of only 16 of the country's teacher training colleges with over 300 students) led to it being chosen for dramatic expansion. A condition, however, was that it should take male as well as female students and the consequence of this was that yet again its accommodation became hopelessly inadequate.

To enable it to cope with both these problems the LCC accepted the suggestion of the Methodist Education Committee that it should rent its training college in Horseferry Road, Westminster, which it was vacating. In this annexe to Avery Hill, from October 1959 to 1962, 180 male students resided and 50 more were taught. They had their own Deputy Principal, Dr C. J. Phillips, and were in effect a college within a college, only very slowly developing staff and student contacts with Avery Hill. It was not until new Avery Hill buildings were ready that the two parts of the College became in reality one.

Throughout the 1960s the Government continued to encourage teacher training colleges to expand. At Avery Hill the male students of the Westminster annexe had raised numbers to 560 by 1963. By 1971 they were 1,500. The most important single contribution to this rise was a second annexe. Like the Westminster annexe, the Mile End annexe was for an entirely new group of students: mature men and women, some perhaps in their late forties, who for one reason or another now wished to become teachers. The LCC believed that, with other experiences of life, they often became better teachers, who were more likely to remain in the profession, and that many needed to be persuaded to attempt this transformation by a training college close to their homes.

Avery Hill in the 1960s

Above: *Music and* (left) *geography lesson in a contemporary classroom.*

The entrance to the Mile End annexe, English Street, 1970. This expansion allowed Avery Hill College to cater for mature students wishing to change to teaching as a career.

It was for this reason that Dr Briault, the ILEA's Education Officer, suggested to Avery Hill that it should establish an annexe for mature students in the English Street buildings of St Paul's Way Secondary School, Mile End, an area in which he believed there were many potential students of this sort, and where there were schools in desperate need of teachers which could subsequently employ them. In the autumn of 1968, 118 students began the first Mile End course. By the early 1970s they had increased to 300.

Numbers at Avery Hill itself had grown partly because of the addition of a third year to courses, partly because of the arrival of the Westminster annexe students. The LCC and its successor the ILEA agreed to a substantial group of new buildings and extensions, most conspicuous of which was a four-storey block intended for day students. By the time these were opened in 1971, however, most of this particular building had been reallocated to other departments, and it was anyway becoming clear that even these additional buildings would be inadequate.

Many solutions to the problem were discussed, including a four-term year, but the one agreed was known as 'box and cox'. Under this a whole year-group at a time would be away from the College on teaching practice, so enabling the College to have approximately a third more students in training at any one time without more accommodation. The box and cox arrangement was first put into practice in 1966. Many students (85 per cent) liked it. The longer periods of practice gave them time to get to know their pupils. They had come to the College to learn to be teachers and the more practice the better. But almost as many (80 per cent) said that it adversely affected their academic work, and 60 per cent that it reduced their interest in the College.

Well before this, from the 1963 Robbins Report onwards, Avery Hill had begun to think more fundamentally about its future. From a succession of reports and Ministry circulars two general suggestions emerged, the first that training colleges should diversify their teaching, the second that they should increasingly provide courses which would lead to a degree rather than a Teacher's Certificate. Briefly, in the late 1960s Avery Hill believed that it might be able to expand to a college of 3,500 students which would, in the words of its Governing Body, 'work towards independent degree and diploma-granting status'. But by 1970 it was also considering an amalgamation of some sort with another college or university. That autumn Mrs Kathleen Jones – its third great Principal in succession, who had succeeded Dr Consitt in 1960 and was to dominate the college for 20 years – visited the University of Sussex to discuss an association. Soon afterwards she also visited Thames Polytechnic, and in 1971 Thames's Director, Godfrey, and Deputy Director, Keith Reed, visited her at Avery Hill on a number of occasions.

In 1973, however, in the ILEA's paper, 'The Future of Colleges of Education' (the paper which led to the merger of Thames Polytechnic and Dartford), Dr Briault wrote about Avery Hill that it was

in a strong position to respond to the changing demands reflected in the White Paper and indeed thinking at the college as to its possible development as a more diversified institution of higher education has been maturing over a period of years. There would, I understand, be widespread support in the college for the introduction of Dip. H.E. and degree courses in addition to the preparation of teachers through the three-and-four-year B. Ed. and one-year training of postgraduates.

Those involved at the time had little doubt that it was not only Avery Hill's standing but Mrs Jones herself who persuaded Dr Briault to take this view.

Sculpture class, 1970s.

Main college building showing the distinctive Honeycomb building, completed in 1961, as an extension to Colonel North's stable block, part of which may be seen in the centre of the photograph.

In October Godfrey wrote to Briault making his disappointment clear. 'I feel that the substantial opportunities which could occur if a College of Education and a Polytechnic work together may now be lost. I can only guess that the strong and understandable desire of the colleges to retain something of their present "image" and to be seen to work with a University has guided them to their present thinking. I believe both of these reasons to be short-sighted.' Thames, he added, was already offering courses in the social sciences and humanities which, in Dr Briault's words, 'Colleges of Education will in future be offering'. Godfrey continued, 'On the basis of your proposal we shall by 1981 have two major and separate institutions of higher education in the south-east of London with foci less than three miles apart.'

Dr Briault's proposal was that the second centre of higher education should consist of some form of association between Avery Hill, Dartford, Rachel McMillan, and perhaps St Gabriel's Church of England College. This did not occur, Dartford merging with Thames and Rachel McMillan and St Gabriel's with Goldsmiths', but for another 12 years Avery Hill retained its independence.

Not, however, without difficulty. The Department of Education, unlike Dr Briault and the ILEA, did not approve of the arrangement, continuing to suggest an amalgamation with Thames, the Secretary of State finally writing that he accepted 'the Authority's strong conviction that Avery Hill should be allowed to attempt to develop as a free-standing, diversified higher education institution, offering courses in teacher education, the arts and social sciences' *despite* his 'strong doubts'. And Avery Hill, which by 1973 was committed to attempting to obtain CNAA approval for all its new courses, found almost as much difficulty in achieving this as Dartford had done. These were also the years of dramatic cut-backs in teacher training, taking the form of threats by the ILEA to close teacher training colleges which were in the wrong place or too small. In November 1976 *The Times* and the *Guardian* both reported that Avery Hill was to be one among some 20 or 30 which the Department of Education was planning to close. The College responded vigorously, Mrs Jones leading a Planning Committee which recruited the support of the local MP, lobbied the ILEA, and prepared a statement detailing the College's past achievements and present qualities. She herself wrote to *The Times*,

> [W]e are concerned by the article in *The Times* of November 30th refer-
> ring to the future of Avery Hill College, which could have an adverse
> effect on the recruitment of students. The College is flourishing; it is
> recruiting vigorously for all 1977 courses. Its reputation and present
> courses give it faith in the success of its future plans. Moreover, it has
> shown considerable adaptability in responding to new local and national
> situations and the needs of the whole community.

The campaign was a success and the ILEA agreed to retain Avery Hill as its one 'free-standing' college of education. By then it had obtained CNAA approval for a B. Ed., and now in succession obtained approval for a B. Ed. degree course (part-time), a B. Ed. (special educational needs), and a BA in theology. The last of these was obtained after Mrs Jones had been succeeded in 1981 by Michael Lovitt, but the first two had been successfully negotiated during her time, and it is she who must be given most credit for Avery Hill's survival and many successes during its last 25 years of independence.

When, in 1983 the ILEA revived the idea of Avery Hill amalgamating with Thames, its arguments were those of ten years earlier. One large institution would be more economical than two smaller ones. Since Avery Hill was predominantly still a teacher training college and therefore a vocational institution, a merger with a polytechnic was appropriate. Furthermore, Thames's connection with Dartford had given it valuable experience in proposing educational degree courses which the CNAA would be likely to approve.

Thames, under Singer, was even keener on a merger than it had been in the 1970s. It asked for safeguards, the most important being that total numbers of students and staff would not be less after amalgamation than they had been before and total funds would not be reduced. But essentially extending Thames's activities into a new area was exactly the sort of expansion which Singer wanted, enabling it not merely to grow in numbers and areas of teaching, but to demonstrate its ability to expand.

Avery Hill was now unable to resist these pressures. It, too, wanted assurances that the merger would be a genuine one and not a demolition, but, with

Facing page: *The Honeycomb and stable block on the Mansion site* (above) *and* (below) *the University Boardroom, Southwood House, on the other side of the park.*

just its one Theology degree course and a Dip. H.E. in Environmental Studies, it was no longer hoping to diversify into a liberal arts college with a broad range of subjects.

A key figure in the merger which followed was Valerie Stead. For the previous two years Stead had worked at the CNAA, where she had become well acquainted with Norbert Singer. She would ask him to be the polytechnic member of CNAA parties which visited other institutions, and rely on him always to be sensible, never whimsical or rude. Now two things happened in quick succession. Bill Stubbs, the ILEA's Education Officer, announced that the ILEA strongly favoured the Avery Hill–Thames merger, which would almost certainly happen; and the position of Vice-Principal at Avery Hill became vacant. Stead applied for this post and was appointed.

She was thus in a difficult position. On the one hand she had been appointed with the ILEA's approval on the understanding that she would work for the merger (a policy which she came to believe best for Avery Hill). On the other hand she owed loyalty to Avery Hill, still at this point independent, and in particular to Michael Lovitt, its Principal. Lovitt, who had only held his post for a year, not only favoured independence, as did many of Avery Hill's staff, but was reluctant so soon to have to take a lesser position in some other institution.

Despite this problem, Stead worked steadily, and openly, to ensure that the merger would take place and that it would be smooth. One of her devices was to meet informally with Singer before any important move, so that she could 'reduce the turbulence' which it might cause at Avery Hill. Another was to invite Thames staff to talk to their equivalents at Avery Hill. Stead was to become a Dean via the merger, so these invitations included Thames Deans, McWilliam being the one Singer told her he thought the best. But none of the dates she suggested for her Deans' strawberry tea suited McWilliam so she had to arrange a separate visit for him. This meeting led to what some have described as Singer's ultimate merger – their eventual marriage.

The merger between Thames and Avery Hill took place on 1 September 1985, when Avery Hill became Thames's Faculty of Education and Community Studies. At the same time a new management structure at Thames was introduced, Singer as Director now to be supported by two Deputy Directors: Reed for Resources, and Lovitt, who was made Deputy Director for Academic Development. In Singer's opinion, however, Lovitt wished to head any organization to which he belonged, and he soon afterwards resigned.

Of all Thames's amalgamations, that with Avery Hill was the most significant, bringing it not only its largest new faculty but a fine new campus with extensive grounds. Furthermore, the amalgamation gave both Thames and Avery Hill secure futures which neither of them would have had on their own.

15

More Expansion and More

1986–1993

IN 1986 JOHN MCWILLIAM, Dean of the Faculty of the Built Environment, succeeded Keith Reed as Assistant Director (Resources), later Deputy Director (Strategy). He, of course, knew Reed well, in particular having worked with him on the Resources Subcommittee (later full Committee) which Reed had chaired for its first 50 meetings and McWilliam was to chair for a further 75 before it was abolished. This was a small committee, consisting, besides the Chairman, of only the Deans and the Polytechnic's Secretary, but one which, despite meeting monthly throughout the year, nobody ever missed because it was here that things happened. It had the authority to turn resolutions of the Academic Council into action without referring them back for confirmation, a power of great importance in getting things done quickly. It had also taught McWilliam a valuable lesson about the running of an institution like the Polytechnic. As a Dean you could not take your own demands to the Committee without considering the effect these would have on others. The institution would only work if everyone considered its interests as a whole.

Successfully as Reed had run this Committee (among his many other duties) McWilliam believed that by 1986 Reed was ready to retire. With the Avery Hill amalgamation he was beginning to feel for the first time that the Polytechnic had outgrown his desire to know its every screw and door-knob. He left McWilliam a first-class secretary, Anne Cook, experienced in staffing and resource issues, a very substantial bank balance, and just two items on his desk (the desk which had been given to the Poly by Sir Thomas Spencer's widow and used by Reed because Spencer was an electrical engineer, the department of which Reed had been head): six pages of handwritten advice about 'how to keep the Poly going as a safe ship'; and a file which gave McWilliam his first opportunity to do the opposite.

The file described approaches Thames had made to Garnett College. Garnett,

Facing page: *The Library or Music Room, Manresa House. The paintings are of the same period as the house.*

195

Facing page: *Mount Clare, Surrey seat of Sir John Dick, Bart. From a picture by G. Robertson, 1784.*

Right: *Staff outside Garnett College, 83 New Kent Road, 1952.*
Below: *Frontage of the same building.*

a technical teacher training college named after William Garnett, who had given valuable support to Woolwich Polytechnic during its financial crisis of 1893–4 and also played a leading role in establishing teacher training in London, ran courses for students training to work in further and higher education. It was thus a suitable expansion for Thames, since Avery Hill was largely concerned with training teachers for primary and secondary schools. It had opened in 1946 at North Western Polytechnic in North London as part of the Ministry of Education's emergency scheme for training teachers.

In 1950 it had become a separate college, maintained by the LCC, and three years later been given its name. In January 1963 it moved to Roehampton (a move delayed because the buildings were not ready), where its premises were of much architectural interest. Ten years earlier Pevsner had written, 'there is nothing like Roehampton anywhere in the County of London to get a live impression of aristocratic Georgian country villas.' Five of these villas survived and Garnett ultimately moved into three of them.

First it was given Mount Clare and Downshire House, Mount Clare to become its residential facility, Downshire House its administrative centre with a teaching-block in the grounds. Mount Clare's land had been bought by George

Mount Clare, picture by the Hassells, father and son, journeyman artists, in about 1820.

Above: *George Clive, cousin of Clive of India and builder of Mount Clare.*

Clive, a cousin of Clive of India, when parts of Putney Park were sold, and the house was probably completed by the architect Robert Taylor in 1773. It may, however, have been a product of the partnership between Capability Brown and his son-in-law, the builder Henry Holland, since many of its details resemble those of Claremont, the house they built for Clive himself at Esher. In the words of Dorothy Stroud, Brown's biographer, Mount Clare 'lasted as a unique example of a country mansion in a London postal district complete with landscaped grounds and cows in its farm buildings until the late 1930s.'

Downshire House had been built slightly later (1790) for an army officer, presently ennobled as Lord Dover. Between then and Garnett's occupation it had had some half-dozen owners before the LCC bought it in 1948 to use its grounds as part of the Alton housing estate.

In 1979 Garnett College was made administratively responsible for Manresa House, with the use of most of the premises for teaching. Putney and Wandsworth Adult Education Institute was allowed to use most of the ground floor and a few other rooms. Of the three separate but adjacent houses, Manresa had the most curious history. It had been built in 1760 by Capability Brown's great enemy,

Entrance hall to Mount Clare. The table is currently being used by the Deputy Vice-Chancellor as his desk.

William Chambers, architect of Somerset House, the Kew pagoda, etc., in Palladian style for the second Earl of Bessborough. In 1861 the fifth Earl sold the estate to the Conservative Land Association for dividing into smallholdings, but this never happened and three years later the Jesuits bought it. It was they who changed its name from Parkstead to Manresa, the name of the Spanish town where the founder of their order, Ignatius Loyola, composed his 'Spiritual Exercises'. For a hundred years the Jesuits remained at Manresa House until driven out by the new flats of the Alton estate which overlooked them. Between then and 1979 Battersea College of Domestic Science had used the house.

Manresa House in the time of the Jesuits. The front block, built in 1951, blocks off this view.

By the 1980s Garnett had become a thriving college, with a total of some 500 students at any one time at Roehampton and about as many studying part-time elsewhere. These attended various colleges in the south of England, or Garnett's own annexe in West Square, close to the Elephant and Castle. It ran a one-year (or equivalent) course leading to a Teacher's Certificate for further education teachers, but its students were of various sorts, some full-time, some sandwich (these attending for one term, returning to teaching for between two and five terms, then attending for a final term), and some day-release students who were able to arrange their teaching to give them a free day a week, usually but not always with their employer's consent and financial support. Students were normally over 25 and were already professionally qualified in the subjects they would teach or were already teaching.

In addition Garnett had developed a full range of pre-service and in-service courses leading to various University of London diplomas, a CNAA B.Ed. or a University of London MA, all these designed by and unique to the College.

Like so many London colleges, it had gradually transferred its courses from the University of London to the CNAA. With both it had had difficulties in obtaining approval, the objections being the usual ones, that its students in, for example, hairdressing, motor mechanics, or coastal navigation were not suffi-ciently academically qualified.

In the years leading to the merger, Garnett was not popular with the ILEA. It was expensive, with a student-staff ratio of about 8 to 1, some of its teaching in the form of individual tutorials. And its standards had fallen to such an extent that approval to recruit to its prestigious MA course had been suspended. As one of only four Further Education teacher training colleges in the country, set far apart, it had lacked a nearby institution with which to compare itself and had become self-referential. John Humphreys, who arrived to teach there in 1984, found it comfortable but old-fashioned, with an old-style senior common room and staff, some of whom were inclined not to leave until they had served out their time. For younger staff seeking interesting responsibility this could be frustrating.

It was in February 1985 that Singer told the Academic Council that the ILEA

The starting point of the Jesuit life. Two novices after taking their first vows, in the garden of Manresa House, where every Jesuit in England had to undergo two years of training.

Facing page: *Temple of Hanover in the grounds of Mount Clare, 1957. It is believed that the temple, previously in the grounds of Manresa House, was rebuilt at Mount Clare. The lake was filled in when building the Garnett College halls of residence. The Temple survives and there are plans to restore it at Manresa.*

Left: *Sketch of Manresa House by Haslop Fletcher, late nineteenth century.*

The Temple of Honour and Virtue, Manresa. The votive figure on top of the temple is not original, but was placed there by the Jesuits, who converted the temple into a shrine to commemorate the Immaculate Conception. Although the temple was dismantled by the GLC, the stonework is safe and awaits restoration.

was encouraging Garnett to merge, and of the approaches made to it by the Polytechnic among some dozen institutions. The ILEA's Education Officer was preparing a paper on the subject. Though Singer was in favour of the amalgamation, he believed that it would only make sense if Garnett moved to one of the Thames sites, where it would require suitable buildings. Since there seemed to be no possibility of this, Thames had concluded that it should no longer pursue the idea in the face of rival offers from institutions which were geographically closer to Garnett. The file McWilliam found on Reed's desk said in effect that the episode was at an end.

To McWilliam this seemed a wasted opportunity, and he worked out a new offer to put to the ILEA. Thames would relieve it of Garnett College if the ILEA would release the three halls of residence behind Southwood House at Avery Hill, two of which were still being used as the Houghton Centre for staff development, so that Garnett's students and courses could be moved there. Towards the cost of the move and refurbishment the ILEA would contribute £300,000, but it would be left in possession of the three potentially valuable Roehampton sites.

Thames' Academic Council discussed the amalgamation at length, members pointing out that, when added to Avery Hill, it would make Thames the largest teacher training institution in the country. It would also increase awareness of the Polytechnic's teacher training activities among London further education colleges – an important source of students for any polytechnic. 'If the amalgamation [of Garnett] were with South Bank Polytechnic, it would reap the harvest.' The Council voted 30 in favour of amalgamation, three against, six not indicating their views.

At this time (June 1986) the ILEA had still not chosen between Thames, South Bank Polytechnic, and Roehampton Institute. The last would probably have been Garnett's choice. It was, after all, adjacent to Garnett's campus. On the other hand it was a direct-grant college consisting of a loose group of

The Jesuits at Manresa House

Right: *The grounds and entrance. Every path was named after a saint, this one being St Aloysius's path.* Below right: *A Jesuit priest in the courtyard, 1930.*

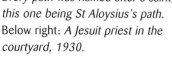

Church of England, Methodist, and Roman Catholic teacher training colleges, as well as the Froebel Institute, and was therefore seen by the ILEA as outside its sphere of influence. Before the end of the year the ILEA had been persuaded to accept Thames's offer rather than South Banks's.

This included, besides the financial arrangements described, an undertaking by Thames thoroughly to reform Garnett. But Thames only agreed to undertake this on certain conditions, the most important of which was that the existing leadership at Garnett should be replaced. Garnett's Principal was therefore given study leave and Valerie Stead was sent to Roehampton to become Acting Principal.

Stead played as important a role in Thames's merger with Garnett as in its merger with Avery Hill, but the situation in which she found herself was significantly different. At Avery Hill she had been able to persuade from the inside. To Garnett she came as an outsider, authorized to shake it out of its self-approving lethargy. Many staff were unhappy about this, considering that someone from outside could not understand Further Education teacher training, and as a result she met stronger resistance. She found allies, however, the most important being Tom Appleton, the Vice-Principal, Bernard Lovell and John Humphreys; and she discovered promising future managers among the younger and frustrated staff; Humphreys one of them.

Typical of the reforms she introduced was the abolition of TOIL (Time Off In Lieu). 'Just about everyone on the staff had time off for some supposedly additional duty he was performing.' Among her early successes was obtaining a reprieve for the MA course (its approval having been suspended by the CNAA, for whom Stead had been an officer) to give Stead the chance to revise it. It is now, as offered by the University of Greenwich, one of the best regarded of its sort in the country.

The plan was for Garnett's part time students to move from its Elephant and Castle site in West Square to Avery Hill's Mile End campus. The ILEA would contribute to the necessary alterations there. Garnett's Roehampton students would move to Avery Hill itself. Garnett would at first become a new Thames

Original ceiling decorations in the Temple. In 1912, with much effort, this ceiling was successfully transported from the Manresa site to Mount Clare.

Left: *Mount Clare in a poor state, 1959. The building was subsequently restored by the ILEA.*

Teacher training at Garnett College

Above: *Science laboratory* (left), *and*
(right) *practical work in the Nautical
Studies Department.*
Below: *Seminar in atomic physics.
As part of the Polytechnic, Garnett
College became the School of Post-
Compulsory Education and Training.*

faculty, then in due course the School of Post-Compulsory Education and Training, of which Humphreys would be head.

By June 1987, however, there had been a complication: planning consent for change of use of the Avery Hill halls of residence had been delayed by the London Borough of Greenwich which demanded more car-parking space. As a result there was time for the draft of the 1988 Education Reform Act to be released and for this to make it clear that increased use of the Mile End annexe by the Polytechnic might mean that the building would become its property. The ILEA therefore asked the Polytechnic to vacate the entire Mile End site. This led Thames to look elsewhere and rent a site at Wapping to which Garnett's part-time students went.

The building at Wapping in Tower Hamlets was the first found by the Polytechnic itself since the original acquisition in Woolwich. Once it was clear that success in acquiring Garnett College depended on vacating the Mile End annexe, McWilliam and Susan Adams (later to become the first Director of the University Estates) set about identifying and acquiring new premises. A site in Docklands with rail or tube links was the preferred choice and the premises of the former Soap Works of London in Wapping owned by the Brideswell Trust seemed an appropriate base!

The 1988 Education Reform Act also affected the transfer of Garnett's Roehampton students to Avery Hill, since it contributed to Thames's decision to prolong its stay at Roehampton so that it should still be working in the properties there, after 'vesting day'. In the end the move was not made until the summer of 1990, in preparation for the next session. That year's annual report described the transfer as 'truly on the "grand scale" – the Southwood Site at Avery Hill was besieged by contractors for all of the summer in order that the building refurbishment would meet the September 1990 deadline. Likewise the Roehampton campus was overtaken by hundreds of packing cases in preparation for the removal from Roehampton to Eltham.'

This was also to be the year in which the two education faculties were integrated, becoming simply the Faculty of Education. During its brief independence at Roehampton the Faculty of Post-Compulsory Education made notable progress. By the end of its first year all its courses had been, or were in the process of being validated; and it had 'broken new ground for the Polytechnic' in so-called 'credit accumulation', by establishing a joint credit-accumulation scheme with the previous Faculty of Education and Community Studies. By 1995, the Faculty of Education was mainly operating from Avery Hill, but the School of Post-Compulsory Education and Training ran its Further Education in-service courses from Wapping, and after its closure in September 1995, from the Sir John Cass Foundation premises in Jewry Street. Humphreys and those who, like him, had been dissatisfied with some features of Garnett found that the amalgamation with Thames brought a breath of fresh air. The ratio of staff to students had to be drastically reduced, but this turned a flabby institution into one which was almost too lean. The new faculty (or school as it became) was able to diversify into the training of other categories of teacher, hence its description as Post-Compulsory Education and Training rather than Further Education.

The success of the merger should not hide the unhappiness it caused some of Garnett's staff. This was in part similar to that felt by the Hammersmith staff when they had been required to move from South-West to South-East London, but some at Garnett felt a more basic regret that a small organization with a character of its own had been swallowed by a large one. They would have felt the same hostility whoever had swallowed them, a point Appleton made at his retirement party.

At first it seemed that Thames's occupation of the three Roehampton properties on vesting day had successfully made these its property, and Wandsworth, the new education authority, soon ceded two of them. Manresa, however, part of which it was using, it claimed. During the dispute which followed and which

The RIBA visiting board examines diploma work of architectural students at Hammersmith in the 1970s. Two of those present, Jacques Paul and Panos Arvanitakis, were both subsequently to become Head of School. The latter has taught at Lime Grove, Hammersmith, Woolwich and finally at Dartford as the School moved.

205

The Rachel McMillan Nursery School (above, left to right):

Rachel and Margaret McMillan (photograph from 1871), initiators of the nursery school movement.

The Rachel McMillan Nursery School opened in Evelyn Street in 1910.

Exterior of Evelyn House in 1911.

In 1914 the Nursery School moved to its present site, in what was then a rough area of Deptford, as seen in this student's snapshot of local people.

Street party in nearby Albury Street for the Silver Jubilee of George V.

Margaret McMillan in her later years.

lasted seven years, Thames even discovered that Wandsworth had registered its ownership of Manresa with the Land Registry, an action which it eventually admitted to have been the result of over zealousness by its staff. During the long dispute Thames spent more than £1 million on repairing Manresa's fabric. Even so, it was only on 1 November 1995 that the Secretary of State finally found in favour of the University of Greenwich, as Thames had by then become.

In an important way the amalgamation with Garnett was a new experience for Thames. Its earlier expansions – Hammersmith, Dartford, Avery Hill – had largely been forced on it. Garnett College was the first one for which it had volunteered. It was therefore unable to claim, as it had been inclined to do, that other people could be blamed for consequent problems.

The first suggestion of a merger between a part of Goldsmiths' and Avery Hill was made in 1984, when Avery Hill was still independent. Nevertheless it was reported to the Thames Governors early that year. The part in question had previously been Rachel McMillan Teacher Training College. During the years when teacher training was being systematized and Dartford had merged with Thames, Rachel McMillan had chosen to merge with Goldsmiths'. Since then

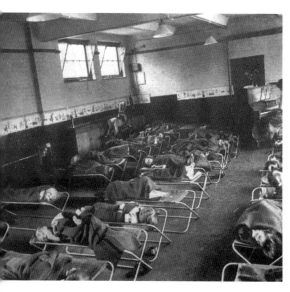

Goldsmiths' had moved it from its own building at Deptford to Goldsmiths' main building a mile away at New Cross.

Staff of Goldsmiths' and Avery Hill had met and discovered advantages which the merger would bring to both colleges. At the same time the South Bank Polytechnic had made counter-proposals to Goldsmiths', a development which Thames's Governors described as 'unhelpful at this stage'. Nothing, however, came of these 1984 proposals.

Goldsmiths' history was curious. In 1890 it had been a rival to Woolwich Polytechnic – this was when the Parochial Church Foundation had refused to contribute to Woolwich because Goldsmiths' was close enough to be used by Woolwich students. Certainly the two were similar, both teaching technical and scientific subjects to evening-class students, Woolwich drawing these mainly from the Arsenal, Goldsmiths' specializing in nautical engineering. But for 14 years there was an important difference: Goldsmiths' was funded almost entirely by the Goldsmiths' Livery Company. Only in 1904 did the Company hand its College over to the University of London – not to the LCC as might have been expected.

Since then its main activities had been teacher training and art, indeed

Aldgate Church and the Sir John Cass Charity School, 18th century.

between 1915 and 1924 it taught no science, its only technical subjects being engineering and building. After the Second World War, however, it developed three science departments: biology, earth sciences, and chemistry.

From 1980 onwards it had been transferring these from its New Cross building to the old Rachel McMillan site in one of the roughest parts of Deptford (close to the lodging-house where, in the seventeenth century, Christopher Marlowe was murdered). Inside this building one of Goldsmiths' biologists remembered finding 'lots of small rooms and dozens of potters wheels' left from Rachel McMillan's occupation. Goldsmiths' swept all this away and undertook a major refurbishment which produced splendid modern laboratories, one of them for 80 students, with high ceilings which dispersed noise and smell. Here it planned to expand science, and for several years the science staff worked with enthusiasm and optimism.

At the same time, however, Goldsmiths', which had *not* become one of Crosland's new polytechnics and was instead one of a dwindling number of directly funded colleges, a category which the Department of Education and Science wanted to eliminate, was under pressure to make more fundamental decisions about its future. One possibility which it discussed at length was an amalgamation with Queen Mary's College, but these negotiations came to nothing because the financial prospects of an amalgamated college seemed too uncertain. Goldsmiths' then returned to the University of London, with which it had always wanted to become more closely connected, and London eventually offered to make it a School rather than an Institute of the University. A condition of the offer, however, was that Goldsmiths' would dispose of its science work, since the University did not want to add to the sites on which it had already decided to concentrate its science teaching.

At about the same time that Goldsmiths' was anxious, because of the University of London's offer, to shed its science work, so too was the City of London Polytechnic. The teaching of science at City had originated at Sir John Cass College. This had a long history. In 1709 Sir John, a Knight and Alderman of the City of London, had offered to take over the management of St Botolph Aldgate Parochial School. A new school for 50 boys and 40 girls was to be built above some shops with, below these a burial vault, the profits of which would partly endow it. The school duly opened in 1710, but eight years later Sir John became anxious that he had provided inadequately for it and drew up a new will in which he abandoned a plan for another school in Hackney in favour of a larger endowment of the Aldgate school.

Unfortunately he suffered a fatal haemorrhage when half-way through signing the five pages of this will, staining the quill with blood. Today boys of the school still wear a red feather in their coats on founder's day. It was 30 years before there was a legal decision in favour of the second will, during which the school temporarily closed.

When it reopened in 1748 it was at first above the Aldgate, then from 1762 to 1869 in Church Row before moving to 25 and 26 Jewry Street. By then its endowment was producing an embarrassingly large annual income and for the next 25 years its trustees and the Charity Commissioners argued about how best to use this. Eventually in 1895 a scheme of the Commissioners was agreed, despite violent objections from the trustees who considered that it diverted money from the school to a purpose never contemplated by Sir John: the founding of a technical institute. In 1902 a new building on the school's Jewry Street site was opened to house both the school and the new institute, and it was not until 1909 that the school moved away and the institute became the sole occupier.

The Sir John Cass Technical Institute never called itself a polytechnic, but this was what in effect it was. It ran part-time courses in science, technology, arts and crafts, and trade subjects. Unlike Woolwich Polytechnic, it did not begin by trying to be a young men's Christian institute, but from the first had education as its purpose. In other ways, however, it resembled Woolwich and the other polytechnics founded in London in the late 1800s. Like Woolwich it was helped by the Technical Education Board. Like Woolwich it grew larger and needed more space. In 1930 the Governors bought 32–35 Jewry Street and built a new wing on this site, opened in 1934. Like Woolwich it soon began to run courses leading to University of London degrees, those at Cass in science and metallurgy. By 1950 its work was so largely of university standard that it was allowed by the Ministry of Education to rename itself Sir John Cass College. It was this college which, as a result of Crosland's binary policy of 1965, had amalgamated with the City of London College (which taught only business, accountancy, and law) to become the City of London Polytechnic. The new Polytechnic which they (together with a school of navigation) formed had 2,000 full-time and 5,000 part-time students. During the next 15 years, however, as one of too many London institutions with science departments competing for too few science students, it steadily began to fail to recruit the numbers it required and its science teaching became an economic liability.

Goldsmiths' and City thus had different reasons for needing to shed their science departments, but from Thames's point of view their need, not its causes, was what mattered, giving Thames a powerful negotiating position. All but two of Thames's scientists supported the acquisitions. Though the faculty believed that its work was of high quality, others considered it dull, and it was certainly small compared either with Thames's other faculties or with competing science faculties elsewhere. The acquisition would provide the funding, equipment, staff, and good-quality space at Deptford which were vital for it to grow and which were to be found in no other way. Furthermore, the science work which Thames would acquire was in areas which complemented its own.

There was a risk: it was no use acquiring new staff and then having to dispose of them for lack of students. But Thames had a good recruitment record, and the acquisitions would eliminate two serious rivals for London's (and the country's) falling number of science students. Put another way, Goldsmiths' and City, if they closed science would be funding their competitor – Thames. McWilliam put proposals to Goldsmiths' and City governors and when Singer finally detailed these to the Academic Council in February 1988 it approved them by a large majority. Next month the Court authorized Singer and the Chairman to conclude a settlement.

Negotiating this was not easy. Thames had to say that it wanted Goldsmiths' Deptford campus and City's at Shadwell (near Wapping), and to overcome City's reluctance to include geology in what it was transferring. In their ultimate form the acquisitions brought Thames not only 290 students from City and 170 from Goldsmiths' and increased its science staff by 65 per cent, but also a phenomenal amount of excellent equipment. John McWilliam estimated the value of property and equipment at Goldsmiths' at £10m. John Parsonage, the new Dean of Science, remembered that on his first visit to the Deptford campus 'it was like Christmas, packing case after packing case, enough for two microscopes for each student'. Much the same was true of City's laboratories which had recently been entirely refurbished with fume cupboards throughout.

In making the acquisitions a success, Thames had advantages. The staff from both institutions came with a dowry in the form of assured funding for their salaries whatever the student–staff ratio for three years during which science would be given its opportunity. The newly acquired staff were also enthusiastic, especially those from Goldsmiths' who had suffered several years' uncertainty about their futures during which they were often unable to get straight answers from their college, in contrast to those they got from Thames. In other ways they found the Thames culture and willingness to delegate responsibility a revelation. One remembered that within an hour of arriving he was made his school's examination officer, and soon afterwards its senior course director, promotions which would have taken years at Goldsmiths'.

But much of the credit must go to John Parsonage. He soon told Singer that he proposed to close the School of Material Sciences in order to release resources for the School of Earth Sciences. 'You know, as Dean, that you're not allowed to do that,' Singer told him. The point made, this was the end of the interview. It was up to Parsonage to make a success of what he had proposed.

Recruitment was the key. On average the Polytechnic was first choice for 40 per cent of its science students. The other 60 per cent came from 'clearing': those, for example, who had got inadequate A-level results for their first choices.

To get the best of these, during the vital two weeks after the results were announced staff would work 12 hours a day, seven days a week. Some prospective students would be offered a 'bridging week'. For a modest fee to cover their accommodation they were taught intensively from early morning till 9 p.m. for four days then on Fridays given an exam. The results of this were less important in themselves than as proof that an applicant was motivated and could learn. The scheme was one of the first of its kind and to test it, a distrustful HM Inspector sat in for a week, but couldn't fault it. Evidence of its usefulness was that the drop-out rate of those recruited in this way was below average.

The acquisitions brought Thames one particular benefit. Previously it had had no geology department, but Goldsmiths' as well as City each had had small ones with four and nine staff respectively. Together they became the School of Earth Sciences and those from Goldsmith's joined those from City at City's campus at Walburgh House, Shadwell. Here, under an ex-City member of staff, Alistair Baxter, its activities grew to such an extent that it had to expand into Thames's Wapping campus close by. From 1993 Thames began to prepare a campus in the former naval quarters (HMS *Pembroke*) at Chatham to which, for the 1994–5 session, Earth Science staff and students from Shadwell moved, followed in September 1995 by the balance of the School from Wapping. Thus from October 1995 Earth Sciences at the University of Greenwich were unified in fine new premises at Chatham, a far cry from Goldsmiths' at Deptford and City Polytechnic's at Shadwell. With over 500 undergraduates it had become the largest such faculty in the country. Meanwhile Goldsmiths' Rachel McMillan campus was occupied by Thames's School of Environmental Sciences, much of which moved from Woolwich to Deptford in 1988/9.

On the same day in September 1990 McWilliam and Valerie Stead made proposals of partnership and merger respectively with two other institutions: West Kent College at Tonbridge and South West London College. The proposal to West Kent had as its aim increasing higher and further education opportunities for the local community. This would be achieved by including West Kent's courses in the Polytechnic's validation and authorization. If West Kent were associated with Thames, successful West Kent students could be guaranteed places at Thames and West Kent could offer Thames's programmes. The proposal added that there were 'different areas of strength in both institutions' which could 'influence curriculum development' and thus increase the choice available to students.

Negotiations with West Kent led to the creation there amongst other programmes of a Higher National Diploma Course in Business and Finance, validated by Thames, and to the granting to it of Associated College status; by 1995 seven other United Kingdom colleges had been granted this status (see below) putting them in the same sort of relationship to the University of Greenwich as Woolwich Polytechnic had once been to the University of London.

McWilliam's proposal to South West London College (a parallel but smaller 'monotechnic' higher education institution in the London Borough of Wandsworth) was the result of a suggestion made a month earlier by the College itself that it might merge with Thames. It suggested this 'principally because of its relatively small size, its narrow subject base (all business related) and its need to offer degree level work if it was to attract more, and better qualified, higher education students.'

Meanwhile, however, South Bank Polytechnic, which had previously denied in its strategic plan that it was seeking any mergers, had made a counter-proposal to South West London College.

We were concerned [Valerie Stead said] to discover that an extensive campaign to undermine our proposal was set in train by the Polytechnic of the South Bank. However, on the evening of 27th September, we attended a meeting of the Governing Body at which both Polytechnics made a formal presentation in support of their proposals. As a result of this process, the Governors of South West London College voted with a very large majority to support this Polytechnic's proposal.

She listed the benefits which the merger would bring to Thames: over 1,200 funded students; staff in business, personnel management, finance, accountancy and law; courses which could be moved to Thames's Roehampton premises, and three additional London sites. Thames was keen to expand its activities in the subject areas in which South West London College specialized.

Four days later South West London College resolved to ask the Secretary of State to provide for the transfer from 13 March 1991 of all its properties, rights, and liabilities to Thames, and on 21 November Singer told the Court that his plan was to move South West London's activities from two of its sites to the Roehampton site (left empty by Garnett College's move to Avery Hill). At the same time working parties were set up to 'consider suitable academic structures' for the merger. All seemed set for another merger of the sort which Thames had managed so successfully before.

Meanwhile, however (13 November), the Department of Education had sent Thames a letter saying that it was bound to take advice about mergers from the Polytechnics and Colleges Funding Council, and that this council 'would need to satisfy itself that an alternative proposal by South Bank Polytechnic to merge with South West London College had been considered'. The immediate result was that the merger date had to be postponed, while the PCFC considered the advice it would give. The Court noted (euphemistically) its 'concern' at the delay and its intention to invoice South West London College for services rendered if the merger was not approved.

Eventually the PCFC advised the minister to base his decision on student preferences at South West London College – a surprising suggestion considering that it had not been made for any of Thames's previous mergers, but one which the Minister accepted. To prepare for this Singer wrote to each South West London College student at home, and sent fact sheets to them via the PCFC, giving information about Thames and the Roehampton campus.

A week later the Minister decided that the merger should not go ahead, but instead South West London College should be dissolved. Students and staff who wished to transfer to Thames could do so, together with proportional amounts of its assets and liabilities.

On 30 October 1991 Singer reported to the Academic Council that the final gain to Thames had been '201 part-time and 284 full-time funded student places, 17 academic and 17 support staff, together with a building in Wandsworth for disposal'. He added that he was 'moderately pleased with the final outcome'. Although not one which had been anticipated, the transfer of staff, students, and assets enabled Thames to set up law degree courses at Avery Hill, and business administration courses at Roehampton, both of which flourished.

The south-west London negotiations taught Thames a lesson: although a proposition may bring academic and economic benefits to all parties, unless all are consulted and involved it may founder. Henceforth Thames paid more attention to the political climate surrounding decision-making in higher education.

Describing the last amalgamation of Singer's time, John Humphreys wrote,

> Some time in the late 1980s, Norbert Singer . . . became interested in the idea of becoming involved in Nurse education. . . . In those days, there were three qualified nurses in the Polytechnic: all in the School of Post-Compulsory Education and Training, and all involved in training nurse tutors. Knowing this, he telephoned the Head of School [Humphreys]. 'Take an interest in this,' he said, 'Let's see how far it can go.' Singer had perceived the possibility of a new market – a major opportunity for his institution. Whereas we had been active in various minor collaborations before, after that telephone call the development of health care education became a strategic priority.

The specific possibility which Singer had identified was a collaboration with the nursing and midwifery training schools of three local health authorities: Greenwich (with schools at the Brook Hospital and Greenwich Hospital); Bexley (with schools at Bexley Hospital and Queen Mary's, Sidcup – the former an old asylum); and Dartford and Gravesham (with schools at Stonehouse Hospital, Dartford, and Gravesend Hospital). With the assistance of Thames, the three schools amalgamated to form the Thames College of Health Care Studies as a prelude to merger with the Polytechnic.

The event which had made an amalgamation with Thames Polytechnic a desirable objective was the publication of the Department of Health's working paper known as Project 2,000. This proposed a major reshaping of the training of nurses, midwives and health visitors, the underlying aim of which would be to make it more academic and less the learning of practical skills. The main feature of the change would be the transformation of trainees from practitioners who were at the same time being trained, to students whose courses consisted both of academic work and of clinical practice. Students would no longer be paid a salary by the NHS, but be given grants like other students – though larger because of their 45-week year.

All over the country colleges of health realized that they needed help in preparing the courses which students of this new sort would have to take. Many of them, as in this instance, turned for this help to polytechnics as institutions with long experience of vocational education.

The School of Post-Compulsory Education and Training responded to Singer's initiative by expanding in as many ways as possible its involvement in health care. Three projects were particularly successful. It took a major interest in physiotherapy by coming to an agreement with the Chartered Society of Physiotherapy under which it credit-rated training which physiotherapists received from their employers; it agreed with the Princess Alexandra and Newham College of Nursing and Midwifery to validate an English National Board Higher Award for its student nurses; and, most originally, it arranged with Macmillan, the publisher, to manage the open learning programme for nurses which *Nursing Times* carried.

This enabled registered nurses in any part of the United Kingdom to accumulate credit leading to a Diploma of Higher Education. Nurses taking the programme were supported by tutors based at 20 hospitals spread throughout the country to whom they could go for guidance. Three Polytechnic (University) staff continually travelled the country supervising such arrangements and approving local study centres. By 1995 more than 3,000 nurses were enrolled in the *Nursing Times* open-learning programme.

Stonehouse Hospital, Dartford, where the nurses' training school became part of the Faculty of Health at the University. Stonehouse was only one of several locations used by the Thames College of Health Care Studies at the time of its incorporation with Thames Polytechnic. These new teaching sites brought those of the University of Greenwich to a total of 20, spread over an area in excess of 500 square miles.

While the School was expanding its own interests in health care education in these enterprising and innovative ways, it was working with Thames College as a part of Greenwich's preparation for merger. In the event the problems which the merger produced were largely the technical ones of transferring the College's staff and sites from the National Health Service to the University. When completed it brought Greenwich 693 full-time students and a large number of part-time post-qualification students, and 140 new staff. The College felt a great sense of achievement when on the official date of the merger, 1 January 1993, it at once became a full faculty of the University. Among its other gains were access to the University's libraries, computers, and recreational facilities.

Since then there have been various changes. At first the student nurses and their courses remained in their previous hospitals, but the faculty quickly withdrew from two sites: Gravesend and Bexley hospitals. And in the summer of 1995 students at Brook Hospital and Greenwich District Hospital moved to Avery Hill.

The central course was a four-year one for pre-registration nurses, and at any one time had some 500 full-time students. But the faculty ran a range of other courses, some part-time for nurses who wanted to upgrade themselves from SEN to SRN, so bringing their qualifications into line with their grading (the work they actually did), others for a growing number of nurses who wanted to obtain awards for special nursing skills (non-invasive surgery for example). The University absorbed the College with few initial problems, its purchasing department soon becoming accustomed to orders for plastic arms, penises, and testicles. Later events, however reminded Singer and McWilliam (both of whom had represented the University on the steering group for the merger) that unless i's were dotted and t's crossed prior to the event, difficulties would follow. The University had not taken sufficient account of the structural changes going on within the NHS, following the creation of trusts and the 'internal market'. The merger agreement meant little to the successors of those with whom it had been agreed, the former feeling free to disclaim things which had been 'understood' but not formalized. Despite these difficulties the merger was a success, bringing the University not only a new area of academic work, but a new funder: the NHS.

16

University at Last

1986–1992

✦ ✦ ✦ ✦ ✦

AT THE SAME TIME THAT the Polytechnic was expanding, as it were, sideways, it was maintaining the standards of teaching and research at the centre for which it already had a decent reputation – but not without difficulties. In his 1986–7 report Singer's exasperation with government parsimony reached a new level.

Session by session, he wrote, the revenue per student had decreased. In recent years the Polytechnic had enormously improved its 'efficiency' and there was now a very much higher student–staff ratio, but a further improvement of this sort would inevitably lead to a reduction in 'the standards to which we have become accustomed and which we wish to maintain'.

Still more serious was the 'ludicrous and continuously reducing' level of funding for capital spending. It was essential that the Polytechnic should have more capital for new space or buildings at Woolwich. Though the National Advisory Board had reduced its overall bid to Government from £8m to £5m the Minister had decided that no capital should be provided for building. 'This appears to be an unbelievable decision in view of the large increase in student numbers in the public sector and the evident shortage of space at Thames Polytechnic.'

Even lack of capital for building works, he continued, did not represent the ultimate problem which faced the Polytechnic. Equally if not more important was the acute shortage of capital for equipment.

The shortfall . . . for . . . computer equipment was so acute during the session, and the threat to the quality of courses . . . so great that arrangements had to be made to purchase, through a leasing arrangement some £700,000 worth of additional computing equipment.

Facing page: Riverside House East, Woolwich. The lower, L-shaped block has been home to many staff and students since the 1960s. In the 1990s, it houses much of the Business Faculty and part of the Library and Media Service. Never designed as a building to be used for teaching, some of the occupants on the upper floors at least have a view of the Thames.

217

Facing page: Mount Clare, Roehampton, was designed, probably by Robert Taylor, as a small, compact villa for summer residence. George Clive paid what was in 1770 the tremendous sum of £6,950 for the whole building. The portico, added later by the second owner, Sir John Dick, was designed by Placido Columbani.

It was fortunate that, because of its corporate status, the Polytechnic was able to make this arrangement. But such arrangements had to be paid for in following years from revenue, and as a result 'activities which should be carried out cannot be carried out because of the need to fund these purchases'.

Certain matters, however, were turning out better than expected. The intake of students for 1987–8 had in the end matched that of the previous year. And the Polytechnic's excellent record in meeting its targets was likely to get it allocations of students (from the National Advisory Board) of the size it wanted and believed it deserved.

The major internal events of the following year were the CNAA's fourth five-yearly review of the Polytechnic's work, and a visit from 17 HM Inspectors to examine all aspects of the Polytechnic's initial teacher training programme.

The CNAA's review had led to a major development in the process of obtaining approval for courses. After it had been established in 1964 with the power to award degrees it had at first validated (and then periodically re-approved) each individual course proposed by institutions like Woolwich Polytechnic (as Thames then was). Gradually, however, this had led to a system described as 'partnership in validation', under which the institution was granted increased discretion in the validation and review of its own courses. Next came the granting by the CNAA to certain institutions of the sole right to review and validate particular courses. This the CNAA gave to Thames in 1986, making it one of only 20 institutions at that time to have such a right. At the same time Thames applied to the CNAA for the final stage in this process of devolvement: the granting to an institution as a whole

View down Wellington Street, with Woolwich Town Hall on the left. Just beyond is the entrance to the University island site, and at the end of the road is Churchill House overlooking General Gordon Square. Churchill House was acquired by the ILEA to house most of the work which transferred from Hammersmith.

of accreditation, this being a general right to create and validate all its courses. Describing the outcome, Singer wrote, that during the CNAA's visit there had been

> a full and frank exchange of views and, as a consequence, the Polytechnic was granted full Accreditation. We are now totally responsible for both the validation and approval of our own courses. This is one more important and significant step in the acknowledgement of the Polytechnic's academic maturity.

Michael Lovitt, Avery Hill's last Principal, subsequently Deputy Director (Academic) had been responsible for processing Thames's application for this important recognition. The following year Thames was also granted accreditation for its research degrees, thus becoming 'one of the very few institutions in the United Kingdom . . . accredited for all its work by the Council of National Academic Awards'.

Meanwhile the 17 HM Inspectors who had visited Avery Hill had reported favourably ('on the whole'), confirming the benefits brought by Avery Hill's amalgamation with Thames.

The year's most important external event was the passing of the 1988 Education Reform Act. Under this the Polytechnic ceased to be a grant-aided institution, funded by the ILEA, and was in future to be funded by a new national body, the Polytechnics and Colleges Funding Council. The full effects of this were still not clear, but were unlikely to be financially helpful. Nor did Singer welcome changes which the Act would probably require to the Court of Governors and the Academic Council, since at Thames these two bodies had been operating 'efficiently and well'. Matters became clearer in 1989 when the PCFC agreed to give institutions 95 per cent of the funds they would have had under previous arrangements (based on student numbers) and let them bid for more. Thames at once began to prepare bids, many to prove successful.

Bidding was more than an academic matter; if Thames chose not to bid, funding for the following year would fall by 5 per cent on the previous year. For institutions like Thames, a 5 per cent reduction would put the budget into deficit with dire consequences for staff levels. On the other hand if a bid were to be successful more students would have to be sought at a lower price than had previously been received. Almost without exception institutions bid against each other with lower prices for more students. This began a new phase of expansion for higher education in England and Wales.

McWilliam remembers well the deadline approaching for the submission of sealed bids.

> Analysis of previous costs and prices, conflicting opinions and advice were all available, but in the end you were left with trying to guess your competitors' bids. Sealing the envelope and posting it to the PCFC at Metropolis House might (and in some cases did) seal your own fate if you got it wrong.

Facing page: *Multi-media and CD-ROM computers in the mezzanine in the Avery Hill library, North Hall. They illustrate the way in which the University has reused to advantage old facilities. The hall was built in the early 1900s as the first gymnasium for Avery Hill Training College. It was refurbished, provided with a mezzanine floor and added to the adjacent library in the mid-1980s.*

The Wolfson Centre for Bulk Solids Handling Technology, opened 1991. A speciality of the School of Engineering for many years, it was eventually moved to Woolwich Dockyard in order to release space at Woolwich. The Wolfson Foundation provided a much-needed grant to allow the move.

A major inspection by a team of HM Inspectors gave the 1989–90 session its character. Inspectors rarely fail to find something to criticize, but the Polytechnic claimed that it was already attending to 'areas where improvement was desirable' and their general verdict was highly favourable. The Polytechnic was 'well led and administered', and its work achieved 'nationally acceptable standards'. They commented in particular on its healthy balance between teaching, research, and consultancy, and on the 'outstanding development of international links'. Research and consultancy were becoming increasingly important activities for the Polytechnic. The following year the Wolfson Centre for Bulk Solids Handling Technology, a speciality of the Polytechnic since it was developed by Stan Mason (see above), subsequently a research and consultancy unit within the School of Engineering, was made an independent unit within the Faculty of Technology located in specially leased accommodation at Woolwich Dockyard. This, besides freeing space for teaching in the island site, would, it was hoped, make the unit self-supporting.

There had been other research work of a fundamental nature, for example into elasticity by Godfrey as head of Mathematics before he became Principal. Vogel's work had also given the Polytechnic a research reputation which still survived 15 years later. On the other hand, teaching, not research, was Singer's priority. 'He was very tolerant of people like me,' Mark Cross remembered, 'and interested in our work, but his attitude was that he wouldn't underwrite research for people who couldn't do it.'

A further problem was that the only research co-ordinating body was the Research Degrees Committee, which was concerned mainly with the processing of higher degrees and so had little time to promote research. In 1992 Mark Cross (head of Mathematics, Statistics and Computing) became chairman of this committee and was appointed Director of Research. Cross had strong views about research and its importance to a university. He agreed with Valerie Pitt that 'all people involved in teaching should be inquisitive about their teaching and involved in scholarship.' A significant component of this was research, undertaken by people at the sharp end of their subjects. His own research had already led to the formation of the Centre for Numerical Modelling and Process Analysis, described in the 1992–3 Annual Report as 'arguably the most successful research group in the University, and one of the largest of its kind in Europe'. The belief which underlay the activities of this group was that 'applied mathematics and computing science could be combined to address significant problems in engineering.' By now the group had four professors and two readers in a team of 13 academics, with nearly 30 research staff and Ph.D. students. To take one project relatively comprehensible to the layman, it has been using computer science to research the way in which liquids distort when they solidify in a mould, extending this to their semi-molten states.

At the time Cross became Director of Research two events coincided, both of much importance to research at the University: the arrival of a new Vice-Chancellor, keener on research; and the transformation of the Polytechnic into a university which gave it access to a wider range of research funding, both from Government and Industry. Until then funding by United Kingdom industry had been so limited (and prejudiced in favour of such universities as Oxford and Cambridge) that the Polytechnic often had to find it abroad, for example in the USA or Australia.

For the 1993 session the Research Committee was split into two, Cross becoming chairman of both new committees. While the Higher Degrees Committee retained the previous committee's main function, a new Research Committee took on its policy-forming and promotional functions. This committee, on which all faculties were represented, began to promote a wider range of projects (until now they had been largely found in the Faculties of Science

Mark Cross, Director of Research since 1993.

Manresa House, Roehampton. The buildings there now form one of the University's main campuses.

221

and Technology). Typical was a research project in the School of Humanities jointly funded by the University and the London Borough of Greenwich to study 'Women's perception of crime in Woolwich town centre'. It also began to suport new projects with small pump-priming monies.

In 1994 the University, in its review of research and consultancy, wrote that its long-term policy was to build world-class research programmes within ten years in at least 12 areas. These areas (drawn from virtually all the University's schools) ranged from applied mathematics to sociology. Two examples suggest the variety of projects already registered. In the School of Architecture and Landscape, Panos Arvanitakis, Head of the School, had been identifying concealed structural damage at 50 St Mary Axe caused by the IRA bombing of the City, while M. Shokoohy was researching the symbolism of the decorative devices in the architecture of the Bahmani Sultanate of the Deccan in the fifteenth century. The bodies providing funds for the research were equally various, including, for example the Whale and Dolphin Conservation society which had given £35,000 to support a M.Sc. Studentship to review the status of the United Kingdom dolphin, and the Nuffield Foundation which was supporting research into Nicaraguan deforestation. Various, too, were the firms with which the University had consultancy contracts. In the School of Engineering, which had 41 such contracts, they included Waste Gas Technology and Mars Confectionery.

The Mansion Site, Avery Hill campus, seen from the park close to the Student Village.

Figures suggest how research at the University in these years expanded. Where in 1992 it had 41 registered and active research projects, in 1995 it had over 300. Where external income had been £2.5m, in 1995 it totalled more than £6m. This was reflected in an increase in the number of postgraduates and in the variety of the research they were pursuing.

During the same period the University began to discuss with the Natural Resources Institute (NRI) another important development of its research and consultancy activities. The Institute, based at Chatham, an executive agency of the Overseas Development Agency, consisted of some 450 research and consultancy staff who undertook projects chiefly concerned with the alleviation of poverty in developing countries by promoting the conservation and sustainable development of renewable natural resources. The NRI, though having an illustrious background dating back to the Imperial Institute of 1887, now found itself a possible candidate for privatization. Unlike other public sector research organizations however, it had no obvious private sector purchaser, so merger with a university was an obvious possibility.

Negotiations with the Polytechnic had come about, like many other things, as a result of a chance meeting, this one between the Institute's Director, Anthony Beattie, and John Parsonage, Dean of Science. Parsonage told Singer what he had learned and suggested that he and Beattie should meet. As soon as Singer heard from Beattie that the Institute might be relinquished by the

Michael Pattison, Secretary-General and Chief Executive of the Royal Institution of Chartered Surveyors until 1995, Director of the Sainsbury Family Trusts thereafter, has been Chairman of the Court and Pro-Chancellor of the University since 1994.

Government he suggested that it might merge with the Polytechnic. Such a merger would relieve the Government of a costly responsibility, while the Polytechnic would be able to improve its research ratings by acquiring a number of world-class scientists already working in the sort of teams which, if recruited from scratch, would take anything from five to ten years to establish. These would continue to be government funded but within about five years would have to become self-supporting. One Saturday morning in early 1994 McWilliam and Parsonage visited the NRI and discussions commenced, but it was to be April 1996 before a settlement was reached (see page 237).

From 1 May 1996, some 360 NRI staff joined the University after a lengthy and complicated bidding process. Greenwich put together a consortium of universities: Imperial College and Wye College of the University of London, together with the University of Edinburgh, to win control of the business and property of the NRI. Suddenly Greenwich became a major force in the world of renewable natural resources. Consultancy and research activity increased threefold at a stroke. David Wills, Dean of the Faculty of the Environment, was appointed as Acting Director of the Natural Resources Institute of the University.

The international links to which the HM Inspectors referred in their report were so numerous that only a few samples can be mentioned. In 1990–1 some two-thirds of the Schools of the Polytechnic were actively involved in creating or sustaining links with other European countries, mostly in the form of staff and student exchanges. The School of Business had been host to a conference of the European Business Studies Network; the School of Architecture and Landscape, where the European Landscape Education Exchange was based, was extending its activities to Eastern Europe, the School of Primary Education had run an induction programme for Dutch teachers who wished to teach in England, and several other Schools were discussing student exchanges with the University of Lille.

During the 1990–1 session the Polytechnic celebrated its 100th anniversary. There were public lectures and seminars, business and industry conferences, and open-days. Old students and staff returned to the Polytechnic for reunions and there was a thanksgiving service at St Mary's, Woolwich, but no repeat of the 1965 anniversary banquet. Its absence symbolized the Polytechnic's transformation during the last 25 years. If Woolwich Poly had then been a little old-fashioned and backward looking, in 1990 Thames was emphatically modern.

The most important academic event of 1991–2 was the launching of a Law School within the Faculty of Business. Legal studies had long been pursued in both the School of Surveying and the Business School. It was also an increasingly important area in, for example, Education and the Social Sciences. Unfortunately, some of the law staff in Business and Surveying had little time for each other and it was the influx of staff and students from the dissolved South West London College that made feasible a law school. The Academic Council approved a £100,000 financial injection to create the nucleus of a law library. Avery Hill was the chosen location and gradually staff transferred there from other parts of the Polytechnic. A lawyer member of staff of the Business School, Paul Vaughan, took on the initial responsibility of launching the School.

Facing page: Grenville, part of the former naval quarters at Chatham, now housing laboratories and offices of the School of Earth Sciences.

Facing page (above): *The disused firework factory, part of the future campus at the London Science Park at Dartford; and* (below) *the Queen Elizabeth II Bridge, a prominent landmark near by.*

Above: *An honorary award presented to Gordon Law, Chairman of the Court 1985–8, who retired as a Member in 1995; and* (below): *students graduating at the 1995 degree ceremonies held at the Barbican. Six ceremonies were held over three days in order to cope with the number of graduands.*

The same year yet another Education Act (The Further and Higher Education Act 1991) had more profound consequences for Thames Polytechnic. The most significant of these was the result of its abolition of Anthony Crosland's binary policy for higher education. In future there would be no practical distinction between a polytechnic and a university. This gave Thames, like other polytechnics, the opportunity to become in name as well as in practice a university.

Singer at once recommended that the Polytechnic should take advantage of this opportunity. Though there was some understanding in this country that polytechnics 'gave the same quality of education' as universities, parents were still inclined to make polytechnics a second choice for their children, and abroad there was less understanding. He remembered visiting Malaya with a group of university and polytechnic staff. When those from universities were taken to Malayan universities, those from polytechnics were taken to secondary technical schools. The name which Thames should take, he suggested, was Greenwich University.

The Court apparently understood him to have said 'University of Greenwich', and in September 1991 noted that this was favoured by most students, and that Thames University was merely the best among other suggestions. Though some Governors wished to retain Thames in the name, Greenwich had the advantage that it would give the University a more definite and memorable connection with a particular place in a part of the country in which the University had always functioned and where it planned to become the foremost institution of higher education. The name which the Privy Council finally agreed was the University of Greenwich.

The meeting at which the Court discussed the new name was also the one at which it was officially told of Singer's wish to retire. The coincidence was appropriate. Though the Polytechnic's elevation to university status was the consequence of a change in government policy, it was Singer more than anyone else who had made it possible for Thames to take advantage of this change.

17

Today and Tomorrow

1993 and onwards

Only a fool will build in defiance of the past. What is new and
significant always must be grafted to old roots, the truly vital roots
are chosen with great care from the ones that merely survive. And
what a slow and delicate process it is to distinguish radical vitality
from the wastes of mere survival, but that is the only way to
achieve progress instead of disaster. (Bela Bartok)

NORBERT SINGER was the University of Greenwich's first Vice-Chancellor for just six months before in March 1993 he retired. His 15-year regime will certainly be seen as the Institution's most significant of the century. Whatever measure is used it shows Thames Polytechnic's transformation from one of the country's smallest polytechnics into one of its most successful new universities. In 1973 it had two campuses and 4,000 students. In 1993 it had seven campuses and over 14,000 students. Such expansion seems now so clearly to have been Singer's aim from the start that the comment of John McWilliam, who as Deputy Director (Strategy) was most closely connected with the Polytechnic's expansion, is a surprising one. Singer, he remembered, had no time for strategic plans but was essentially pragmatic, his policies invariably a response to a particular problem.

The new Vice-Chancellor was David Fussey, for the previous three years Deputy Vice-Chancellor of Coventry University. Fussey had trained as an engineer and worked for the Central Electricity Board before becoming an academic. From Nottingham University he had moved to Australia, to Papua New Guinea and then to Plymouth Polytechnic where he had become Dean of the Faculty of Technology.

When Fussey encountered Bartok's words he felt that they closely resembled his idea of what he wanted to do for the University of Greenwich and how he

Facing page (above): *A quadrangle in the Avery Hill student village, the first phase of which opened for the 1993–4 session.*
Below: *The new library at Dartford, created in 1993 from the former dance studio, following a fire started by a disgruntled student.*

David Fussey, Vice-Chancellor since 1993.

227

The installation of Baroness Young of Farnworth as the Chancellor of the University, at the Royal Naval College, Greenwich, 13 May 1994.

Valerie Stead, Deputy Vice-Chancellor since 1994, who joined Avery Hill College as Vice-Principal in 1983.

should do it. Under Singer the University had acquired half a dozen other institutions or parts of institutions, each with its own special expertise and traditions. From these he must select for cultivation 'the truly vital roots', and weld them into a whole. He must not only bring the varied traditions together but, equally important, give them a sense of where they were going. Greenwich must treat the traditions of the old universities similarly, not aping them but choosing from them what was best for it.

A tradition which the University had already decided to adopt was the appointment of a Chancellor: it chose Baroness Young of Farnworth. Though never in the House of Commons, Baroness Young had served on Oxford City's Council for 15 years, been made a life peer in 1971 and since then held a number of government and opposition posts under Heath and Thatcher, among them becoming the first woman leader of the House of Lords and first woman Lord Privy Seal. Several of her non-political positions had been educational, and she was a member of the Court of Cranfield Institute of Technology. In a statement after her appointment she said, 'children as young as five . . . should be helped to realize that education is something essential that will affect them for the rest of their lives.' Those who had 'missed out' should have the chance to 'catch up and to train or retrain'.

By now the expansion of the University had acquired a momentum which seemed unstoppable. A typical if relatively small new venture was the launching of Greenwich University Press. This was suggested by Clive Seymour, one of the biologists who had transferred from Goldsmiths' to Thames in 1988, a man who described himself as continually bothered by ideas which he liked to get rid of by passing them on to someone else. Having not sent any to McWilliam for a while he passed him this one, was surprised soon afterwards to hear that he had been mentioned at a Governors' meeting and more surprised to be given the job of starting the press.

Its main publications at first were so-called Greenwich Readers. These gathered together in one volume the sort of articles and extracts from books which a lecturer would be likely to give students as a reading list on a particular subject, so protecting the library from sudden demands which it could not possibly meet. The subjects covered were in the field of social studies, Greenwich Reader No. 1 titled *Drugs and Drug Use in Society*, edited by Ross Coomber.

The Press soon also began to publish monographs on special subjects; and by 1995 it had ventured into commercial publishing with *Shadow of the Titanic*, the autobiography of Eva Hart who, at the age of seven, was one of the survivors, and four *Bridge Reader* videos. Asked who were his salesmen, Seymour replied, 'You're looking at one of them.'

New developments had also quickly followed the merger with Thames College of Health Care Studies (see Chapter 15). In 1993 the University, together with the Bexley and Greenwich Commissioning Agency, made its first clinical appointment, Dr Barry Evans, to be Director of Health Needs for Bexley and Greenwich. The appointment was intended to increase the University's involvement in public health. Neither Dr Evans nor the subject itself could be assigned to any particular school; besides its obvious connection with the Faculty of Health, it had implications for environmental science, social science, technology, and the built environment. The School of Environmental Science already ran undergraduate degree courses leading to degrees in Environmental Health and Occupation Safety and Health. The University now planned a Master's Degree in Public Health. The same year it appointed Professor Robert Douglas as Visiting Professor in Occupational Health and Hygiene.

Yet another new academic venture was the introduction of full-time degree courses in Sports Science and Psychology, both launched in 1994–5.

Long overdue and therefore a most welcome development in 1994 was the acquisition of the Woolwich public swimming-baths (closed for many years) for a new Students' Union headquarters. The transformation of the building, which stands in Bathway, a turning off the old Lower Market Street where Woolwich Polytechnic built the first of its important extensions, was a daunting task, the licence for the bars only being obtained on the morning it was due to open. The Union was now able to move from the 'hopelessly inadequate' accommodation it had had to use on the island site (the old Den) and in its new premises could employ 40 full-time staff to give advice to students on every subject, from their grants and health to their courses.

Here the President of the Union has her office, shared with four vice-Presidents, the five of them elected annually and known collectively as the sabbaticals. Each has different responsibilities. One, for example, is primarily concerned with sports clubs or societies, numbering 17 and 22 respectively in 1995. Another organizes support for campaigns, intern and external – which can still arouse passion, though nothing like the mass support of the 1970s.

From 1992 another was much concerned with the Student Leadership Programme. This, with the support of the Enterprise in Higher Education Steering Committee, encourages students to take part in extra-curricular activities and so 'leave university with more than a degree'. One such activity

John McWilliam, Deputy Vice-Chancellor since 1994, joined Thames Polytechnic in 1979 as Head of the School of Surveying.

The Union building, as it was in 1894 on its opening as a public baths. One hundred years later, after a closure of some eight years, the baths were purchased by the University to provide facilities for Woolwich students.

Aerial view of model of the proposed development of the Avery Hill Mansion Site: by 1994–5 planning consents had been obtained and land purchased to allow sufficient development for over 3,000 students, a far cry from the first intake at the beginning of the century. (By kind permission of Nick Evans Architects.)

became more significant in the mid-1990s – participation in the Student Representative Council. This body, consisting of the sabbaticals, the non-sabbatical Union officers and elected representatives from each of the University's schools, now became the governing body of the Union.

Singer may have disliked strategic planning, but by the 1980s this had become inescapable, in particular to enable the Polytechnic to provide the accommodation which it would need for the number of students which it expected in the years ahead. The first result, in 1989, was the commencement of the building of a new student village on the Southwood site at Avery Hill. This would eventually consist of brick-built blocks of 4–5 bedroom flats to house in total 2,000 students, standing round seven courtyards named after Henry VIII and his six wives – the ruins of his Palace at Eltham were a mile away. In September 1993 the first 650 students moved into the completed first phase of the village.

The Avery Hill student village led directly to the first of a succession of strategic plans which considered more generally the University, its role in society, and its future, the 1992–6 strategic plan leading to annually updated plans, in turn looking one year further ahead.

Each began with a so-called 'mission statement'. In simplified form the 1994/5–1998/9 mission statement described the University's aims as follows:

To provide high-quality teaching, scholarship and research.
To make it easy for students who would benefit to obtain this.
To help them to gain academic and professional awards.
To establish partnerships with other institutions in the United Kingdom and abroad for the same purposes.
To contribute to the economic, environmental and social regeneration of its region.

Four of these had always been the Polytechnic/University's aims, but the fourth – the development of partnerships – was comparatively new. If the years from 1976 to 1993 had been those of merger and take-over, the years from 1990 onwards were to be those of partnership. Ivor Jones, head of the Partnership Unit from its foundation in 1992, considered that the unit was assisting in the transformation of the University into a truly regional institution.

In the United Kingdom partnership had begun in 1990 with an association between the University and West Kent College at Tonbridge in which West Kent became an Associate College (see page 211). This had been followed by the establishment of similar connections with seven more colleges of further education in south-east London, Kent, and Essex. Working closely with the colleges the University approved offerings by the colleges of the early years of university awards on their own premises. Often new university awards were created by collaboration with the colleges, drawing on their specialist knowledge and skills. On finishing their college-based years students would transfer to the University to complete their Higher Education awards. Exceptionally the University would approve a college to offer the whole of an undergraduate award.

From the colleges' point of view such arrangements enabled them to move into higher education, this improving their reputation and status, so befitting their further education activities. From the point of view of the students, they were often able to live at home during the early years of degree courses, something many found important now that student grants had dwindled, and they obtained automatic places at the University provided they completed their studies satisfactorily at the colleges. From the University's point of view the arrangement helped to emphasize its connections with its chosen regions, and to offer access to students who might otherwise have not been able to attend.

The University also developed linking arrangements of a looser kind with other colleges – eight of them by 1995. These differed from its arrangements with

Phase 1 of the proposed expansion at Avery Hill (Nick Evans Architects), looking north-east into the rose garden.

Mansion site at Avery Hill: design detail of phase 2 of the 'Nursery' extensions.

Cross-section showing part of the proposed campus in the London Science Park at Dartford. Master plan by Skidmore, Owings and Merrill. Most of the car parking will be under ground as the campus is in the London green belt.

associate colleges in that linked colleges could have the same sort of arrangements with other universities, and the arrangements with Greenwich were not meant necessarily to be permanent, but in other ways they were similar. One example was an M.Sc. course in osteopathy, jointly developed with the European School of Osteopathy, Maidstone. In 1990–1 there were in total about 50–60 students at associated and linked colleges reading for University of Greenwich awards. By 1994–5 there were over 1,700 – both full- and part-time.

Another form of partnership was 'credit-rating'. The University had, for example, developed a partnership of this sort with the Lantern Trust, a charity approved by the Department of Health, the main work of which was counselling the bereaved, those diagnosed as HIV/AIDS positive, and others in distress. For the Trust Greenwich accredited several courses which it ran for its staff, up to Master's level. More generally the University developed arrangements with various businesses and other organizations, for example with a consortium of Social Work Departments of London Boroughs, under which it credit-rated the training they gave their staff, i.e. determined what this was worth in progress towards an award. Sometimes the University alone carried out the credit-rating, sometimes as one of a group of universities, an example of such a group being the Mount Clare Consortium formed by four of the new universities, based at Mount Clare on the University's Roehampton campus, to credit-rate Continuing Professional Development awards in the construction industry.

Yet another form of United Kingdom partnership consisted of an access programme, under which the University established compact arrangements with some 17 secondary schools, guaranteeing their students places at Greenwich provided they obtained required standards. The University hoped in this way to create a steady stream of applicants from within its region, while the schools gained close links with a local university (including visits to and from the university by staff and students) which would encourage their pupils to enter higher education, especially as the University undertook to look closely at 'records of achievement' as well as A-level scores.

While other universities were expanding in similar ways, Greenwich believed that it was ahead if not unique in helping with the development of awards in subject areas which it did not teach. In 1995, for example, it was helping West Kent College with the development of an HNC course in television production skills – in response to a shortage of 20- to 30-year-old men and women trained in these skills which arose when the BBC ceased to provide training courses.

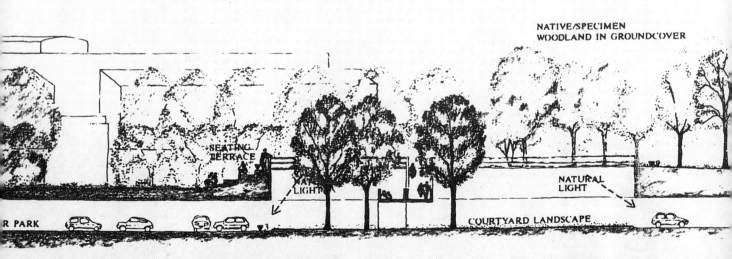

NATIVE/SPECIMEN
WOODLAND IN GROUNDCOVER

SEATING TERRACE

NATURAL LIGHT

NATURAL LIGHT

CAR PARK

COURTYARD LANDSCAPE

Abroad the University also expanded its partnership arrangements, though more cautiously. It would validate degree proposals and approve their delivery at foreign institutions, these leading to the students acquiring University of Greenwich degrees. Typically it had validated an M.Sc. degree in Environmental Science and in Agribusiness Management for two consortia of Dutch Polytechnics which, because they were not universities, were unable to give postgraduate awards under the Dutch educational system.

Other arrangements came into a category known as 'Local Delivery Mode'. The University would co-operate with foreign institutions to enable them to run early years of Greenwich degrees, so enabling their students to obtain university degrees with a shorter and less costly stay in Britain. The University would send staff to the foreign institution where they would take charge of such programmes. Typical were a first-year programme in surveying at Sunway College, Malaysia, and an MA in primary and secondary education at Malmö, Sweden. In April 1995 the Vice-Chancellor attended awards ceremonies in Malaysia and in Hong Kong. In all cases the programmes would be based on University of Greenwich awards, but would sometimes be modified to take account of local conditions or requirements.

The Partnership Unit also promoted a wide range of student exchanges, not only in Europe but elsewhere. One recent development was the University's membership of the International Student Exchange Programme, which enabled students to complete part of their awards in the United States.

The 1994/5–1998/9 strategic plan also included a new section on Information Strategy. From 1995–6 a Campus Wide Information Service would be developed, to provide staff and students with all kinds of information, from academic to social. It would allow them to access such external databases as SuperJanet, library services, and Internet. This would produce an important change in the way in which information was obtainable throughout the University. 'The management of information', the plan noted, 'provides the key challenge to the University over the next five years.'

More fundamentally, the same strategic plan gave details of the new division of the University into four large faculties: Human Sciences, Science and Engineering, Business, and the Environment. Each of the 16 schools was placed within one or other of these faculties. This was more than an exercise in tidiness, since it redefined the functions of the four new Deans of the Faculties and of the Heads of the Schools. The primary responsibility of the Deans was for the quality of the teaching and research in the schools. They were to have somewhat the function of internal inspectors. The Heads of the

AVENUE TREES

SECTION

Schools, on the other hand were responsible for the actual achievement of quality in their schools.

To emphasize the nature of the Deans' position and suggest that, from the schools' point of view, they were part of management, each Dean was given a special responsibility: information strategy, Europe, beyond Europe, and academic development.

Connected with this new arrangement, in the sense that it was the ultimate aim of the University to bring the schools of each of the four faculties together on one campus, was the Polytechnic/University's most intractable problem, its accommodation.

On the one hand it simply did not have enough. This shortage had been serious since its foundation in the 1890s. Though by 1992 it had 77,000 sq. m. of teaching space, the number of students it was teaching required in theory 120,000 sq. m.

On the other hand an equally serious problem was the vast area over which it was operating. Briefly, after the merger with Thames College of Health Care Studies, it had no fewer than 20 teaching-sites, and though several of the smaller hospital schools were soon closed, by 1994 it still had 13 campuses, spread over some 500 sq. miles, reaching from Roehampton in the west to Chatham in the east.

This was highly inefficient. In 1989 it had been calculated that even a seven-campus university would cost £1.6m a year more to run than one on a single site. An equally serious consequence was that it had ceased to have any clear identity. The name, Greenwich, was an improvement on Thames, but one for which there was little justification, since it had not a single shed or acre in Greenwich town itself. Closest was its Rachel McMillan campus at Deptford, but this was not close enough.

Behind the numerous changes in the University's sites which took place in the 1990s lay three aims. First, retaining or acquiring campuses in the areas in which it intended to become the principal institution of higher education: south-east London and Kent. Second, justifying its name by acquiring premises in Greenwich itself. Third, reducing the number of its campuses, if possible to four, but at the same time increasing the accommodation each of them would provide.

In pursuit of the first aim it made an extensive search of Kent, but was only able to find two sites. Neither would accommodate the whole university, but, together with Woolwich and Avery Hill, they would enable it to abandon all other sites so achieving the desired four campuses.

The first and smaller of the Kent sites, King's Hill, West Malling, is a major Business Park near Maidstone, once an airfield. Here the University was offered land by the developers for a campus and by September 1994 it had already converted ex-RAF buildings to create teaching space. The type of education it was offering was postgraduate in level and largely Continuous Professional Development in character. Its first courses were for a Diploma in Management Studies, Health, and an MA in Employment Strategy; these were followed by an MA in Marketing. The new centre also had conference facilities and was to be the guinea-pig for an investigation into the virtual campus – ways in which students working at home might be computer-linked to everything they would find in a real campus classroom from the lecturer to their fellow students. King's Hill would continue to concentrate on postgraduate-level work, extending the subjects covered to all those the University offered and becoming one of its main campuses.

Facing page: *Part of the library at Chatham, formerly the Wardroom of HMS Pembroke.*

The site at King's Hill, West Malling, earmarked for further expansion by the University.

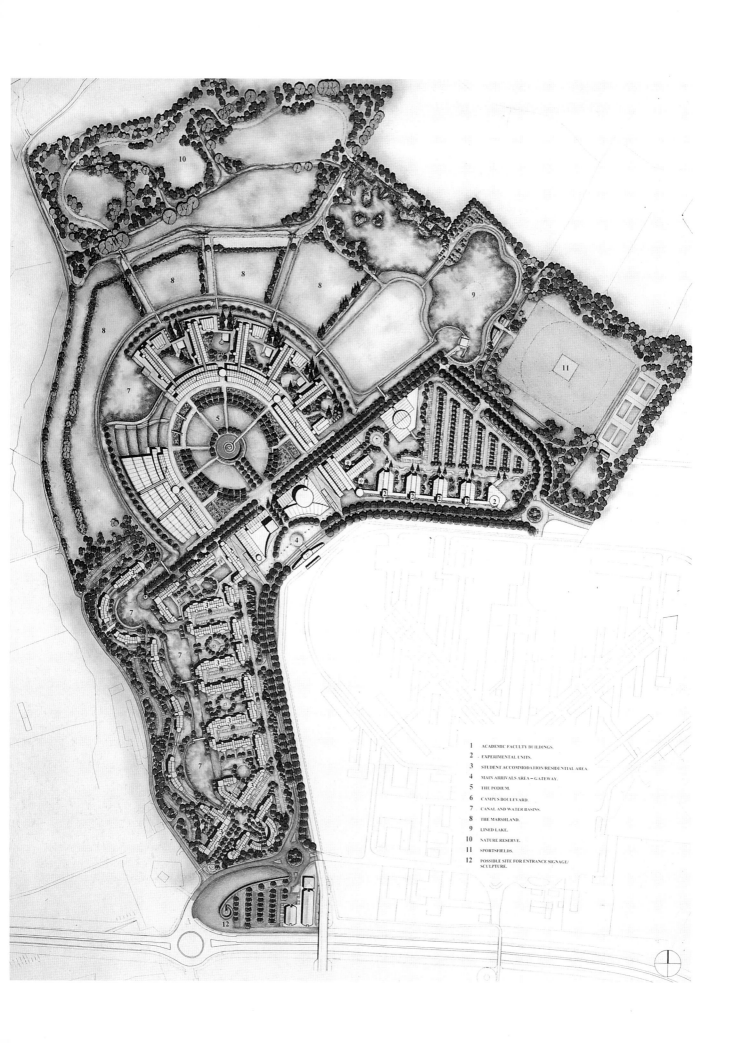

1   ACADEMIC FACULTY BUILDINGS.

2   EXPERIMENTAL UNITS.

3   STUDENT ACCOMMODATION/RESIDENTIAL AREA.

4   MAIN ARRIVALS AREA – GATEWAY.

5   THE PODIUM.

6   CAMPUS BOULEVARD.

7   CANAL AND WATER BASINS.

8   THE MARSHLAND.

9   LINED LAKE.

10 NATURE RESERVE.

11 SPORTSFIELDS.

12 POSSIBLE SITE FOR ENTRANCE SIGNAGE/
    SCULPTURE.

The second new site in Kent was at North Dartford, close to the Queen Elizabeth II bridge. Dartford Borough Council backed the University's plan to build a campus here and resolved to give planning permission, but the site was in the green belt and the Secretary of State, Michael Howard, reacted to fears of opposition by sending the proposal to a planning inquiry. This took place in January 1993 and it was after Easter before the Chief Planning Inspector recommended its rejection.

The Secretary of State, however, considered that the development of the East Thames Gateway (intended to encourage London to expand east rather than west as it had traditionally done) could be as important as the preservation of the green belt and, issuing a letter rejecting his inspector's advice, indicated that he was minded to grant consent. He asked the University, however, to show that in the meanwhile no alternative site outside the green belt had become available. When it successfully did this, and also showed that at Dartford it would stimulate the London Science Park, he formally overrode the Planning Inspector's recommendation and gave planning consent.

It was the University's intention to spend some £90m on a 135-acre campus, sited next to Joyce Green Hospital, itself due to close. This would eventually provide teaching for 5,000 students and living accommodation for 2,000, the first of whom would move there before the year 2000. The campus was to be part of the London Science Park – expected to become a development of national significance over the years.

Meanwhile one of the south-east London campuses which was to become part of the four-campus university – Avery Hill – was to be expanded with new buildings on the mansion site and an extension of the student village; and the other – Woolwich – might ultimately move into the Arsenal, which the Ministry of Defence had declared 'surplus to requirements'.

Now, however, new opportunities which could not be ignored arose to upset the tidy four-campus plan. One of these led to the leasing (already mentioned) by the University of the premises at Chatham to which the Faculty of Earth Sciences moved. This had occurred as a result of negotiations with the Government about the acquisition of the Natural Resources Institute, from which the University was in fact leasing its Chatham buildings. At the same time it had formed a consortium with Imperial College, Wye College, London, and the University of Edinburgh to bid for the whole Institute, the result being that all of its staff, property, and contracts transferred to the University of Greenwich on 1 May 1996. Since the NRI property was adjacent, a sizeable new campus would be created here, and in anticipation of this the University negotiated a lease of several additional buildings including the former gymnasium and the Chief Petty Officers' Mess of HMS *Pembroke*, which it turned into a sports hall/examination room and a teaching space, with some facilities for staff and students.

At around the same time there occurred an opportunity to pursue the second of the University's general aims – the creation of real links with Greenwich town. This took the form of a proposal that the former Dreadnought Seaman's Hospital be handed over to the University by the National Health Service to house the former College of Health Care Studies. Much water was to flow

Facing page: *Master plan by Skidmore, Owings and Merrill in association with Derek Lovejoy Partnership, for the development of London Science Park at Dartford campus. The area of the site is 135 acres and the development will be home to some 5,000 students. There will be a second student village (the first being at Avery Hill) as part of the campus. Students will be able to take a boat around the canals to the lakes.*

Field trip in Spain by members of the School of Earth Sciences, Chatham, for the Geography degree.

under that particular bridge before the idea became a reality, but, subject to the Armed Forces Bill reaching the statute book, the University finally expects to acquire a long leasehold interest in the former hospital in 1996.

The third and most exciting opportunity bids fair to justify beyond any doubt the University's name: the leasing of the former Royal Greenwich Hospital following the decision by the Ministry of Defence to move the Royal Naval College to Camberley. The Hospital's buildings (of which the Dreadnought Seaman's Hospital is only one) had a long and complicated history having been built by or for half a dozen kings and queens, employing as many different architects. The oldest of which any substantial part survives is the Queen's House, begun by James 1 in 1613 for his Queen, Anne of Denmark, designed by Inigo Jones. Though completed in 1637 by Charles I for his queen, Henrietta Maria, it did not finally become the perfect square which survives today until after the Restoration (1660) when two more bridges over the Dover Road were added. Today it forms part of the National Maritime Museum.

At this time an older brick Royal Palace built in Tudor times by Henry VIII still survived, but Charles II pulled that down and employed John Webb to build a grander affair, the King Charles block, in line with the Queen's House but consisting of a courtyard with one side open to the river. Begun in 1664, this was not in fact completed until 1769.

Meanwhile in 1690 the Queen's House had become the residence of the Ranger of Greenwich Park and the Governor of the Naval Hospital, an institution for naval pensioners similar to today's Chelsea Hospital. And to prepare for their move to Greenwich Palace (William and Mary had moved to Hampton Court which they thought healthier) Wren built, from 1698 onwards, the King William Building, with domes and colonnades, the Queen Mary Building, and the Queen Anne Building – Hawksmoor, Vanburgh, and Ripley

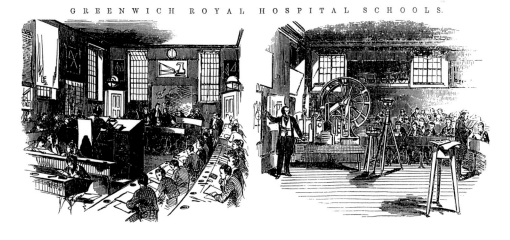

The Royal Greenwich Hospital's previous involvement with education included a school for the children of Navy personnel. Mathematics and optics class (left), and (right) lesson on steam machinery (picture from 1848).

all taking a hand in their completion. The whole group has been described as 'the most stately procession of buildings we possess'. 'The most curious thing about them,' Pevsner added, 'is that they are indeed a procession, that is the space between them is more telling than the architecture itself in spite of Wren's two twin domes and colonnades.'

In 1705 the pensioners began to arrive, by 1708 they numbered 350, by 1755 1,550, and by 1815 2,718. It was not until 1873 that the Royal Naval College at Portsmouth was moved to Greenwich after the last pensioners had left.

By 1994 it had become a victim of the economies which followed the end of the cold war, one of them the Ministry of Defence's plan to close two of its staff colleges. Again the University learned of this at an unplanned meeting when McWilliam (now Deputy Vice-Chancellor) spoke to the Minister at a reception. During 1995 the Government initiated a marketing campaign to find new tenants for the Naval College properties; a campaign which provoked something of a national outcry, protesting at 'selling the family silver'. By the end of the year, the University had made a bid. Meanwhile it had had wide discussions with the Borough of Greenwich and English Heritage, about the work on this historic building which would be required to make it meet Health and Safety Regulations.

At the end of March 1996, the Secretary of State for Defence announced in the House of Commons that the University's proposals for the Royal Naval College were the preferred solution for future occupation. The University will be the dominant occupier, with both the National Maritime Museum and the Maritime Trust having minority occupational leases. An over-arching trust will be established to assume financial responsibility for maintainance of the historic buildings. The University expects to take up occupation from Summer 1997 onwards.

From its foundation the Polytechnic has served above all the people of towns on the south bank of the Thames. The bid for the Royal Naval College, if successful, will emphasize this 100-year connection, bringing the University the best-known building on the lower Thames. At the same time the Royal Naval College would become the University's flagship under its new name. There could be no more appropriate event to end this history.

Executive Officers

Chairmen of the Governing Body

Woolwich Polytechnic

1891–1894	T. A. Denny
1895–1903	Quintin Hogg
1904–1907	Revd Canon Escreet
1908–1909	Henry J. Butter
1910–1913	William Calderwood
1914–1917	J. T. La Brooy
1918–1920	George Whale
1921–1923	Revd C. H. Grinling
1924–1926	Revd A. M. Pickering
1927–1929	Menzies A. Stapley
1930–1934	William Calderwood
1935–1938	Menzies A. Stapley
1939–1941	E. G. Dixon
1942–1944	E. G. Stevenson
1945–1947	G. Leslie Wates
1948–1949	Percy Dunsheath
1949–1952	Sir Thomas G. Spencer
1952–1955	Brian Manning
1955–1959	Henry E. Helwig
1959– 1962	Douglas H. Mizen
1962– 1965	Edward F. Burford
1965–1968	G. Ainsworth Wates

Thames Polytechnic (from 1970)

1968–1973	Leslie S. Crutch
1973–1976	L. G. Taffs
1976–1979	E. Norman Harris
1979–1982	Ingwald Kraft
1982–1985	Alec A. Grant
1985–1988	Gordon M. Law
1988–1991	Fredrick W. Styles

University of Greenwich (from 1992)

1991–1994	Dame Joan Varley
1994	Michael A. Patterson

Principals of Woolwich Polytechnic

1893–1895	Frederick C. Garrett
1895–1899	Andrew G. Ashcroft
1899–1903	Dr John Ryan
1903–1912	William Gannon
1912–1932	Alexander F. Hogg
1932–1950	Dr Edward Mallett
1951–1956	Dr James S. Tait
1957–1967	Dr Harold Heywood
1967–1970	Dr Derrick E. R. Godfrey

Directors of Thames Polytechnic

1970–1978	Dr Derrick E. R. Godfrey
1978–1992	Dr Norbert Singer CBE

Vice-Chancellors of the University of Greenwich

1992–1993	Dr Norbert Singer CBE
1993–	Dr David E. Fussey

Principals of Avery Hill College
(formerly Avery Hill College of Education)

1906	Mary Bentinck Smith
1906–1907	Miss A. B. Collier
1907–1908	Philippa Fawcett *(Acting Principal)*
1908–1922	Emily M. Julian
1922–1938	Freda Hawtrey
1939–1960	Dr Frances Consitt
1960–1981	Kathleen E. Jones
1981–1985	Michael Lovitt *(continuing as Deputy Director (Academic) of Thames Polytechnic)*

Principals of Dartford College of Education

(formerly Kingsfield College of Physical Training, and The Bergman-Österberg College of Physical Education)

1885–1915	Madame Martina Bergman-Österberg
1916–1917	Miss H. Meade
1917–1919	Helen C. B. Greene
1919–1921	Hilda C. Walton
1922–1930	Eva Lett
1930–1939	Miss R. Hope Greenhall
1939–1949	Grizel MacLaren
1950–1962	Edith Alexander
1962–1975	Margaret Chamberlain
1975–1978	Kenneth Challinor

Principals of Garnett College

(formerly North-Western Polytechnic)

1946–1963	Dr James C. Docherty
1963–1971	C. Jameson
1971–1976	E. J. Brent
1976–1978	L. S. Powell
1978–1987	J. Talbot

(Valerie A. Stead, now Deputy Vice-Chancellor of the University, was Acting Principal during the merger period)

Past Presidents of the Students Union

Thames Polytechnic

Sept. 1965	Brian Chalkley (resigned)
Jan. 1965	Adrian Perry
1966–7	Dick Lodge
1967–8	D. L. Yorath
1968–9	A. J. Britton
1969–70	D. W. J. Cruikshank
1970–71	R. M. Hinkley
1971–2	S. Winstanley
1972–3	A. Mathison
1973–4	J. Laxton
1974–5	Hugh Kelly (resigned)
July 1975	Erik Shopland
1975–6	Vacant
1977–8	John Ford
1978–9	Lesley Day
1979–80	Ray Daniel

1980–81	Simon Hubbard
1981–2	Ken Stratford
1982–3	Ken Stratford
1983–4	Peggy Eagle
1984–5	Martin Banham (resigned)
June 1985	David Lee
1985–6	David Lee
1986–7	David Lee
1987–8	Carl Blackburn
1988–9	Steve Sparks
1989–90	Robert Pitt
1991–92	Chris Herriot

University of Greenwich

1992–3	Paul Thomas
1993–4	Russell Cole
1994–5	Russell Cole
1995–6	Lisa MacDonald-Brown

Bibliography

Collin Brooks, *An Educational Aventure. A History of the Woolwich Polytechnic*, 1954.

Walter Besant, *All Sorts and Conditions of Man*, 1882.

Michael Locke, *Traditions and Controls in the Making of a Polytechnic: Woolwich Polytechnic 1890–1970*, 1978.

J. May, *Madame Bergman-Österberg*, 1969.

Albert Pomfret, *Dartford College 1885–1985*, (1985).

David Shorney, *Teachers in Training 1906–1995. A History of Avery Hill College*, 1989.

Sidney Webb, *London Education*, 1904.

Ethel Wood, *The Polytechnic and its Founder Quentin Hogg*, 1932.

Evolution of the University

1890–1970	WOOLWICH POLYTECHNIC
1953	Woolwich College of Commerce reconstituted as the Department of Commerce and Management Studies
1970–1992	THAMES POLYTECHNIC: designation
1975	Dartford College of Physical Education merger
	(formerly Kingsfield College of Physical Training and The Bergman-Österberg College of Physical Training)
1985	Avery Hill College amalgamation (formerly Avery Hill College of Education)
1987	Garnett College incorporation
1989	Incorporation of Science Courses from City of London Polytechnic and Goldsmiths' College and acquisition of Rachel McMillan College buildings
1991	Transfer of parts of South West London College
1992	Thames College of Health Care Studies Merger
1992	UNIVERSITY OF GREENWICH: Designation

Facing page: The grand library in the Avery Hill Mansion, originally Col. North's picture gallery and ballroom. It was completely refurbished by the University in the early 1990s.

242

Chronology

1845: Quintin Hogg is born.

1845	Quintin Hogg, founder of the polytechnic movement, born.
1849	Martina Bergman (later Madame Österberg), founder of the physical training college at Dartford, born.
1864	Quintin Hogg and Lord Kinnaird launch a Ragged School near Charing Cross Jesuits buy Parkstead, Roehampton, for use as a training college, naming it Manresa House after the home town of the founder of the Jesuits.
1870	Education Act (1870) establishes school boards and makes elementary education available to all.
1871	Hogg establishes Young Men's Christian Institute, Castle Street.
1881	Brook Green School of Art (to become Hammersmith College of Art and Building) founded as a small evening class in Hammersmith. Madame Österberg becomes London's Superintendent of Physical Education in Girls' and Infants' Schools
1882	Young Men's Christian Institute moves and becomes the Regent Street Polytechnic Institute, the inspiration of all subsequent British polytechnics.
1884	Francis (Frank) Didden, a former Institute student, becomes a fitter at the Woolwich Arsenal and works towards founding a polytechnic there.

1882: Regent Street Polytechnic Institute.

1885   Madame Österberg opens Hampstead Gymnasium, the precursor of Dartford College.

1887   Francis Didden and Quintin Hogg find two suitable premises in Woolwich for a polytechnic, but neither scheme succeeds.

1888   Polytechnic Athletic Club raises funds for the proposed polytechnic with a sports meeting at Charlton.
Colonel North, the Nitrate King, buys Avery Hill mansion.

1889   Didden approaches the City Parochial Foundation for funding but is rejected.

1890: Woolwich Polytechnic founded.

1890   Woolwich Polytechnic founded, in the former house of Samuel Barnes, 47 William Street, bought with money largely contributed by T. A. Denny, at a special price on the understanding that it be used for the Polytechnic. Didden and his family move in, alterations are made and a gym built in the garden.
Polytechnic Athletic Club holds second fund-raising meeting, and is given official status by Hogg.

1891   First session of study at the new Woolwich Polytechnic. 38 subjects, 625 students and members of the Institute.

1892   80 subjects on offer. 49 William Street bought by Polytechnic and new labs built.

1893   Woolwich Polytechnic finally obtains City Parochial Foundation funds. Also LCC Technical Education Board support on condition Educational Principal appointed. F. C. Garrett chosen.

1890s: Engineering lab at Woolwich Polytechnic.

1894   Announcement that Woolwich Polytechnic to close (July) due to lack of money, but able to reopen (September) with expanded control by Technical Education Board. New Governing Body takes over.

1896: Avery Hill mansion up for sale.

1895   A. J. Naylor becomes Clerk to the Governors of Woolwich Polytechnic. Didden demoted to head of Social Side, and Garrett resigns as Principal after long dispute with Didden. Andrew Ashcroft appointed Principal.
Madame Österberg moves Hampstead College to Kingsfield House, Dartford, and renames it the Bergman-Österberg Physical Training College.

1896   Woolwich Polytechnic buys houses in Lower Market Street (later Polytechnic Street) backing on to William Street gardens, for expansion.
Colonel North dies, and his family puts his mansion at Avery Hill up for sale.

1897   New buildings at Woolwich Polytechnic. Day School for Boys opened.

1895: Kingsfield House, Dartford, becomes the Bergman-Österberg Physical Training College

1902: LCC buys Avery Hill.

1899   Girls admitted to Woolwich Polytechnic Day School. Engineering Society established. Ashcroft unexpectedly resigns. John Ryan appointed Principal.

1900   Boer War disrupts the Polytechnic, as students from the Woolwich Arsenal have problems attending classes.

1901   Penfold medal established to commemorate the former Governor, Abel Penfold.

1902   Avery Hill bought by LCC.
Quintin Hogg dies.
Board of Education inspection criticizes Polytechnic School of Art, which is subsequently derecognized then rerecognized. Canon Escreet (later Archdeacon) appointed Chairman of Governing Body.
Education Act gives local authorities power to fund teacher-training colleges.

1903   William Gannon appointed Principal.

1904   Education Act of 1902 extended to London, and LCC takes charge of Woolwich Polytechnic.
Didden dismissed from Woolwich Polytechnic. Gannon reorganization leads to dismissal of all but two of the previous part-time staff.

1905   Gannon reorganisation of Polytechnic Institute (social side) and dismissal of Head of the Polytechnic Day School (now Secondary School).

1906: Woolwich Polytechnic Electrical Engineering department.

1906   Avery Hill opens as the LCC's first residential teacher training college, with 45 resident and 115 day students. Mary Bentinck Smith first Principal.
Student numbers at Woolwich Polytechnic exceed 1,800, with nearly 4,400 class entries for the 1906–7 session. Two Trade Schools established, and School of Dressmaking.

1906: Avery Hill becomes LCCs first teacher training college.

1907   Brook Green School of Art relaunched in Lime Grove, Shepherd's Bush.
Philippa Fawcett appointed Acting Principal of Avery Hill Teacher Training College, before spending the rest of her career at the LCC.

1908   Emily Julian appointed Principal of Avery Hill Teacher Training College.

1910   William Calderwood appointed Chairman of the Governing Body at Woolwich, and is involved in arranging courses for the Arsenal Trade Lads, and new building, as well as being a member of the Board of Governors at Avery Hill Teacher Training College.
Rachel McMillan Nursery School, the first of its kind, launched by Rachel and Margaret McMillan.

1910s: Physical training at the Bergman-Österberg Institute.

1912 Alexander Hogg (no relation to Quintin) appointed Principal at Woolwich

1913 City Parochial Foundation loan allows Woolwich Polytechnic to buy freehold of Polytechnic buildings, and grant from LCC allows further expansion.

1914 First World War leads to reduction in number of Arsenal Trade Lads at Woolwich Polytechnic.
Rachel McMillan Nursery School moves to Church Street, Deptford.

1914: McMillan nursery school at Deptford.

1915 Woolwich resolves that 'all resources of the Polytechnic be placed at the disposal of the Arsenal for manufacture of munitions'. Classes in War economy cooking started. Avery Hill Roper Hall extension commandeered by War Office for wounded.
Madame Österberg, founder of Dartford College, dies.

First World War: Women worker at the Arsenal.

1916 New Woolwich Polytechnic buildings and entrance on Thomas Street/William Street corner built.
Completion of hostels at Avery Hill Teacher Training College allows for expansion to 250 residential students.

1920 LCC London Education Scheme envisages Woolwich Polytechnic remaining largely devoted to evening classes. Woolwich Polytechnic School of Domestic Economy closed.

1921 Memorial tablet to Woolwich Polytechnic deaths in the war – 8 staff and 53 former students – erected.

1922 Freda Hawtrey appointed Principal of Avery Hill Teacher Training College; her great interest in McMillan sisters nursery school at Deptford.

1923 Burnham Committee recommends closer links between training colleges and universities, resulting in universities conducting the exams for Teacher's Certificates.

1925: Woolwich Town Hall site on Wellington Street and Polytechnic Street.

1928 Avery Hill Teacher Training College begins association with University of London in wake of Burnham Committee proposals.

1929 Oakfield Hall and hostel built at Dartford College.

1930 Brook Green School of Art renamed Hammersmith College of Building, Arts and Crafts. Expands to include Technical School of Building.

1929: Oakfield Hall built at Dartford.

1931 LCC takes over Rachel McMillan Nursery School.

1932 Woolwich Polytechnic expands in Thomas Street. Alexander Hogg retires as Principal after 20 years, and Naylor as Secretary and Clerk to the Governors after 37 years. Edward Mallett appointed Principal, Joseph Halliwell Secretary.

1934   Sandwich courses in engineering introduced.
Athletic Club absorbed into Polytechnic Union along
with other Woolwich Polytechnic societies.

1936   Island site in Woolwich recognized by Governors as area
for expansion. Further purchases made in 1937–8.
Dartford College associated with University of London
according to Burnham Committee proposals, and
introduces Diploma in Theory and Practice of Physical
Education.

936: Natural dance movement,
artford College.

1938   University of London inspectors of Woolwich
Polytechnic favourably impressed.

1939   Second World War leads to evacuation of Woolwich
Polytechnic junior schools, and numbers attending
evening classes falling from 4,635 to 1,570 in one year.
Military personnel start courses at the Polytechnic.

1940   First bombs fall on Woolwich Polytechnic (January).
Bergman-Österberg Physical Training College evacuated
from Dartford to Cornwall; changes its name to Dartford
College of Further Education. Kingsfield House bombed.

1941   Serious bomb damage at Woolwich Polytechnic.
Avery Hill Teacher Training College evacuated to
Yorkshire. Many buildings at Avery Hill damaged by
bombing.

Second World War: Bomb damage at Woolwich Polytechnic.

1944   Flying bomb destroys Somerville Hall of Residence at
Avery Hill.

1945   Celebration of VE day (June) at Woolwich Polytechnic,
at which Chanticleer is adopted as the Union mascot.

1946   Predecessor of Garnett College opened at North
Western Polytechnic as part of the post-war emergency
scheme for teacher training.

1947   Hammersmith College of Building, Arts and Crafts
renamed.

1945: Chanticleer, adopted as the Woolwich Polytechnic mascot at the VE Day celebrations.

1948   Memorial gates erected at Well Hall sports ground to
mark dead of both world wars.
LCC buys Downshire House, Roehampton.

948: War Memorial gates.

1949   Avery Hill Teacher Training College officially reopened
after return.

1950   Diamond Jubilee of Woolwich Polytechnic. Mallett,
Principal for 18 years, dies in office. Student Board
formed, subsequently renamed Students' Union Society.

1951   James Tait appointed Principal of Woolwich Polytechnic.

1953   Garnett College named in honour of William Garnett,
who helped establish teacher training in London under
the LCC (1893).

1954: Mount Clare bought by LCC, occupied by Garnett College nine years later.

1954   Mount Clare (built for cousin of Clive of India) bought by LCC
Girls' Technical School transferred from Woolwich Polytechnic to LCC.

1955   Government announces formation of national Council for Technological Awards. Woolwich Polytechnic starts Diploma of Technology awards.

1956   Government selects Colleges of Advanced Technology. Woolwich Polytechnic *not* chosen.
Boys' School and Junior Arts School transferred from Woolwich Polytechnic to LCC.
Woolwich Polytechnic designated a Regional College.
Students' Union Society produces first *Student's Handbook*.

1957   Harold Heywood appointed Principal of Woolwich Polytechnic.

1959   RIBA recognizes Diploma course at Hammersmith College of Art and Building.
Methodist Training College in Horseferry Road, Westminster, rented to Avery Hill.

1960   Dartford College transferred to LCC. General teacher training started.
Kathleen Jones becomes Principal of Avery Hill.

1961   Woolwich Polytechnic School of Art closed. Department of Domestic Science closed.

1962   LCC buys Manresa House, Roehampton after Jesuits move out following plans for adjacent high-rise flats.

1963   Robbins Report leads to establishment of Council for National Academic Awards. Woolwich Polytechnic starts to transfer degree courses from University of London to CNAA. Students' Union Society becomes independent Students' Union. Former Society becomes Polytechnic Union, effectively an old students' club.
Wellington Street block completed – first new building since 1939.
Garnett College moves to Roehampton.

1964   Thomas Street block completed.
Woolwich Polytechnic's move to Thamesmead first suggested.

1965   Woolwich Polytechnic 75th anniversary celebrations.
Anthony Crosland, Secretary of State for Education, makes 'Woolwich Speech' describing binary policy on further education: no new universities for 10 years, but 30 new polytechnics.
Woolwich Polytechnic rents Riverside House.
Halliwell retires as Secretary to the Governors after 33 years.

1959: Diploma course at Hammersmith College recognised by RIBA.

1962: Jesuits leave Manresa House.

1960s: New buildings – Churchill House for Woolwich Polytechnic.

*969: Hammersmith College of
*rt and Building merges with
Voolwich Polytechnic.

1967   Derrick Godfrey, Vice-Principal, appointed Principal of
Woolwich Polytechnic.

1968   Hammersmith College of Art and Building starts
Landscape Architecture Department, and this moves
with Architecture to Vencourt House, Hammersmith.
Mile End annexe of Avery Hill opened for mature
students wishing to become teachers.

1969   Merger of Hammersmith Departments of Architecture,
Landscape Architecture and Surveying with Woolwich
Polytechnic.

1970   Woolwich Polytechnic and Hammersmith Departments
together designated Thames Polytechnic. Godfrey
becomes Director.

1971   Thames Polytechnic's first hall of residence opened;
named Thomas Spencer Hall in honour of long-serving
Governor and Chairman of Governing Body.
Avery Hill numbers rise to 1,500. Day student block
opened.

1972   Government White Paper sets out aim to reduce
number of teacher training colleges.
First student occupation at Thames Polytechnic, in
campaign for higher grants.

1975   Thamesmead plan disappears 'for foreseeable future'.

1976   Thames Polytechnic and Dartford College merge.
Teacher training at Dartford ceases within 10 years.
Avery Hill retained by ILEA as only free-standing
teacher training college.

1978   Norbert Singer appointed Director of Thames
Polytechnic. Churchill House, Woolwich, rented for
Hammersmith Architecture and Surveying Departments.
Landscape department goes to Dartford.
18-day student occupation of the Polytechnic in protest
against cuts in places for overseas students.

1979   Garnett College becomes administratively responsible for
Manresa House.

1981   Architecture school moves to Dartford.

1983   Modular teaching units introduced throughout
Polytechnic.

1985   Thames Polytechnic merges with Avery Hill College of
Education.
Faculty of Built Environment created at Dartford site.

1987   ILEA abolished, Polytechnics and Colleges Funding
Council established.
Thames Polytechnic merges with Garnett College.

*1971: Thomas Spencer Hall,
Thames's first hall of residence.*

1970s: Student marches.

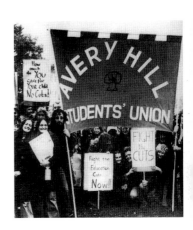

1979: Manresa House becomes responsibility of Garnett College.

1995: Wardroom, Chatham, becomes library of School of Earth Sciences.

1988   Science teaching transferred from Goldsmiths' (McMillan building, Deptford), and from City Polytechnic to Thames Polytechnic, which establishes the School of Earth Sciences. Garnett College becomes Faculty of Post-Compulsory Education, and (1990) students move from Roehampton to Avery Hill. West Kent College, Tonbridge, becomes first Associate College.

1990   Celebration of Polytechnic's 100th anniversary.

1991   Further and Higher Education Act abolishes Anthony Crosland's binary policy for higher education, and enables polytechnics to become universities. South West London College, Wandsworth dissolved; many staff and students transferred to Thames Polytechnic. Law School in Faculty of Business launched.

1992   Thames Polytechnic becomes University of Greenwich. Singer becomes Vice-Chancellor. Discussions with Natural Resources Institute at Chatham begin.

1993   David Fussey appointed Vice-Chancellor and Baroness Young Chancellor of the University. Student numbers reach 13,000. Thames College of Health Care Studies merges with University and becomes a faculty. First stage of new student village on Southwood site, Avery Hill, opened.
Secretary of State gives planning consent for new campus at the London Science Park, Dartford, to cater for 5000 students.

1994   University of Greenwich part of consortium bidding for whole of Natural Resources Institute. New campus opened at King's Hill Centre, West Malling. Woolwich former public swimming baths bought for student union. Division of whole University into four faculties: Human Sciences, Science and Engineering, Business, and Environment.

1995   University campus at Chatham (HMS *Pembroke*) established for School of Earth Sciences. Long leasehold obtained of Dreadnought Seamen's Hospital, Greenwich. University bids for the Royal Naval College.

1996   Natural Resources Institute becomes an Institute within the University. Government announces that University of Greenwich's proposals for Royal Naval College are the preferred solution.

1993: Part of the proposed development of the Avery Hill Mansion Site. (Nick Evans Architects)

Index